Lecture Notes in Computer Science 8570

Commenced Publication in 1973
Founding and Former Series Editors:
Gerhard Goos, Juris Hartmanis, and Jan van Leeuwen

T0183288

Martina Seidl · Nikolai Tillmann (Eds.)

Tests and Proofs

8th International Conference, TAP 2014
Held as Part of STAF 2014
York, UK, July 24-25, 2014
Proceedings

 Springer

Volume Editors

Martina Seidl
Johannes Kepler University
Institute for Formal Models and Verification
Altenbergerstr. 69, 4040 Linz, Austria
E-mail: martina.seidl@jku.at

Nikolai Tillmann
Microsoft Research
One Microsoft Way, Redmond, WA 98052, USA
E-mail: nikolait@microsoft.com

ISSN 0302-9743   e-ISSN 1611-3349
ISBN 978-3-319-09098-6   e-ISBN 978-3-319-09099-3
DOI 10.1007/978-3-319-09099-3
Springer Cham Heidelberg New York Dordrecht London

Library of Congress Control Number: 2014942868

LNCS Sublibrary: SL 2 – Programming and Software Engineering

Typesetting: Camera-ready by author, data conversion by Scientific Publishing Services, Chennai, India

Printed on acid-free paper

Springer is part of Springer Science+Business Media (www.springer.com)

Foreword

Software Technologies: Applications and Foundations (STAF) is a federation of a number of leading conferences on software technologies. It was formed after the end of the successful TOOLS federated event (http://tools.ethz.ch) in 2012, aiming to provide a loose umbrella organization for practical software technologies conferences, supported by a Steering Committee that provides continuity. The STAF federated event runs annually; the conferences that participate can vary from year to year, but all focus on practical and foundational advances in software technology. The conferences address all aspects of software technology, from object-oriented design, testing, mathematical approaches to modelling and verification, model transformation, graph transformation, model-driven engineering, aspect-oriented development, and tools.

STAF 2014 was held at the University of York, UK, during July 21-25, 2014, and hosted four conferences (ICMT 2014, ECMFA 2014, ICGT 2014 and TAP 2014), a long-running transformation tools contest (TTC 2014), eight workshops affiliated with the conferences, and (for the first time) a doctoral symposium. The event featured six internationally renowned keynote speakers, and welcomed participants from around the globe.

The STAF Organizing Committee thanks all participants for submitting and attending, the program chairs and Steering Committee members for the individual conferences, the keynote speakers for their thoughtful, insightful, and engaging talks, the University of York and IBM UK for their support, and the many ducks who helped to make the event a memorable one.

July 2014   Richard F. Paige

Preface

This volume contains the papers presented at the 8th International Conference on Tests and Proofs (TAP 2014), held during July 24–25, 2014 in York, UK, as part of the Software Technologies: Applications and Foundations (STAF) federated event.

TAP 2014 is the 8th event in a series of conferences devoted to the synergy of proofs and tests. Abandoning the traditional separation of formal verification and testing as orthogonal research fields, TAP aims at the identification of common grounds of the different research communities. In particular, both follow the goal to improve the quality of software and hardware, but with different means. Therefore, TAP provides a forum for the cross-fertilization of ideas and approaches from the formal verification community and the testing community in order to drop earlier dogmatic views on the incompatibility of proving and testing. TAP offers a meeting place for researchers who combine proofs and tests in an interdisciplinary manner by taking the best from both worlds.

Since its first edition at the ETH Zürich in 2007, TAP has been organized annually with great success. TAP was hosted by the Monash University Prato Centre near Florence in 2008, the ETH Zürich in 2009, the University of Malaga in 2010, the ETH Zürich in 2011, the Czech Technical University in Prague in 2012, and the Budapest University of Technology and Economics in 2013. From 2010 to 2012, TAP was co-located with the TOOLS conference series on advanced software technologies. In 2013, TAP became part of the STAF federated event, which was formed after the end of the TOOLS conference series.

For the 8th edition of the TAP conference hosted by the University of York, UK, we initially received 33 submissions from which 27 were considered for reviewing. After a rigorous reviewing process and an intensive discussion phase, we finally accepted 10 long papers and 4 short papers as well as 2 tutorial presentations. For each paper, we required at least three reviews from the Program Committee or from subreviewers assigned by Program Committee members. The overall quality of the submissions was very high. The accepted papers are contributions related to the following four research topics: test generation, bridging semantic gaps, integrated development processes, and bounded verification.

We wish to sincerely thank all authors who submitted their work for consideration. Further, we would like to thank the Program Committee members as well as the additional reviewers for their energy and their professional work in the review and selection process. Their names are listed on the following pages. The lively discussions during the paper selection were extremely vital and constructive.

We are very proud that TAP 2014 features a keynote by Ben Livshits on "Finding Malware on a Web Scale". As the core of several very large scale malware-finding tools for JavaScript code is an interesting interplay of static and runtime analysis, this keynote perfectly fits within the scope of TAP. Besides the two submitted tutorials selected by the Program Committee, we are very happy to host an additional invited tutorial by Margus Veanes on "Symbolic Automata", a toolkit for efficiently manipulating and analyzing regular expressions, symbolic finite automata and transducers, combining efficient representations of large concrete sets and symbolic reasoning.

Finally, we would like to thank the organizers of the STAF event, in particular the general conference chair Richard Paige, for their hard work and their support in making the conference success, we thank the University of York for providing the facilities, and we thank Springer for publishing these proceedings.

May 2014   Martina Seidl
                                                                   Nikolai Tillmann

Organization

Program Committee

Dirk Beyer	University of Passau, Germany
Achim D. Brucker	SAP AG, Germany
Robert Clarisó	Universitat Oberta de Catalunya, Spain
Marco Comini	University of Udine, Italy
Catherine Dubois	ENSIIE-CEDRIC, France
Juhan Ernits	Tallinn University of Technology, Estonia
Gordon Fraser	University of Sheffield, UK
Angelo Gargantini	University of Bergamo, Italy
Christoph Gladisch	Karlsruhe Institute of Technology, Germany
Martin Gogolla	University of Bremen, Germany
Arnaud Gotlieb	SIMULA Research Laboratory, Norway
Reiner Hähnle	Technical University of Darmstadt, Germany
Bart Jacobs	Katholieke Universiteit Leuven, Belgium
Jacques Julliand	Université de Franche-Comté, France
Thierry Jéron	Inria Rennes - Bretagne Atlantique, France
Gregory Kapfhammer	Allegheny College, USA
Nikolai Kosmatov	CEA LIST Institute, France
Victor Kuliamin	Russian Academy of Sciences, Russia
Karl Meinke	Royal Institute of Technology Stockholm, Sweden
Michal Moskal	Microsoft Research, USA
Alexandre Petrenko	Computer Research Institute of Montreal, Canada
Holger Schlingloff	Fraunhofer FIRST and Humboldt University, Germany
Martina Seidl	Johannes Kepler University Linz, Austria
Nikolai Tillmann	Microsoft Research, USA
T.H. Tse	The University of Hong Kong, China
Margus Veanes	Microsoft Research, USA
Luca Viganò	King's College London, UK
Manuel Wimmer	Vienna University of Technology, Austria
Burkhart Wolff	University Paris-Sud, France

Additional Reviewers

Baruzzo, Andrea
Bill, Robert
Bouquet, Fabrice
Bubel, Richard
Chai, Ming
Dangl, Matthias
Dury, Arnaud
Gerlach, Jens

Guardini, Davide
Hilken, Frank
Kääramees, Marko
Lackner, Hartmut
Langelier, Guillaume
Nguena Timo, Omer Landry
Niemann, Philipp
Ulbrich, Mattias

Table of Contents

Model-Based Mutation Testing
of an Industrial Measurement Device

Bernhard K. Aichernig[1], Jakob Auer[2], Elisabeth Jöbstl[1], Robert Korošec[2],
Willibald Krenn[3], Rupert Schlick[3], and Birgit Vera Schmidt[2]

[1] Institute for Software Technology, Graz University of Technology, Austria
{aichernig,joebstl}@ist.tugraz.at
[2] AVL List GmbH, Graz, Austria
{jakob.auer,robert.korosec,birgitvera.schmidt}@avl.com
[3] AIT Austrian Institute of Technology, Vienna, Austria
{willibald.krenn,rupert.schlick}@ait.ac.at

Abstract. *MoMuT::UML* is a model-based mutation testing tool for
UML models. It maps UML state machines to a formal semantics and
performs a conformance check between an original and a set of mutated
models to automatically generate test cases. The resulting test suite is
able to detect whether a system under test implements one of the faulty
models instead of the correct, original model. In this work, we illustrate the whole model-based mutation testing process by means of an
industrial case study. We test the control logic of a device that counts
the particles in exhaust gases. First, we model the system under test
in UML. Then, *MoMuT::UML* is used to automatically generate three
test suites from the UML test model: one mutation-based test suite, one
set of random test cases, and a third test suite combining random and
mutation-based test case generation. The test cases are executed on the
system under test and effectively reveal several errors. Finally, we compare the fault detection capabilities of the three test suites on a set of
faulty systems, which were created by intentionally injecting faults into
the implementation.

Keywords: test case generation, model-based testing, mutation testing,
automotive industry, UML.

1 Introduction

Testing of complex systems is a challenging and labour-intensive task. Approximately 50% of the elapsed time and costs of a software project are spent on
testing [24]. Furthermore, the later a software error is detected, the higher are
the costs for fixing it [18]. Hence, tools and techniques to assist testers are de-
manded by industry. In this work, we present a formal approach to software
testing and demonstrate its applicability in an industrial setting.

Figure 1 gives an overview of our approach, which we refer to as *model-based
mutation testing*. Yellow parts highlight the aspects of mutation testing that we

M. Seidl and N. Tillmann (Eds.): TAP 2014, LNCS 8570, pp. 1–19, 2014.
© Springer International Publishing Switzerland 2014

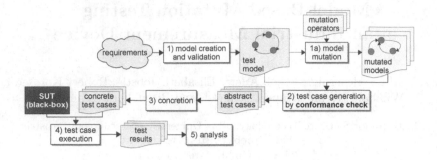

Fig. 1. Overview of model-based mutation testing

integrate into model-based testing, which is depicted in grey. Model-based testing (MBT) is a black-box testing technique requiring no knowledge about the source code of the system under test (SUT). Only the interface to the SUT has to be known. A test engineer creates a formal model that describes the expected behaviour of the SUT (Step 1). Test cases are then automatically derived from this test model. A crucial matter in MBT is the choice of the test criterion. It specifies which test cases shall be generated and hence, has a great influence on the quality of the resulting test suite. Exhaustive testing, i.e., using all of the test cases that can possibly be created from the test model, is impractical. Examples for commonly used test criteria are coverage criteria, random traversals, equivalence classes, or specified testing scenarios (test purposes). We follow a fault-centred approach, i.e., use mutations for test case generation (TCG). We syntactically alter the original test model producing a set of mutated models (Step 1a). We then automatically generate test cases that *kill* the model mutants, i.e., reveal their non-conforming behaviour. This is accomplished by a conformance check between the original and the mutated models (Step 2). As the test model is an abstraction of the SUT, also the derived test cases are *abstract*. Hence, they have to be concretised, i.e., mapped to the level of detail of the SUT (Step 3). Finally, the concrete test cases can be executed on the SUT (Step 4) and the test results can be analysed (Step 5). A particular feature of the generated test suites is their fault coverage. The generated tests will detect whether a faulty model has been implemented instead of the correct, original model. Hence, the generated test suite covers all of the modelled faults expressed by the model mutation operators and has a high chance of covering many additional similar faults (cf. coupling effect [14]).

Tool support for our model-based mutation testing approach is provided by the *MoMuT::UML* test case generator. It takes a UML model of the SUT, automatically creates mutated models, and subsequently uses these models for the automatic generation of abstract test cases. For model creation, we rely on external UML modelling tools like *Visual Paradigm*. The concretion and execution of the abstract test cases has also not been integrated in *MoMuT::UML* as these tasks highly depend on the SUT.

We already presented and applied the model-based mutation testing approach previously [2]. However, this earlier work relied on an enumerative TCG engine. One contribution of this work is the application of a new and more efficient TCG engine based on SMT solving techniques. Underlying research has already been presented in [3–5]. However, these earlier tool versions did not yet support the full language required for the UML approach and additionally used Prolog's constraint solver instead of the SMT solver Z3. Hence, this is the first time that we apply our SMT-based TCG tool to a UML model.

The main contribution is a comprehensive case study: we demonstrate the whole model-based mutation testing process on an industrial use case from the automotive domain incl. modelling, test generation, concretion, as well as execution and analysis of the test results. Moreover, we evaluate the fault detection capability of the mutation-based tests on a set of faulty SUTs and compare it with random tests and a test suite combining random and mutation-based tests.

The rest of this paper is structured as follows. Section 2 presents the SUT and describes how it has been modelled in UML. Section 3 deals with test case generation with *MoMuT::UML* and Section 4 reports on test execution. Finally, we discuss related work in Section 5 and conclude the paper in Section 6.

2   System under Test: A Particle Counter

The SUT is a measurement device for the automotive domain produced by AVL[1] which is used to measure particle number concentrations of diluted exhaust gas in compliance with UNECE-83 and PMP[2]. The particle counter consists of a conditioning component (volatile particle remover VPR) and the actual particle number counter (PNC). The VPR consists of the first dilution step, an evaporation tube, and a secondary dilution step.

In order to count non-volatile particles, a pump draws the exhaust gas into a sampling probe which eliminates all particles >2.5 µm. The sampled exhaust gas is then diluted with cleaned hot air to stabilize the particle number concentration. After the hot primary dilution, the diluted exhaust gas is further heated up in the evaporation tube in order to convert all volatile particles into the gaseous phase. Afterwards, a secondary dilution is performed to prevent further condensation or adsorption of volatile substances and to ensure that the maximum inlet temperature of the particle number counter (PNC) is not exceeded. Within the PNC the particles are enlarged due to the condensation of butanol and detected and counted using the light-scattering method.

In this paper we are concerned with testing the control logic of the particle counter, which offers several different operation modes to the user. For example, the user can choose between continuously measuring the current particle concentration or accumulating the number of particles counted over a period of time. During the measurement, the ratio by which the exhaust gas is mixed with particle-free dilution air can be adjusted. Additionally, there is a command

---

[1] https://www.avl.com/particle-counter, 18.03.2014
[2] http://www.unece.org/, 14.05.2014

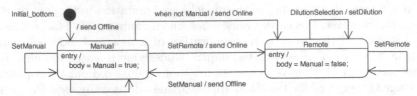

Fig. 2. The orthogonal region modelling the communication mode changes

to measure pure, particle-free air to check whether the sensors are calibrated correctly. Other commands are provided for necessary maintenance tasks like a leakage test, a response check, or for purging the sampling line.

In total, the particle counter distinguishes between eight different operating states that can be triggered via the testing interface. They include two idle states (*Pause* and *Standby*) as well as states like *Measurement* or *Purging*. Additionally, there are two different communication modes: *Manual* for controlling the particle counter directly via the buttons at the device and *Remote* for controlling the system remotely via a client, which will be tested. Furthermore, the system may switch from a *Ready* to a *Busy* status when processing a command.

The device receives commands from the user interface and shows its current state and each change between different internal modes. Commands from the user may be rejected (a) if the command is not available in the current operating state, (b) if the system is in the wrong communication mode, or (c) if the system is busy. In each case, the system returns an appropriate error message.

Initially, the system is idle (*Pause* operating state), *Ready* to accept commands, and expects *Manual* communication. In order to receive commands via our testing interface, it has to be set into the *Remote* communication state.

Every system update must be tested on a testbed that is equal to the customer's setup. However, this is complex and expensive when physical devices are used. A solution are virtual testbeds, where the combustion engine as well as the measurement device are simulated by real-time software. The simulation of the particle counter is basically a Matlab Simulink[3] model, which is compiled to a real-time executable. Thus, only two computers are required: one runs the simulation, the other one the test driver and the client for communication with the simulated SUT. In this work, we test the simulation of the particle counting device. However, the generated test cases can of course also be executed on the physical device. For more details on our test execution setup, see Section 4.

Test Model. The test model has been created with the UML editor *Visual Paradigm* 10.2. It comprises a class diagram for specifying the testing interface, i.e., possible input and output events, and a state machine for modelling the behaviour of the SUT. The state machine consists of three orthogonal regions. One for the operating state, one for switching between busy/ready, and one for

---

[3] http://www.mathworks.co.uk/products/simulink, 18.03.2014

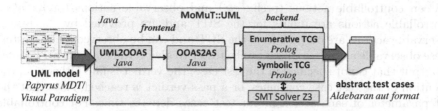

Fig. 3. Architecture of the *MoMuT::UML* tool chain

the communication modes. The latter is shown in Fig. 2. It is the simplest of the three regions. The whole state machine consists of 19 states (5 nested into the top-level states and further 7 nested into these) and 39 transitions (excluding initial transitions). Transitions are triggered by signal receptions from the outside, by changes of internal variables, or by progress of time. OCL[4] expressions are used for expressing guards on variable values and on states of other regions. Transition effects and entry/exit actions send outgoing signals or change the value of internal variables. We use AGSL [35] as action language.

3 Test Case Generation with *MoMuT::UML*

MoMuT::UML automatically generates test cases from UML models. Figure 3 gives an overview of the inputs, outputs, and the architecture. As input, it requires (1) a class diagram and (2) a state machine modelling the SUT. Although there exist plenty of UML modelling tools, most of them work with a very specific or proprietary format. Hence, it is not feasible to support all possible UML modelling tools and we concentrated on support for Papyrus MDT[5] (an Eclipse plugin) and *Visual Paradigm* for UML 10.2[6]. Like all model-based testing tools, *MoMuT::UML* delivers *abstract* test cases, which describe sequences of events on the model's level of abstraction. *MoMuT::UML* uses the Aldebaran format[7] to represent test cases. It is a very simplistic and straightforward format for Labelled Transition Systems (LTS). The format is also supported by other tools, e.g., the popular CADP toolbox[8].

An exemplary abstract test case for the particle counter's control logic is depicted in Fig. 4. It is a direct graphical representation of the textual test case in Aldebaran format produced by *MoMuT::UML*. Note that we deal with positive test cases, i.e., they only contain desired behaviour as specified in the original test model. Fail verdicts are implicit: every reaction from the SUT that is not specified in the test case leads to a fail verdict. In the test case, we distinguish

---

[4] http://www.omg.org/spec/OCL/, 13.05.2014
[5] http://www.eclipse.org/papyrus, 18.03.2014
[6] http://www.visual-paradigm.com/product/vpuml, 18.03.2014
[7] http://www.inrialpes.fr/vasy/cadp/man/aldebaran.html#sect6, 18.03.2014
[8] http://cadp.inria.fr, 18.03.2014

between controllable actions (prefix *ctr*) and observable actions (prefix *obs*). Controllable actions are inputs for the SUT and are provided by the tester. Observable actions are outputs from the SUT and can be observed by the tester. These observable actions are used by the tester to give verdicts. If the SUT issues an output that is not specified in the test case, the verdict is fail. Otherwise, the execution of the test case continues, or a pass verdict is reached. Note that the first parameter of each action in our test cases denotes time. For controllable actions, it states the number of time units the tester has to wait before sending the input to the SUT. For observable actions, it denotes the period of time in which the SUT may deliver a specified output.

obs StatusReady(0)

obs SPAU_state(0)

obs Offline(0)

ctr SetStandby(0)

obs StatusBusy(0)

obs STBY_state(0)

obs Online(0)

obs StatusReady(30)

ctr StartMeasurement(0)

obs StatusBusy(0)

obs SMGA_state(0)

obs StatusReady(30)

ctr StartIntegralMeasurement(0)

obs SINT_state(0)

ctr SetStandby(0)

obs STBY_state(0)

pass

Fig. 4. A sample test case

Initially, the system is ready, in operating state *Pause – SPAU*, and offline. This is reflected by the first three events in the test case depicted in Fig. 4. Then, it requests the system to switch to the *Standby* operating state. This entails a sequence of outputs from the system: it becomes busy, moves to operating state *Standby (STBY)*, switches to the remote mode (online), and finally becomes ready within 30 seconds. The next input to the SUT starts the measurement of the current particle concentration. Again, a sequence of observations similar to the previous one is triggered. Being ready and in operating state *measurement (SMGA)*, the system must accept the command that starts integral measurement, i.e., cumulative particle measurement. In this case, the system does not become busy, but directly switches to the according operating state *(SINT)*. Finally, measurement is stopped by returning to the *Standby (STBY)* state.

As shown in Fig. 3, *MoMuT::UML*'s architecture distinguishes between *frontend* and *backend*. The frontend is implemented in Java, the backend relies on native code.

Frontend. The frontend is responsible for converting the UML model into a representation suitable for the backend, i.e., the actual test case generator. First, the UML model is transformed into a labelled and object-oriented action system (OOAS [23]). This executable intermediate representation has formal semantics and is based on a generalisation of Dijkstra's guarded command language [25] and Back's action system [9] formalism. Most UML elements can be directly mapped to the corresponding OOAS structures, e.g., classes, member fields, and methods. Transitions of the state machine are - roughly speaking - mapped to actions. Only the time- and event semantics of UML needs to be expressed by more complex OOAS structures. Second, the

Table 1. Number of model-mutants per mutation operator

Mutation Operator	#	Upper Bound	
Set Guard to False	22	$O(t)$	t ... # transitions[9]
Set Guard to True	21	$O(t)$	t ... # transitions with guard
Set OCL Sub-Expr. False	115	$O(e)$	e ... # boolean OCL sub expressions
Set OCL Sub-Expr. True	115	$O(e)$	e ... # boolean OCL sub expressions
Invert Change Expr.	2	$O(t)$	t ... # transitions with change trigger
Invert Guard	21	$O(t)$	t ... # transitions with guard
Invert OCL Sub-Expr.	115	$O(e)$	e ... # boolean OCL sub expressions
Remove Change Trigger	2	$O(t)$	t ... # transitions with change trigger
Remove Effect	28	$O(t)$	t ... # transitions with effect
Remove Entry Action	11	$O(s)$	s ... # states with entry actions
Remove Exit Action	2	$O(s)$	s ... # states with exit actions
Remove Signal Trigger	44	$O(t)$	t ... # transitions with signal trigger
Remove Time Trigger	6	$O(t)$	t ... # transitions with time trigger
Replace Effect	2044	$O(t \cdot t_e)$	t ... # transitions, t_e ... # transitions with effects
Replace Signal Event	528	$O(t \cdot sg)$	t ... # signal triggered transitions, sg ... # signals
Replace OCL Operator	27	$O(o)$	o ... # of $and, or, <, \leq, >, \geq, =, \neq, +, -, *, div$

OOAS is lowered to a non-object-oriented, but still labelled action system (AS) the backend can work with.

The frontend is also home to the mutation engine that injects faults to construct model mutants. Mutations are inserted at the UML level. The mutation operators (cf. Table 1) are applied to the following state machine elements: triggers, guards, transition effects, entry- and exit actions. The elements are either removed or replaced with another element of the same type from the model. This leads to $O(n)$ mutants for the removals and $O(n^2)$ mutants for the replacements (with n being the number of considered elements in the model). Additional operators exist for change-trigger expressions, for guards expressed in OCL and for effect, entry-/exit action and method bodies. The modifications made here are: exchange operators, modify literals, fix (sub-)expressions to literals. They all lead to $O(n)$ mutants. After all model mutants have been generated, they are converted into action systems similarly to the original UML model.

Backend. These action systems serve as input for the TCG backend. There exist two alternative implementations: an enumerative and a symbolic TCG engine. The enumerative backend is called *Ulysses*. It is a conformance checker for action systems and performs an explicit forward search of the state space. This process yields the labelled transition system (LTS) semantics of the UML models. The conformance relation in use is input-output conformance (*ioco*). Informally, ioco conformance is given if for all input/output traces of the specification the implementation does only produce output allowed by the specification. Notice that an implementation may react arbitrarily to unspecified inputs, which means that ioco supports partial specifications. Partial-model support is an important feature as incorporating all aspects of a complex SUT in one monolithic model is hard. When executing *Ulysses* during TCG, the original model is treated as the specification, while the mutated models are considered implementations. For

---

[9] Due to a bug in the mutation engine only one guard-less transition was mutated.

a formal definition of ioco and LTSs, we refer to Tretmans [32]. For further information on the enumerative backend, see our previous work [2].

Experiments have shown that the performance of the explicit conformance checker *Ulysses* is lacking when the tool is applied to complex models. Therefore, a second backend exploiting SMT solving has been implemented. It interfaces with Microsoft's SMT solver Z3[10]. In this paper, we concentrate on this *symbolic* TCG engine. It supports two conformance relations: ioco and refinement. Our refinement relation is defined similarly as in [19], i.e., the mutated action system must imply the original action system for all possible observations, which are defined via a predicative semantics. Intuitively, it states that an implementation must not reach states or events that are not allowed by the specification. For a formal definition, we refer to [5, 21].

The basic idea of our refinement checking approach is to encode the transition relation as well as a condition that decides about refinement as SMT formulas [4]. We then use Z3 to see whether non-refinement can be proven and if so, proceed with test case generation. Since the refinement check is the corner stone of our test-case generation approach, it needs to be quick. Here we benefit from the SMT solver as it solves the constraints in general more efficiently than is possible by simple enumeration-based approaches. One particular example is the progress of time where the discrete time domain typically ranges over some bounded set of positive integers: only at certain points in time, defined by the time triggers in the UML model, some action will be enabled. Enumerating all positive integer values to find the right point in time where some action is enabled is much more time consuming (for high bounds) than symbolically solving the constraints. While the refinement check is fully symbolic, the reachability check (finding a trace to the point of non-refinement) relies on explicit state enumeration, which itself uses the SMT solver and the symbolic encoding of the transition relation to compute the states. We optimised our basic approach and achieved significant performance gains [3,5]. However, in these earlier publications we did not support all elements of the action system language required for the integration with the *MoMuT::UML* frontend. Adding the missing features and working with more complex models meant that we had to give up on SICStus Prolog's built-in constraint solver and switch to Z3.

Our refinement relation is rather strict as it disallows differences of internal states. In addition, it does not distinguish between inputs and outputs. Hence, additional inputs in the SUT lead to non-refinement and partial models become useless. Therefore, the symbolic backend also offers an ioco check: it uses the SMT solver to repeatedly solve the transition relation of the action systems, thereby gaining the underlying LTSs. This implementation is more efficient compared to the enumerative backend – particularly in terms of memory consumption. However, an ioco check between complex models is still expensive.

To counteract, our symbolic TCG engine offers a third option that combines the strict, but efficient refinement check with an ioco check. We consider the refinement check as *weak mutation testing*, where a wrong internal state already

---

[10] http://z3.codeplex.com, 18.03.2014

Table 2. TCG details for mutation (M), random (R), and the combined (C) test suites

	Test Suite		
	M	*R*	*C*
Max. Depth [ref/rand + ioco]	18 + 7	25 + 0	20 + 5
Model Mutants [#]	3103	3103	3103
Model Mutants Killed By Rand. TC [#]	-	2173	1819
Model Mutants Surviving [ref/rand + ioco]	375 + 177	930 + 0	375 + 308
Gen. TCs [# unique (+ dupl./invalid)[11]]	67(+9)	238(+2)	57(+7)
Max. TC Depth [steps]	19	25	20
Overall Gen. Time [#workers, hh:mm:ss]	21, 44:08:49	1, 1:43:39	21, 67:34:35
Gen. Time Mutants [mm:ss]	14:12	-	15:32
Gen. Time AS [mm:ss]	13:03	00:01	11:57
Avg. Time - Generate TC [mm:ss]	12:43	00:26	26:47
Avg. Time - Equiv. Mutant [mm:ss]	22:42	-	24:26
Avg. Time - Kill Mutant w. TC [mm:ss]	2:59	-	2:42

kills a mutant. In contrast, *strong mutation testing* additionally requires that this wrong internal state propagates to a wrong observation, which is checked by ioco. Hence, we first perform a refinement check. Only if non-refinement is identified, we append an ioco check. Note that this ioco check does usually not start at the initial state, but at a deeper state. This allows for higher exploration depths and hence longer test cases.

In addition to the mutation-based TCG, both backends offer random traversals of the test model to generate a random test suite of a given size (in terms of the number of generated tests and their length). *MoMuT::UML* also allows the combination of random and mutation-based testing. This TCG strategy first generates a set of random tests and runs them on the mutated models to see which model mutants are killed. In a second step, the surviving mutated models are used as input for the more complex mutation-based TCG.

Before generating a new test case, both backends check whether an already existing test case kills the new model mutant. This check is done to avoid generating duplicate test cases and to minimise the size of the generated test suite. Finally, we want to point out that the mutation-based TCG lends itself to parallel processing, as each model/mutant pair is independent. Hence *MoMuT::UML* supports TCG with multiple, parallel running workers: the user states the desired number of workers and the tool partitions the set of model mutants such that mutants are processed in parallel.

3.1 Test Case Generation for the Particle Counter

Using the symbolic backend, we generated three test suites: the first test suite, denoted *M*, is mutation-based, the second, called *R*, is randomly generated, and the third one, referred to as *C*, is a combined random/mutation test suite. To

---

[11] M and C: Number of duplicate tests due to parallel TCG.

R: Number of invalid tests due to the abstraction of time in the model.

generate M and C, we used our combination of refinement and ioco as explained before. All test suites were generated on a computer equipped with about 190 GB RAM and two 6-core Intel Xeon processors (3.47 GHz), running a 64-bit Linux (Debian 7.1). The system supports hyper-threading, hence 24 logical cores were available and allowed the exploitation of $MoMuT{::}UML$'s multi-worker capability. The approximate complexity of the model can be estimated when considering the bounded integer types of the 87 state variables. Theoretically, the state space consists of about $2.7 \cdot 10^{36}$ states. However, not all of these states are reachable from the initial system state by applying the 139 actions of the model.

Table 2 presents the most important figures for each of the three test suites. The first row shows the maximum exploration depth that was kept a constant 25 steps with M and C differing in the balance of the refinement and ioco depth. This was done in order to explore the relative effect of these two bounds. In total, 3103 model mutants were generated. Strategies R and C, both employing random tests, are able to kill 70% and 59% of the model mutants with the random tests only. The difference in the effectiveness is explained by the differences in depth (25 vs. 20) and number (238 vs. 20) of the random tests. After TCG, we have a total of 552, 930, and 683 model mutants not covered by test cases for strategies M, R, and C respectively. Examining the difference between M and C, we found that this is due to the reduced ioco-depth, which prevented C from finding 6 test cases M was able to find. The three strategies produce test suites differing in size and maximum depth of the test cases: M comprises 67, R 238, and C 57 unique tests that can be executed on the SUT. Duplicates in M and C are due to the race condition between multiple worker threads generating tests in $MoMuT{::}UML$, while R generated a small number of tests not applicable to the SUT due to the abstraction of time in the model. Looking at the maximum length of the generated test cases, we can see that M has the shortest tests with a maximum depth of 19, while in R and C the maximum depths, determined by the random strategy, are 25 and 20 respectively. The overall generation times in Table 2 include model-mutant generation, UML to OOAS to AS mapping, and the actual TCG process. The latter takes advantage of 21 parallel workers for test suites M and C. Note that the generation times for M and C are not comparable due to the different exploration depths. Times for mutant generation and OOAS to AS mapping are also given separately in the table. The last three rows give average values for the time required for creating one new test case, for processing a mutant that is equivalent up to the given depth, and the time needed for checking whether an existing test already kills a model mutant.

Although we allowed for a refinement search depth of up to 20, none of the tests has a refinement-depth greater than 17. Changing the maximum ioco-depth had a bigger influence. While almost all tests were found with an ioco-depth of less than three, there were four tests that needed a depth of seven. Further analysis of the data indicates that our bounds were not high enough to find all possible test cases. For example, in some instances the random tests of C were able to kill mutants deemed equivalent by M.

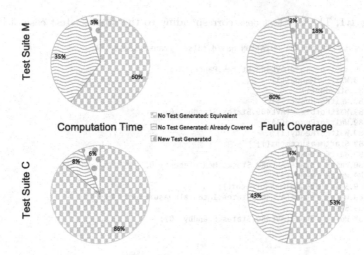

Fig. 5. Breakup of computation time and final fault coverage

Figure 5 shows a detailed breakup of the computation time and fault coverage for test suite M and the mutation-part of test suite C. The figures on the computation time prove that we spend more than 60% of the total TCG time checking equivalent model mutants. Note that this percentage is even higher for strategy C since the 20 random tests already kill many non-equivalent mutants. The data also demonstrates that our mutation engine needs to be improved to generate more meaningful mutants as in test set M 80% of the model mutants are covered by test cases generated for two percent of them. The combined strategy C has a better ratio due to the random tests removing a lot of model mutants.

We also attempted to generate test suite C using the enumerative backend but otherwise using the same setup. While the symbolic backend proved to be CPU-bound, i.e., we were never in danger of running out of RAM, the enumerative backend was unable to finish the task due to excessive memory consumption. Even with many of the parallel computations being prematurely aborted, the computation time exceeded 144 hours.

4   Concretion, Test Execution, and Analysis of Results

Before the abstract test cases, which have been generated by *MoMuT::UML*, can be executed on the SUT, the tests need to be concretised and brought to the level of abstraction of the SUT. This can either be accomplished by a translation of the abstract test cases into executable test cases or by a special test driver, which performs this adaptation on the fly during execution. As the existing test infrastructure of AVL is based on concrete unit tests, we chose the first option and mapped the abstract test cases to valid NUnit[12] test methods.

---

[12] http://www.nunit.org, 18.03.2014

Listing 1.1. The C# test case corresponding to the abstract test case of Fig. 4

```
1    public void CMB_AVL489_MUTATION_guard_false__transition_9() {
2      avl489.WaitForReady(1);
3      avl489.WaitForState(AVL489.States.Pause, 0);
4      avl489.WaitForManual(1);
5      avl489.Standby();
6      avl489.WaitForBusy(1);
7      avl489.WaitForState(AVL489.States.Standby, 0);
8      avl489.WaitForRemote(1);
9      avl489.WaitForReady(1);
10     avl489.StartMeasurement();
11     avl489.WaitForBusy(1);
12     avl489.WaitForState(AVL489.States.Measurement, 0);
13     avl489.WaitForReady(1);
14     avl489.StartIntegralMeasurement();
15     avl489.WaitForState(AVL489.States.IntegralMeasurement, 0);
16     avl489.Standby();
17     avl489.WaitForState(AVL489.States.Standby, 0);
18   }
```

Transforming the events of the abstract test cases into concrete method calls in the NUnit tests proved to be straightforward and has been implemented via simple XML-configured text substitutions. For example, the test case shown in Fig. 4 is mapped to the C# test method shown in Listing 1.1. Controllable events are directly mapped to method calls of the SUT's interface. Observable events are not as simple to map. Because the SUT does not actively report state changes, observable actions like *WaitForManual* have to be implemented via repeated polling of the system's state. If the desired state is not reached within a specified time span, the method throws an exception leading to a fail verdict. Unfortunately, repeated polling of the complete SUT state turned out too expensive. We therefore had to *weaken* our testing approach and only poll the state variables of the SUT related to the expected observable event. This means that the execution of a test will yield a pass verdict although the SUT produces additional, unspecified outputs to the expected one. This change, which we could not avoid, limits our ability to find faults via the coupling effect and means that we cannot guarantee that the ioco relation holds between the SUT and the model - not even with exhaustive testing. For details on the mapping between abstract and concrete tests and the test execution setup, we refer to [8].

We would like to remark that the concretion of abstract test-cases can not always be automated as easily as in our case. The more abstract the model, the more work has to be done during the mapping and the more likely it is to introduce bugs. However, running the resulting test cases is an effective means of finding bugs in the concretion step. Also, code reviews of test driver and/or a sample of concrete test cases in connection with test-runs on known-to-be-wrong SUT mock-ups will further increase the confidence in a correct mapping.

4.1   Execution Results for the Particle Counter

The generated test cases were executed on the simulation of the device as described above and effectively revealed several errors. Although the simulation

Table 3. SUT Mutants

Number	Description
1	Operation SetManual disabled in state *Measurement*
2	Operation SetManual disabled in state *IntegralMeasurement*
3	Operation SetManual disabled in state *Purging*
4	Device will not become *Busy* when changing to state *Pause*
5	Device will not become *Busy* when changing to state *Standby*
6	Device will not become *Busy* when changing to state *Leakage*
7	Operation SetRemote disabled in state *Zerogas*.
8	Operation SetRemote disabled in state *Purging*.
9	Operation SetRemote disabled in state *Leakage*.
10	Duration the device stays *Busy* divided in half.
11	Duration the device stays *Busy* doubled.
12	Operation StartMeasurement disabled.
13	Operation StartIntegralMeasurement disabled.
14	Operation SetPurge disabled.
15	Operation Zerogas disabled.
16	Device becomes *Busy* after SetPause in state *Pause*

was in use for several years already, these tricky bugs had not been identified so far. In the following, we give an overview of the errors.

One class of errors relates to changes of the operating state, which should not be possible when the device is busy. In the first case, the simulation allowed a switch from the operating state *Pause* to *Standby*, although the device was busy. The second issue concerned the activation of the integral measurement of the number of particles over a period of time. If the device is measuring the current particle concentration and is still busy, the system must reject the request for cumulative measurement. However, the simulation accepted the command. Further issues in the simulation were encountered when sending multiple inputs to the SUT in a short period of time. The simulation accepted them without any error messages, creating the impression that the inputs were processed. In reality, however, the inputs were absorbed and ignored. The correct behaviour is to emit appropriate error messages.

Not only the simulation of the device was erroneous but also the client for remote control of the device. The client did not correctly receive all error messages from the simulation. Normally, if the device is offline and receives the command to change the dilution value, it returns the error message *RejectOffline*. In this particular case, the error messages were not recorded.

4.2   Evaluation of the Test Suites

After the bugs described in the previous section had been fixed, a set of artificial faults were injected to evaluate the fault detection capabilities of the test suites. In total 16 faulty implementations (cf. Table 3) with a varying likelihood of detection were prepared by AVL. In the following, we refer to these faulty implementations as *SUT mutants*, in contrast to the *model mutants* we use to derive test cases. Two computers, running Windows 7 (64-bit), were needed for

Table 4. Test case execution results

| | Test Suite | | |
	M	R	C
TCs [#]	67	238	57
Exec. Time on Original SUT [hh:mm]	00:29	01:36	00:29
Exec. Time on All Faulty SUTs [hh:mm]	07:53	27:24	08:07
Survived Faulty SUTs [#]	4	6	3
Mutation Score [%]	75	62.5	81.25

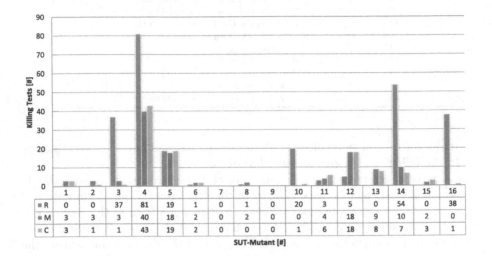

Fig. 6. Evaluation Results

test case execution. The first one was simulating the particle counter and ran the real-time simulation of the device, using about 300 MB RAM, while the second one ran the test driver communicating with the simulated device. The test driver and the client for remote communication with the simulated measurement device required one core and about 1 GB of RAM.

Table 4 summarises the test suite evaluation runs. As can be seen, running the random test suite R took roughly three times as long as any of the two remaining test suites. Besides being most expensive when run, it also has the lowest mutation score. The *mutation score* measures the effectiveness of a test suite in terms of its mutation detection ability. It is defined as the ratio of killed mutants to the number of non-equivalent mutants. Note that there are no equivalent SUT mutants as we did not apply mutation operators, but deliberately injected faults in the SUT. The combination of random and mutation tests achieved the best results in this evaluation: test suite C does not only have the lowest number of test cases, but also the highest mutation score. The execution time on the faulty SUTs varied depending on how many tests failed, i.e., did not have to be fully executed.

Figure 6 highlights the results in more detail. In particular, the figure shows that two of the SUT mutants (7 and 9) were not found by any of the tests. These two artificial faults disable the ability to switch the system online in specific operating states that can only be reached within a sequence of at least 8 and 9 steps. The faulty SUT no. 8 shows the same behaviour but in an operating state that is easier to reach. Since the affected functionality is split across multiple regions of the UML model, there is no simple model mutation directly emulating this type of problem. Hence, we identified a weakness in our set of model-mutation operators that causes *MoMuT::UML* to miss test cases that cover these errors. The faults were very unlikely to be found by random tests as they were buried deep in the model. Comparing test suites M and C reveals that C could even have a higher killing rate if we had not restricted the ioco-depth below the value of M (cf. SUT mutant 8). We also checked whether the test environment's inability to observe the full state of the SUT had adverse effects on test suites M and C. We found this, indeed, to be the case. One example is SUT mutant 16. It is not killed by test suite M due to the test execution setup. Given full observability of the SUT's state, test suite M would kill this SUT mutant. Test suite C kills this mutant despite the restricted observations as one random test detects the fault.

General threats to the validity of this case study can be summarised as follows: (1) The set of manually prepared SUT mutants might be a sample too small. To guard against this, the experts at AVL came up with a diverse set of SUT mutants representing typical faults they consider as being relevant. (2) The limitation of the test environment to snapshot the full state of the device might weaken our testing approach. This is indeed the case but we still get a very good detection rate. (3) We only run one set of random tests and, hence, one might argue that a different set might have done better. We are aware of this issue, which was caused by the limited amount of time we had in the lab. We tried to mitigate it by creating a sufficiently large and deep (the random tests are the deepest) test suite. Finally, (4) the style of modelling limits the test cases that can be generated. This is an issue only in very specialised cases of the presented case study and does not weaken the general outcome.

In summing up, the results corroborate that, while fault-based TCG is expensive, it leads to high-quality test suites. This is in line with previous results reported by others, cf. [29]. Also, our combined random and mutation strategy really combines the best of two worlds: cheap random tests with directed, fault-based tests and the guarantee to cover certain faults.

5   Related Work

To our knowledge, this is the first test case generation approach that deals with UML state machines, uses mutations, and is based on constraint/SMT solving.

A lot of research has been conducted on automated test case generation from UML state machines. However, none of these works is mutation-based. Indeed, there has been previous work on mutation testing of UML state machines but in terms of model validation [15]. It seems that we are the first who actually generate test cases from mutated UML state machines. One of the first tools for test case generation from UML state machines was based on various coverage criteria [27]. Following this lead, many other approaches also concentrated on coverage-based test case generation, e.g., [16,22,36]. Apart from coverage criteria, also test purposes/specifications are a popular way to derive test cases. This approach has also been employed in several works on test generation from UML state machines, e.g., [12,17,30]. Besides academia, commercial companies provide tools for test case generation from UML state machines [33], e.g., Smartesting CertifyIt[13], IBM's Rational Rhapsody[14] with the add-on for Automatic Test Generation (ATG), or Conformiq Designer[15]. Finally we want to point to other industrial-sized MBT case studies in [2,33] and refer to a brief literature review on test case generation from UML state machines [1].

Regarding model-based mutation testing, one of the first models to be mutated were predicate-calculus- [13] and Z specifications [31]. Later on, model checkers were used to check temporal formulae expressing equivalence between original and mutated models. Model checkers work very similar to our approach. In case of non-equivalence, they produce counterexamples that serve as test cases [7]. In contrast to our work, which can cope with non-deterministic models, most test case generation approaches using model checkers solely deal with deterministic systems. Nevertheless, there also exist work considering non-determinism and the involved difficulties, e.g., [10,28]. In addition, [26] considers non-determinism, but does not work with mutations. For a survey on mutation testing incl. mutation-based test case generation, we refer to [20]. The idea of using an ioco checker for mutation testing comes from Weiglhofer, who tested against Lotos specifications [6]. Like our enumerative backend *Ulysses* [11], Weiglhofer's ioco checker relies on enumerative techniques. A general taxonomy of model-based testing approaches can be found in [34].

6 Conclusion

We gave an overview of our formal testing approach called model-based mutation testing and its implementation in *MoMuT::UML*. We combine model-based testing with mutation testing to generate a test suite that guarantees the coverage of certain modelled faults. We conducted a comprehensive case study on an industrial use case from the automotive domain: a particle counter. We began with the modelling of the system under test in UML. This test model has subsequently been used for test case generation with *MoMuT::UML*, resulting in three test suites: a mutation-based test suite, a random test suite, and a combined random- and mutation-based test suite. We showed how the resulting abstract tests were mapped to concrete tests before being executed on the system under test. Our test cases effectively revealed subtle errors that have neither

---

[13] http://www.smartesting.com/en/product/certify-it, 18.03.2014
[14] http://www-03.ibm.com/software/products/en/ratirhapfami, 18.03.2014
[15] http://www.conformiq.com/products/conformiq-designer, 18.03.2014

been found by manual testing nor by the operation of the system over several years.

After fixing these bugs we deliberately injected faults to assess the fault detection capabilities of our three test suites. It turned out that the random test suite, although it is the largest with 238 test cases, achieved the lowest mutation score (62.5%). In contrast, the combination of random and mutation-based tests resulted in the smallest test suite (57 test cases) with the best detection rate (~81%). The mutation-based test suite was of similar size (67 test cases), but achieved a lower mutation score (75%). Our case study demonstrates that the combination of random and mutation-based test case generation is beneficial. Random tests are generated with relatively low effort and mutation-based test case generation completes the test suite to guarantee coverage of the modelled faults. This confirms our earlier work, where we came to the same conclusion based on two further case studies [2].

Nevertheless, none of our three test suites was able to detect all injected faults. We identified two possible reasons. First, the test execution environment was restricted due to technical reasons that we could not circumvent. We could only check for outputs expected by a test case but not for unexpected ones. This restriction decreased the fault detection capabilities of our tests. Second, we identified a weakness in our set of model mutants that failed to cover a particular faulty system. Hence, the implemented model-mutation operators need to be extended. Having said that, an analysis of the existing model mutants showed that we generate too many similar mutations as 80% of our model mutants were killed by test cases generated from only 2% of our model mutants. Finally, and as with most mutation testing approaches, equivalent mutants are hindering: They consume 60% of the overall computation time. Future work includes further analysis of the applied mutation operators to improve the situation.

Acknowledgments. Research herein was funded by the Austrian Research Promotion Agency (FFG), program line "Trust in IT Systems", project number 829583, TRUst via Failed FALsification of Complex Dependable Systems Using Automated Test Case Generation through Model Mutation (TRUFAL).

References

1. Aggarwal, M., Sabharwal, S.: Test case generation from UML state machine diagram: A survey. In: ICCCT, pp. 133–140. IEEE (2012)
2. Aichernig, B.K., Brandl, H., Jöbstl, E., Krenn, W., Schlick, R., Tiran, S.: Killing strategies for model-based mutation testing. Software Testing, Verification and Reliability (2014)
3. Aichernig, B.K., Jöbstl, E.: Efficient refinement checking for model-based mutation testing. In: QSIC, pp. 21–30. IEEE (2012)
4. Aichernig, B.K., Jöbstl, E.: Towards symbolic model-based mutation testing: Combining reachability and refinement checking. MBT. EPTCS 80, 88–102 (2012)
5. Aichernig, B.K., Jöbstl, E., Kegele, M.: Incremental refinement checking for test case generation. In: Veanes, M., Viganò, L. (eds.) TAP 2013. LNCS, vol. 7942, pp. 1–19. Springer, Heidelberg (2013)

6. Aichernig, B.K., Peischl, B., Weiglhofer, M., Wotawa, F.: Protocol conformance testing a SIP registrar: An industrial application of formal methods. In: SEFM, pp. 215–224. IEEE (2007)
7. Ammann, P., Black, P.E., Majurski, W.: Using model checking to generate tests from specifications. In: ICFEM, pp. 46–54. IEEE (1998)
8. Auer, J.: Automated Integration Testing of Measurement Devices - A Case Study at AVL List GmbH. Bachelor's thesis, Graz University of Technology (2013)
9. Back, R.J., Kurki-Suonio, R.: Decentralization of process nets with centralized control. In: PODC, pp. 131–142. ACM (1983)
10. Boroday, S., Petrenko, A., Groz, R.: Can a model checker generate tests for non-deterministic systems? ENCTS 190(2), 3–19 (2007)
11. Brandl, H., Weiglhofer, M., Aichernig, B.K.: Automated conformance verification of hybrid systems. In: QSIC, pp. 3–12. IEEE (2010)
12. Briand, L.C., Labiche, Y., Cui, J.: Automated support for deriving test requirements from UML statecharts. Software and System Modeling 4(4), 399–423 (2005)
13. Budd, T., Gopal, A.: Program testing by specification mutation. Comput. Lang. 10(1), 63–73 (1985)
14. DeMillo, R.A., Lipton, R.J., Sayward, F.G.: Hints on test data selection: Help for the practicing programmer. IEEE Computer 11(4), 34–41 (1978)
15. Fabbri, S.C.P.F., Maldonado, J.C., Masiero, P.C., Delamaro, M.E., Wong, W.E.: Mutation testing applied to validate specifications based on Statecharts. In: ISSRE, pp. 210–219. IEEE (1999)
16. Fröhlich, P., Link, J.: Automated test case generation from dynamic models. In: Bertino, E. (ed.) ECOOP 2000. LNCS, vol. 1850, pp. 472–492. Springer, Heidelberg (2000)
17. Gnesi, S., Latella, D., Massink, M.: Formal test-case generation for UML statecharts. In: ICECCS, pp. 75–84. IEEE (2004)
18. Grub, P., Takang, A.A.: Software Maintenance: Concepts and Practice, 2nd edn. World Scientific Publishing (2003)
19. Hoare, C., He, J.: Unifying Theories of Programming. Prentice Hall (1998)
20. Jia, Y., Harman, M.: An analysis and survey of the development of mutation testing. IEEE Trans. Software Eng. 37(5), 649–678 (2011)
21. Jöbstl, E.: Model-Based Mutation Testing with Constraint and SMT Solvers. Ph.D. thesis, Graz University of Technology, Institute for Software Technology (2014)
22. Kansomkeat, S., Rivepiboon, W.: Automated-generating test case using UML statechart diagrams. In: SAICSIT, pp. 296–300 (2003)
23. Krenn, W., Schlick, R., Aichernig, B.K.: Mapping UML to labeled transition systems for test-case generation - a translation via object-oriented action systems. In: de Boer, F.S., Bonsangue, M.M., Hallerstede, S., Leuschel, M. (eds.) FMCO 2009. LNCS, vol. 6286, pp. 186–207. Springer, Heidelberg (2010)
24. Myers, G.J.: The Art of Software Testing. Wiley (1979)
25. Nelson, G.: A generalization of Dijkstra's calculus. ACM Trans. Program. Lang. Syst. 11(4), 517–561 (1989)
26. Nogueira, S., Sampaio, A., Mota, A.: Guided test generation from CSP models. In: Fitzgerald, J.S., Haxthausen, A.E., Yenigun, H. (eds.) ICTAC 2008. LNCS, vol. 5160, pp. 258–273. Springer, Heidelberg (2008)
27. Offutt, J., Abdurazik, A.: Generating tests from UML specifications. In: France, R.B. (ed.) UML 1999. LNCS, vol. 1723, pp. 416–429. Springer, Heidelberg (1999)
28. Okun, V., Black, P.E., Yesha, Y.: Testing with model checker: Insuring fault visibility. In: 2002 WSEAS Int. Conf. on System Science, Applied Mathematics & Computer Science, and Power Engineering Systems, pp. 1351–1356 (2003)

29. Paradkar, A.: Case studies on fault detection effectiveness of model based test generation techniques. SIGSOFT Softw. Eng. Notes 30(4), 1–7 (2005)
30. Seifert, D.: Conformance testing based on UML state machines. In: Liu, S., Araki, K. (eds.) ICFEM 2008. LNCS, vol. 5256, pp. 45–65. Springer, Heidelberg (2008)
31. Stocks, P.A.: Applying formal methods to software testing. Ph.D. thesis, Department of computer science, University of Queensland (1993)
32. Tretmans, J.: Test generation with inputs, outputs and repetitive quiescence. Software - Concepts and Tools 17(3), 103–120 (1996)
33. Utting, M., Legeard, B.: Practical Model-Based Testing: A Tools Approach. Morgan Kaufmann Publishers (2007)
34. Utting, M., Pretschner, A., Legeard, B.: A taxonomy of model-based testing approaches. Software Testing, Verification and Reliability 22(5), 297–312 (2012)
35. Weissenbacher, G. (ed.): D 3.2b - modelling languages (final version). Tech. rep., MOGENTES (2010)
36. Weißleder, S.: Test Models and Coverage Criteria for Automatic Model-Based Test Generation with UML State Machines. Ph.D. thesis, Humboldt Universität zu Berlin (2009)

Computing with an SMT Solver

Nada Amin[1], K. Rustan M. Leino[2], and Tiark Rompf[1,3]

[1] EPFL, Lausanne, Switzerland
{first.last}@epfl.ch
[2] Microsoft Research, Redmond, WA, USA
leino@microsoft.com
[3] Oracle Labs, Lausanne, Switzerland
{first.last}@oracle.com

Abstract. Satisfiability modulo theories (SMT) solvers that support quantifier instantiations via matching triggers can be programmed to give practical support for user-defined theories. Care must be taken to avoid so-called matching loops, which may prevent termination of the solver. By design, such avoidance limits the extent to which the SMT solver is able to apply the definitions of user-defined functions. For some inputs to these functions, however, it is instead desireable to allow unadulterated use of the functions; in particular, if it is known that evaluation will terminate.

This paper describes the program verifier Dafny's SMT encoding of recursive user-defined functions. It then describes a novel encoding that, drawing on ideas from offline partial evaluation systems, lets the SMT solver evaluate "safe" function applications while guarding against matching loops for others.

1 Introduction

The collections of cooperating decision procedures in modern satisfiability modulo theories (SMT [3]) solvers provide a powerful reasoning engine. This power is harnessed in numerous applications where logical constraints are involved, including program verification, program analysis, program testing, program synthesis, constraint-based type inference, and theorem proving. While some of the theories supported (*e.g.*, the theory of uninterpreted functions) have complete decision procedures, the SMT solver may support other theories (*e.g.*, integer linear arithmetic) only by semi-decision procedures, either because of theoretical limitations or because of practical time or space compromises. It would be unreasonable to expect the SMT solver to provide support for all theories of interest. Luckily, many theories can be axiomatized in the input to the SMT solver, using logical quantifiers that give some interpretation to otherwise uninterpreted function symbols.

Quantifier support in an SMT solver was first implemented in Simplify [12], based on an idea from Greg Nelson's PhD thesis [26]. The idea is to give each universal quantifier a *matching pattern*, a.k.a. a *trigger*, that guides the instantiation of the quantifier. For example, consider the following fragment of input to an SMT solver:

```
Fib(0) = 0 ∧ Fib(1) = 1 ∧
∀ n: int {:Fib(n)} • 2 ≤ n ⟹ Fib(n) = Fib(n-2) + Fib(n-1)
```

M. Seidl and N. Tillmann (Eds.): TAP 2014, LNCS 8570, pp. 20–35, 2014.
© Springer International Publishing Switzerland 2014

where we have written $\{:M\}$ to use the list of expressions M as the matching pattern for the enclosing quantifier. This instructs the SMT solver to instantiate the quantifier with n:=E whenever in its proof search the current set of ground terms includes a subexpression of the form Fib(E). The approach of using triggers does not, in general, give a complete decision procedure, but the approach fits well into the SMT approach and has been used effectively in practice.

Understanding and making good use of matching patterns is a crucial part of the design of a system built on top of an SMT solver. Using triggers that are too liberal and hence allow too many instantiations can be a source of inefficiency in the proof search. A particular worry is that of non-termination among instantiations, a condition known as a *matching loop*. Therefore, it is necessary to use triggers to curb instantiations. On the other hand, using triggers that are too specific can be a source of incompleteness, since they may prevent instantiations that are needed in the proof. Both of these extremes are common mistakes.

In this paper, we explain and solve a problem with quantifiers that skirts the edge between the two extremes. While instantiations must in general be curbed, there are some instantiations where it is desireable to let the instantiations "run loose". For example, if Fib(k), which matches the trigger, is a ground term in the proof search, then the resulting instantiation produces two new terms, Fib(k-2) and Fib(k-1), and these terms also match the trigger. If nothing else is known about the term k, a neverending series of instantiations n:=k-d, one for each natural number d, could arise. We want to prevent the proof search from considering all of these, so some curbing is necessary. On the other hand, if the proof exploration produces a fact like k=12, then we would wish for the SMT solver to instantiate the quantifier enough times to figure out Fib(k)=144, as if it used the axiom to *compute* the value of Fib(12). The problem we solve in this paper is to find an encoding that provides curbing in the general case and computation in the case where functions are involved on literals. We do the encoding as part of the input to the SMT solver, using appropriate matching patterns; no modification of the SMT solver itself is needed, assuming the SMT solver supports quantifiers via matching patterns in the first place.

We encountered this problem while using the Dafny program verifier [21], where occasionally it is necessary to compute or partially evaluate expressions that contain some literals. For example, we may wish for the SMT solver to compute Fib(12) above. As another example, given

```
∀ n: int, t: T •
   (n = 0 ⟹ iter(n, t) = t) ∧
   (n > 0 ⟹ iter(n, t) = iter(n-1, f(t)))
```

we may wish for the SMT solver to partially evaluate iter(5,x) as f(f(f(f(f(x))))). The need for computation also arises when one wants to statically *test* the outcome of a given function. For example, one can use Dafny to define the formal semantics of a language, say some form of the lambda calculus[1], and one may then want to test that

---

[1] Full example, which we will revisit in Sec. 5, at http://rise4fun.com/Dafny/CXCK.

the evaluation of a particular term reduces to the expected value. For instance, verifying the formula

```
n > 0 ⟹ reduces_to(
  Appl(LambdaOf(0, Var(0)), Const(29)),
  Const(29),
  n)
```

is a test that $(\lambda x_0.\ x_0)$ 29 reduces to 29 in no more than n reduction steps.

Throughout the paper, we use Dafny as the context for explaining the problem and solution. What we say is likely to apply to any language or notation with user-defined functions that in some form are encoded as SMT input. In Sec. 2, we give a primer on matching patterns in an SMT solver. We describe how Dafny uses matching patterns to curb instantiation of user-defined functions in Sec. 3. This account of curbing represents the current encoding used in Dafny, which is more uniform and flexible than its previously described encodings [21]. In Sec. 4, we then give our encoding that allows literal arguments to be treated differently. We have implemented our encoding in Dafny and report on our experience in Sec. 5, through examples that show both full evaluation of functions and partial evaluation of functions.

2   A Primer on Matching Patterns

A simplified view of the operation of an SMT solver, suitable for our purposes, is the following. The solver is asked to check the validity of a conjecture P, often of the form A ⟹ Q where A is a conjunction of axioms and Q is some proof goal. During the proof search, the *proof state* at any time is (some bookkeeping information and) a conjunction of atomic formulas, some of which consist only of ground terms and others of which are universal quantifiers. The ground terms are represented in an *E-graph* [26], a data structure that represents the *congruence closure* of a set of terms (that is, equalities between terms, with the built-in knowledge that two terms f(x) and f(y) are equal if the terms x and y are).

At opportune times, the SMT solver considers the quantifiers in the proof state and looks in the E-graph for ground terms that match the triggers of the quantifiers. The matching ground terms are used to instantiate the quantifiers. This yields more formulas and the proof search continues.

Logically, a universal quantifier holds for all values of the bound variables, but uninformed instantiations are not likely to be useful in the proof search. Therefore, matching patterns are used to limit the instantiations that can take place. Syntactically, a matching pattern is a set of terms whose free variables include all the bound variables of the quantifier. For example, a possible matching pattern for a quantifier $\forall$ x,y • ... (here and elsewhere, we omit types of bound variables when they are obvious or irrelevant for the example) is $\{: f(x), g(x,y)\}$. It says that the quantifier can be instantiated with x,y:=E,F in a proof state where the E-graph contains both the terms f(E) and g(E,F). The terms given in a matching pattern are typically subterms of the body of the quantifier. Since the role of the matching pattern is to limit instantiations, terms that do not discriminate are not allowed; for example, $\{: f(x), y\}$ is not a legal trigger for the quantifier above, since it places no constraints on the ground terms that could be used for y.

Since matching is performed in the E-graph, which represents uninterpreted function symbols in the SMT solver, a matching pattern cannot use symbols that are interpreted by some theory; for example, a matching pattern cannot make use of arithmetic inequalities like $\leq$[2]. One quantifier can contain several matching patterns; a match for any one of them can cause an instantiation.

As an example, suppose we want to define in the SMT input a function ff that applies a particular function f twice. Function ff's defining axiom is the following:

$$\forall \; x \; \bullet \; ff(x) = f(f(x))$$

It is instructive to consider different choices of triggers for this quantifier.

Probably the best trigger for this quantifier is $\{: ff(x)\}$, because it will in effect make ff into something of a macro—as soon as an ff term arises among the ground terms, it will become equated with its definition. It is useful to think of quantifier instantiations as having a *direction*. The direction implied by the trigger $\{: ff(x)\}$ is to go from a higher-level function ff to a more primitive function f. Such a direction is also what one would have in mind when designing effective input for a term rewriting system (*e.g.*, Maude [8]), but note that term rewriting systems and macros replace a source term with a target term, whereas instantiating a quantifier conjoins the instantiated quantifier body to the proof state.

Suppose there is a number of interesting properties that hold for values in the functional image of ff, but not necessarily for all values in the functional image of f. Then, we may want to produce ff terms whenever possible and to axiomatize the other properties in terms of ff. For this purpose, $\{: f(f(x))\}$ may make a suitable trigger. Note that this trigger goes in the other direction from $\{: ff(x)\}$.

Let us consider what may happen if we choose the trigger to be $\{: f(x)\}$. Suppose a proof state contains the ground term f(k). It will cause the quantifier to be instantiated for x:=k, giving us (an equality between) two new terms, ff(k) and f(f(k)). The existence of the latter among the ground terms now gives rise to the instantiation x:=f(k) and before we know it, the SMT solver will spend all its time instantiating the quantifier with longer and longer terms x:=f(f(..f(k)..)). This situation is known as a *matching loop* and is one that we want to avoid[3].

For a larger example that highlights typical trigger considerations and gives guidance on trigger design, see [23].

3   User-Defined Functions and Curbing in Dafny

Dafny is a programming language that includes support for specifications and proofs. This built-in support makes the language suitable for reasoning about imperative and functional programs as well as some formalized mathematics. Dafny programs are translated into the Boogie intermediate verification language, which the Boogie verification engine then turns into input for the SMT solver Z3 [1,20]. For our purposes in

---

[2] Because of this restriction, adding a new theory to the SMT solver comes at the considerable expense of not being able to match on its symbols.

[3] Boogie code for the matching loop example discussed here:
http://rise4fun.com/Boogie/mH23.

this paper, the most relevant part of the Dafny language is its (possibly recursive) user-defined functions, and we consider their translation into axioms for the SMT solver.

Let us give some motivation by considering an example. Suppose we want to encode as SMT input a Dafny function that defines triangle numbers:

```
function Triangle(n: nat): nat
{
  if n = 0 then 0 else n + Triangle(n-1)
}
```

To encode this for the SMT solver, we introduce a function `Triangle` on the integers and supply an axiom like this:

$$\forall\ n:\ \textbf{int}\ \bullet\ 0 \leq n \Longrightarrow$$
$$\text{Triangle}(n) = \textbf{if}\ n = 0\ \textbf{then}\ 0\ \textbf{else}\ n + \text{Triangle}(n\text{-}1)$$

How do we want this quantifier to be triggered? Whenever a proof search involves a term `Triangle(k)` for some subterm k, then it seems useful to instantiate the quantifier with n:=k, so we may consider the straightforward trigger *{:Triangle(n)}*. However, such a trigger would lead to a matching loop, because lacking any information about k, the SMT solver would explore both branches of the if expression, and the successive exploration of the else branch would lead to new instantiations of the quantifier[4].

To curb such instantiations, the Dafny verifier adds an extra parameter to the SMT encoding of the function. Borrowing a recent name from discussions about co-induction in the type-theory community, we will refer to this parameter as "fuel". The fuel parameter specifies how many unrollings of the function we want to allow the SMT solver to do. Note, the value of the function does not actually depend on the fuel parameter; it is used only to control the SMT solver's instantiations.

Since matching is performed in the E-graph, it is important that non-zero fuel values be recognizable structurally, with no theory reasoning and without interpreted symbols like 0 and +. Thus, we make use of Peano arithmetic (that is, unary arithmetic) and provide the following declarations in the SMT input:

```
type Fuel
function Z(): Fuel
function S(Fuel): Fuel
```

These declarations can be thought of as an inductive datatype like

```
datatype Fuel = Z | S(Fuel)
```

but we do not bother to say anything about Z and S, beyond fact that they are functions with the given signatures.

We can now encode the Dafny function `Triangle`. We declare it in the SMT input as follows:

```
function Triangle(fuel: Fuel, n: int): int
```

---

[4] http://rise4fun.com/Boogie/Agsl

Next, we produce three axioms. The "synonym" axiom that says that the value of the fuel parameter is irrelevant:

$\forall$ fuel: Fuel, n: **int** • *{:Triangle(S(fuel), n)}*
Triangle(S(fuel), n) = Triangle(fuel, n)

The "definition" axiom encodes the function body:

$\forall$ fuel: Fuel, n: **int** • *{:Triangle(S(fuel), n)}* $0 \leq$ n $\Longrightarrow$
Triangle(S(fuel), n) = **if** n $=$ 0 **then** 0 **else** n + Triangle(fuel, n-1)

Finally, the "consequence" axiom states properties that come from the signature and specification of the function:

$\forall$ fuel: Fuel, n: **int** • *{:Triangle(S(fuel), n)}* $0 \leq$ n $\Longrightarrow$
$0 \leq$ Triangle(S(fuel), n)

This encoding provides curbing because the matching patterns will cause the quantifiers to be instantiated only when the fuel parameter is non-zero (more precisely, when it has the form S applied to something) and because recursive (and mutually recursive) calls in the right-hand side of the definition axiom use a smaller fuel value than the left-hand side.

The verifier translates other Dafny uses of the function with some default value for the fuel parameter. In Dafny, this default value is usually 1 (that is, S(Z())), but it is 2 in certain proof-obligation positions (like when a user-supplied assertion or postcondition needs to be verified). Although we currently do not provide it as a feature, the default fuel value could in principle be set by the user, globally or for particular functions or particular proof obligations.

We end this section with an example that both illustrates the technique and serves as a segue to the next section. Consider a lemma that proves, by induction, that Triangle(n) is at least twice as big as n, provided n is at least 3. In Dafny, this is done as follows:[5]

```
lemma TriangleProperty(n: nat)
  ensures 3 ≤ n ⟹ 2*n ≤ Triangle(n);
{
  if n ≤ 3 {
    assert Triangle(3) = 6;  // the crucial property of the base case
  } else {
    TriangleProperty(n-1);   // invoke the induction hypothesis
  }
}
```

The "postcondition" of the lemma, given by the **ensures** clause, states the conclusion of the lemma. The body of the lemma is some code, where all control paths are verified to lead to the postcondition. The recursive call to TriangleProperty essentially obtains the inductive hypothesis, applied for n-1.

---

[5] We ignore the fact that Dafny has some support for automatic induction [22] and here give the proof explicitly.

To detail the proof obligations for this lemma, we view the lemma as a pre/post-condition pair and write the following pseudo code (which is representative of what the intermediate form in Boogie will look like):

```
assume 0 ≤ n;   // assume precondition of lemma
if n ≤ 3 {
  assert Triangle(S(S(Z())), 3) = 6;   // fuel = 2
} else {
  assert 0 ≤ n-1;   // check precondition of call
  // assume postcondition of call:
  assume 3 ≤ n-1 ⟹ 2*(n-1) ≤ Triangle(S(Z()), n-1);   // fuel = 1
}
// check postcondition of lemma:
assert 3 ≤ n ⟹ 2*n ≤ Triangle(S(S(Z())), n);   // fuel = 2
```

Note that the fuel argument is passed in as 2 in proof-obligation positions and as 1 elsewhere. The verification condition for this pseudo code is the following first-order formula, which is given to the SMT solver:

```
0 ≤ n ⟹
  (n ≤ 3 ⟹ Triangle(S(S(Z())), 3) = 6) ∧   // check then branch
  (3 < n ⟹ 0 ≤ n-1) ∧   // check else branch (trivial)
  // prove the postcondition from what is learnt in both branches:
  ( (n ≤ 3 ∧ Triangle(S(S(Z())), 3) = 6) ∨
    (3 < n ∧ 0 ≤ n-1 ∧ (3 ≤ n-1 ⟹ 2*(n-1) ≤ Triangle(S(Z()), n-1)))
    ⟹ 3 ≤ n ⟹ 2*n ≤ Triangle(S(S(Z())), n))
```

To prove the postcondition of the lemma, there are two cases. If $n = 3$, the postcondition follows from what is learnt from the then branch. If $4 \leq n$, the postcondition follows from the definition axiom and the induction hypothesis. In more detail, since the fuel parameter of the last call to Triangle has the form S(...), the definition axiom is triggered and thus the final inequality becomes:

```
2*n ≤ n + Triangle(S(Z()), n-1)
```

This inequality follows from what is learnt from the else branch (that is, the induction hypothesis).

As we just saw, we had more fuel than necessary to complete the proof of the postcondition in this example. But what about the proof of the then branch? The fuel supplied in its call to Triangle is enough for two instantiations of the definition axiom, which reduces the proof goal to:

```
3 + 2 + Triangle(Z(), 1) = 6
```

Since there is no fuel left, the SMT solver is unable to complete this proof (so a verification error will be reported to the user). In the next section, we describe how we extend the encoding to handle cases like this.

4   Enabling Computation

We enable computation by allowing unfolding steps that do not decrease the fuel parameter in chosen cases, picked at compile time. Dafny generates SMT input that allows unfolding for two kinds of function applications: (a) when *all* function arguments are known to be constants, and (b) when all arguments that are part of the decreasing measure for termination (maintained internally by Dafny) are constants. In the first case, the result of the function application is known to be a constant as well. In the second case, the result is not necessarily a constant, but evaluation (via E-matching for the instantiations) is still guaranteed to terminate. If it is known which function arguments are part of the decreasing measure (which it is in Dafny), then (b) is typically more useful; however, we nevertheless also generate SMT input for case (a), because one can construct examples where handling (a) is useful and (b) does not apply.[6] Dafny propagates which expressions will definitely evaluate to constants and uses this information for further unfolding decisions; a technique known as *binding-time analysis* in the context of partial evaluation [18].

Our encoding for computation relies on an identity function, provided in the SMT input, to mark constant expressions as "literals":

```
function Lit<T>(x: T): T { x }
```

For each user-defined function, we add extra "computation" axiom(s) that trigger on literal argument(s) and that do not consume any fuel. For the `Triangle` function, we provide the following extra axiom:

$$\forall \text{ fuel: Fuel, } n: \textbf{int} \bullet \{ :Triangle(fuel, Lit(n)) \}$$
$$0 \leq n \implies$$
$$Triangle(fuel, Lit(n)) =$$
$$\quad \textbf{if } n = 0 \textbf{ then } 0 \textbf{ else } n + Triangle(fuel, Lit(n-1))$$

To enable computations, the Dafny compiler wraps all concrete values, such as 2, with the `Lit` marker. The compiler also lifts simple operations on literal expressions: `Lit(x)+Lit(y)` becomes `Lit(x+y)`, since adding two constant values will produce a constant again. This lifting mechanism is also what enables recursive computations, since `Triangle(fuel, Lit(n)-Lit(1))` becomes `Triangle(fuel, Lit(n-1))`. Note that the variable n is wrapped as a literal expression `Lit(n)` because it is a formal parameter fixed as a literal in the trigger of the axiom.

For computations to be composable, we also `Lit`-wrap each function application on all literal arguments. Hence, `Triangle(fuel, Lit(3))` is tagged as a constant expression `Lit(Triangle(fuel, Lit(3)))`. This propagation of binding-time information is essential to enable computation on nested expressions, such as `Triangle(Triangle(3))` in Dafny.

Finally, a word of caution: we don't always want to compute. The SMT solver can prove `Fib(1000)≠1000` on its own without computing `Fib(1000)`, but if we provide a "computation" axiom for `Fib` and give it too much importance, then the solver hangs instead. We resolve this tension by giving a low priority to the "computation" axioms.

---

[6] http://rise4fun.com/Dafny/J1Im

Also, as a small tweak that matters in practice, we also let if-then-else expressions act as a "barrier" for literals, so that we unwrap any top-level literals following the if, then or else expressions. This is why the computation axiom above does not return Lit-wrapped expressions in the then and else branches.

5 Experience

We re-iterate the necessity of the fuel parameter with a complete Dafny example [7] which correctly verifies using the encoding described in Sec. 3 but enters a matching loop when the fuel parameter is ignored. The example proves the equivalence of the recursive and iterative definitions of the factorial function.

```
function Factorial(n: nat): nat
{
   if n = 0 then 1 else n*Factorial(n-1)
}
function FactorialIter(n: nat, acc: nat): nat
{
   if n = 0 then acc else FactorialIter(n-1, acc*n)
}
function Factorial'(n: nat): nat
{
   FactorialIter(n, 1)
}
lemma lemmaFactorialStep(n: nat, acc: nat)
   ensures acc*Factorial(n) = FactorialIter(n, acc);
{
}
lemma theoremFactorialEquiv(n: nat)
   ensures Factorial(n) = Factorial'(n);
{
   lemmaFactorialStep(n, 1);
}
```

This example demonstrates that curbing is sometimes essential when proving universally quantified theorems in Dafny. Now, we show that controlled relaxation of the curbing, described in Sec. 4, is also very important in practice.

Just like one would write tests in conventional languages, in Dafny, one can write out examples with their expected results, with the hope that they will be automatically verified. Thanks to our novel encoding that enables computation, this hope is now often materialized.

For example, in an implementation of the simply typed lambda calculus[8], we may wish to check that $\lambda(x : T).\lambda(f : T \rightarrow T).f(f(x))$ has type $T \rightarrow (T \rightarrow T) \rightarrow T$. This example now verifies automatically, while it previously required 5 intermediate

---

[7] http://rise4fun.com/Dafny/EHG1
[8] http://rise4fun.com/Dafny/SUOW

statements to verify. Note that we represent variable names directy as numbers (0 is x and 1 is f):

```
lemma example_typing()
  ensures has_type(map[],
      Lambda(0, T, Lambda(1, Arrow(T, T),
      Appl(Var(1), Appl(Var(1), Var(0))))))
    =
      Some(Arrow(T, Arrow(Arrow(T, T), T)));
{
  /* This manual proof is no longer necessary, thanks to computation.
  var c := extend(1, Arrow(T, T), extend(0, T, map[]));
  assert find(c, 0) = Some(T);
  assert has_type(c, Var(0)) = Some(T);
  assert has_type(c, Var(1)) = Some(Arrow(T, T));
  assert has_type(c, Appl(Var(1), Appl(Var(1), Var(0)))) = Some(T); */
}
```

We now illustrate the utility of generating a computation axiom which triggers merely when decreasing formal parameters are literals. Even when the typing context is left abstract, Dafny automatically verifies type-checking of the example $\lambda(f : T \rightarrow T).f(f(x))$ provided a context with at least $(x : T)$:

```
lemma example_typing_m(m: map<int,ty>)
  requires 0 in m ∧ m[0]=T;
  ensures has_type(m,
      Lambda(1, Arrow(T, T),
      Appl(Var(1), Appl(Var(1), Var(0)))))
    =
      Some(Arrow(Arrow(T, T), T));
{
}
```

Even though the context m is not a literal, computation is possible because only the term parameter (that is, the second parameter to has_type) is part of the decreasing measure of the has_type function, and that argument is a literal in this example application.

Here is another example [9], inspired by an exercise in the Coq-based textbook *Software Foundations* [28]. This example shows that our encoding of computations plays well with function applications in complex expressions.

```
datatype Nat = 0 | S(Nat) // Peano numbers
function plus(n: Nat, m: Nat): Nat
{
  // ...
}
function mult(n: Nat, m: Nat): Nat
```

---

[9] http://rise4fun.com/Dafny/AtWK

```
{
  // ... in terms of plus
}
function factorial(n: Nat): Nat
{
  // ... in terms of mult
}
function toNat(n: nat): Nat
{
  if n=0 then 0 else S(toNat(n-1))
}
lemma test_factorial0()
  ensures factorial(toNat(3)) = toNat(6);
{
}
lemma test_factorial1()
  ensures factorial(toNat(5)) = mult(toNat(10),toNat(12));
{
}
```

With the previous encoding of user-defined functions that implements curbing without computation, proving `test_factorial1` would be very tedious and require many intermediate steps.

5.1   Limitations

Since we need to make the computation axioms low priority to avoid hanging computations, we also prevent some larger (tractable) computations. This is a matter of degree: we may not want to allow `Fib(1000)`, but what about `Fib(40)`?

We chose to make unfolding decisions at compile time, when generating SMT input in Dafny, as opposed to delegating to the SMT solver to make such decisions on-the-fly, at run time—in particular, we chose not to provide the SMT solver with any axioms that would create fresh applications of the `Lit` marker. Clearly, such a static binding-time analysis is approximate by nature and cannot always deduce that an expression will evaluate to a constant. Hence, we miss some easily computable expressions, as we show next. We extend the previous sample code with an example that Dafny cannot auto-verify:

```
function returnFst(a: nat, b: nat): nat
{
  if b=0 then a else returnFst(a, b-1)
}

lemma test_factorial_indirect(n: nat)
  ensures factorial(toNat(returnFst(5, n)))=mult(toNat(10),toNat(12));
{
}
```

Note that we use a convoluted definition of returnFst. Otherwise, the function would be inlined by the Dafny compiler, and the example reduced to test_factorial1. The problem here is that the Dafny compiler does not detect that returnFst(5, n) is in fact equivalent to 5, and hence fails to recognize at compile time that the argument to factorial is indeed a literal. Interestingly, it is enough guidance for verification to provide this fact:

```
lemma eqReturnFst(a: nat, b: nat)
  ensures returnFst(a, b) = a;
{
}
lemma test_factorial_indirect_ok(n: nat)
  ensures factorial(toNat(returnFst(5, n)))=mult(toNat(10),toNat(12));
{
  eqReturnFst(5, n);
}
```

We leave a closer investigation of online techniques to future work, where the SMT solver would make unfolding decisions on the fly. The benefit would be an increase in precision, but in general, ensuring termination is harder in an online setting. We conjecture that the additional information about termination measures that is available in Dafny could be put to use here as well, possibly at the expense of a more involved encoding.

6 Related Work

Partial Evaluation. Partial evaluation [18] denotes a class of program transformations that aim to pre-compute parts of a program that do not depend on dynamic input values. The result of partial evaluation is a residual program, where expressions that only depend on statically known values are evaluated to constants. Partial evaluation is usually applied to improve performance, as the residual program performs less work. In our case, we are interested in the simplification aspect: in a verification context, evaluating an application of a user-defined function means that we can directly reason about the result value and need not reason about the function definition.

Partial evaluation comes in two flavors: online [5,29,30] and offline [7,9,15,16]. In an online setting, decisions whether to evaluate or to residualize an expression are made on the fly. If a function is called with only static arguments, the function will be evaluated. If a subset of the arguments is static, a specialized function may be generated. A well-known problem in online partial evaluation is that it is difficult to ensure termination (and even a terminating computation might take a long time). The second flavor of partial evaluation is offline. Here, a binding-time analysis first classifies each expression as static or dynamic. A second pass then evaluates all expressions classified as static.

In our case, evaluation is a special case of proof search in an SMT solver. Conceptually, evaluation corresponds to unfolding of functions and simplifying. On the SMT level, unfolding means instantiation of the corresponding quantifier. Without further directions, the SMT solver will make decisions online, whether or not to unfold quantifier definitions, based on heuristics like a global instantiation depth. Since the SMT solver knows nothing about user-defined functions apart from their axiomatization, it cannot know whether a particular function will terminate or not, and whether unfolding is profitable. On the Dafny level, however, this kind of information is readily available. Our encoding serves the purpose of communicating this information to the solver. In essence, we implement a classic offline partial evaluation scheme. We perform a simple binding-time analysis to identify static expressions within Dafny. We tag those expressions with a Lit(.) marker, and we emit axioms that direct the SMT solver to unfold functions if they are called with Lit(.) arguments. But we also get some of the effects of an online scheme, because the SMT solver may end up combining results from our simple binding-time analysis. For example, given the Dafny program snippet

```
var y := 12;
assert y ≤ k ∧ k < y + m ∧ m = 1 ⟹ Fib(k) = 144;
```

our simple binding-time analysis will classify only 12 as "static" (that is, it will Lit-wrap it). But after the SMT solver's theory reasoning concludes $k = y = 12$, that "static" classification is in effect transferred to k, and thus the term Fib(k) will be fully evaluated.

A different approach is taken by the Leon verification system [19]. Instead of mapping user-defined functions to quantifiers and invoking the SMT solver only once, Leon invokes the solver interactively, while successively unfolding function definitions in the solver input. This is an example of a practical online approach, but crucially one that circumvents the brittle solver heuristics.

Computation in Proof Assistants. Many interactive proof assistants rely on computations. For example, uses of Coq [6] and PVS [27] routinely need computation as part of type checking. These computations are not set up using trigger-based quantifiers, but are instead based on custom tactics or other heuristics or mechanisms.

Quantifiers and Triggers. The SMT solver Simplify [12] was the first to give comprehensive support of trigger-based quantifiers. As DPLL(T)-style architectures became popular, experimental SMT solvers [14,24] and mature SMT solvers [2,4] also added support for quantifiers. For our purposes, the efficient implementation of matching in the SMT solver Z3 [11] took quantifier support to a heightened level [10].

More information about how triggers work can be found in the descriptions of Simplify [12] and Z3 [11], as well as in Michał Moskal's PhD thesis [25]. Dross *et al.* have studied a logical semantics for triggers [13]. Leino and Monahan [23] convey the artform of typical trigger design through a particular example.

Curbing by Constructor Cases. In the current version of Dafny, curbing is achieved as we have described in Sec. 3. In a previous version, functions whose body consisted of a **match** expression would get translated "Haskell style" into one axiom per constructor **case**. Inspired by VeriFast [17], this translation attempts to curb instantiations by including the name of a constructor in each trigger, which means that the axioms will not be applied unless it is already known which case applies. With this approach, computation and partial evaluation do not need our Lit encoding and axioms. The approach does not guarantee termination [17], but it seems to do well in practice. The main limitation is that the approach only applies to functions defined by `match` expressions. We have found that we no longer need the "Haskell style" translation for curbing, so the only curbing that Dafny now uses is what we described in Sec. 3. In fact, our current curbing allows more examples to be verified, because of the more liberal triggering.

7 Conclusions

Proper attention to the design of matching triggers is crucial for any tool that wants to harness the power of an SMT solver with trigger-based quantifiers. The Dafny program verifier simultaneously uses two techniques to encode the user-defined functions that it has to reason about. While one technique curbs instantiations and thus limits the use of function definitions, the other technique is designed to give unadulterated use of the function definitions. The first technique is useful because many inductive program proofs need only one unfolding of functions, and the curbing prevents matching loops in the SMT solver. The other technique is useful because it allows the SMT solver to perform computations and partial evaluations, and axioms are set up in such a way that they apply only when the function arguments are literals. The two techniques come together automatically in Dafny, and there is no need for users do anything special to obtain the benefits.

Using our design, we have profited from the use of computation in Dafny. For example, we have transcribed into Dafny examples from two chapters of the Coq-based *Software Foundations* book by Pierce *et al.* [28], which uses many examples to test the given definitions. Our design and implementation of the two simultaneous techniques in Dafny now make it possible to benefit from computation while doing proofs within the comfort of the automation provided by an SMT-based program verifier.

Acknowledgments. We thank Nik Swamy for useful comments on an earlier draft of this paper.

References

1. Barnett, M., Chang, B.-Y.E., DeLine, R., Jacobs, B., Leino, K.R.M.: Boogie: A Modular Reusable Verifier for Object-Oriented Programs. In: de Boer, F.S., Bonsangue, M.M., Graf, S., de Roever, W.-P. (eds.) FMCO 2005. LNCS, vol. 4111, pp. 364–387. Springer, Heidelberg (2006)
2. Barrett, C.W., Berezin, S.: CVC Lite: A New Implementation of the Cooperating Validity Checker Category B. In: Alur, R., Peled, D.A. (eds.) CAV 2004. LNCS, vol. 3114, pp. 515–518. Springer, Heidelberg (2004)
3. Barrett, C., Stump, A., Tinelli, C.: The SMT-LIB standard: Version 2.0. In: Gupta, A., Kroening, D. (eds.) Proceedings of the 8th International Workshop on Satisfiability Modulo Theories (2010)
4. Barrett, C.W., Tinelli, C.: CVC3. In: Damm, W., Hermanns, H. (eds.) CAV 2007. LNCS, vol. 4590, pp. 298–302. Springer, Heidelberg (2007)
5. Berlin, A.A., Weise, D.: Compiling scientific code using partial evaluation. IEEE Computer 23(12), 25–37 (1990)

6. Bertot, Y., Castéran, P.: Interactive Theorem Proving and Program Development — Coq'Art: The Calculus of Inductive Constructions. In: Texts in Theoretical Computer Science. Springer (2004)
7. Bondorf, A.: Automatic autoprojection of higher order recursive equations. Sci. Comput. Program. 17(1-3), 3–34 (1991)
8. Clavel, M., Durán, F., Eker, S., Lincoln, P., Martí-Oliet, N., Meseguer, J., Quesada, J.F.: Maude: Specification and programming in rewriting logic. Theoretical Computer Science 285(2), 187–243 (2002)
9. Consel, C.: A tour of Schism: A partial evaluation system for higher-order applicative languages. In: Schmidt, D.A. (ed.) Proceedings of the ACM SIGPLAN Symposium on Partial Evaluation and Semantics-Based Program Manipulation, PEPM 1993, pp. 145–154. ACM (June 1993)
10. de Moura, L., Bjørner, N.S.: Efficient E-Matching for SMT Solvers. In: Pfenning, F. (ed.) CADE 2007. LNCS (LNAI), vol. 4603, pp. 183–198. Springer, Heidelberg (2007)
11. de Moura, L., Bjørner, N.S.: Z3: An Efficient SMT Solver. In: Ramakrishnan, C.R., Rehof, J. (eds.) TACAS 2008. LNCS, vol. 4963, pp. 337–340. Springer, Heidelberg (2008)
12. Detlefs, D., Nelson, G., Saxe, J.B.: Simplify: a theorem prover for program checking. Journal of the ACM 52(3), 365–473 (2005)
13. Dross, C., Conchon, S., Kanig, J., Paskevich, A.: Reasoning with triggers. In: Fontaine, P., Goel, A. (eds.) 10th International Workshop on Satisfiability Modulo Theories, SMT 2012. EasyChair 2013 EPiC Series, pp. 22–31 (2012)
14. Flanagan, C., Joshi, R., Ou, X., Saxe, J.B.: Theorem proving using lazy proof explication. In: Hunt Jr., W.A., Somenzi, F. (eds.) CAV 2003. LNCS, vol. 2725, pp. 355–367. Springer, Heidelberg (2003)
15. Gomard, C.K., Jones, N.D.: Compiler generation by partial evaluation: A case study. Structured Programming 12(3), 123–144 (1991)
16. Gomard, C.K., Jones, N.D.: A partial evaluator for the untyped lambda-calculus. J. Funct. Program. 1(1), 21–69 (1991)
17. Jacobs, B., Piessens, F.: The VeriFast program verifier. Technical Report CW-520, Department of Computer Science, Katholieke Universiteit Leuven (August 2008)
18. Jones, N.D., Gomard, C.K., Sestoft, P.: Partial evaluation and automatic program generation. Prentice-Hall, Inc. (1993)
19. Kneuss, E., Kuraj, I., Kuncak, V., Suter, P.: Synthesis modulo recursive functions. In: Hosking, A.L., Eugster, P.T., Lopes, C.V. (eds.) Proceedings of the 2013 ACM SIGPLAN International Conference on Object Oriented Programming Systems Languages & Applications, OOPSLA 2013, pp. 407–426. ACM (October 2013)
20. Rustan, K., Leino, M.: Specification and verification of object-oriented software. In: Broy, M., Sitou, W., Hoare, T. (eds.) Engineering Methods and Tools for Software Safety and Security. NATO Science for Peace and Security Series D: Information and Communication Security, vol. 22, pp. 231–266. IOS Press (2009), Summer School Marktoberdorf 2008 lecture notes.
21. Leino, K.R.M.: Dafny: An automatic program verifier for functional correctness. In: Clarke, E.M., Voronkov, A. (eds.) LPAR-16 2010. LNCS, vol. 6355, pp. 348–370. Springer, Heidelberg (2010)
22. Leino, K.R.M.: Automating induction with an SMT solver. In: Kuncak, V., Rybalchenko, A. (eds.) VMCAI 2012. LNCS, vol. 7148, pp. 315–331. Springer, Heidelberg (2012)
23. Rustan, K., Leino, M., Monahan, R.: Reasoning about comprehensions with first-order SMT solvers. In: Shin, S.Y., Ossowski, S. (eds.) Proceedings of the 2009 ACM Symposium on Applied Computing (SAC), pp. 615–622. ACM (March 2009)

24. Leino, K.R.M., Musuvathi, M., Ou, X.: A Two-Tier Technique for Supporting Quantifiers in a Lazily Proof-Explicating Theorem Prover. In: Halbwachs, N., Zuck, L.D. (eds.) TACAS 2005. LNCS, vol. 3440, pp. 334–348. Springer, Heidelberg (2005)
25. Moskal, M.J.: Satisfiability Modulo Software. PhD thesis, Institute of Computer Science, University of Wrocław (2009)
26. Nelson, C.G.: Techniques for program verification. Technical Report CSL-81-10, Xerox PARC (June 1981)
27. Owre, S., Rajan, S., Rushby, J.M., Shankar, N., Srivas, M.K.: PVS: Combining specification, proof checking, and model checking. In: Alur, R., Henzinger, T.A. (eds.) CAV 1996. LNCS, vol. 1102, pp. 411–414. Springer, Heidelberg (1996)
28. Pierce, B.C., Casinghino, C., Gaboardi, M., Greenberg, M., Hriţcu, C., Sjöberg, V., Yorgey, B.: Software Foundations. In: Electronic textbook (2013), http://www.cis.upenn.edu/~bcpierce/sf
29. Sahlin, D.: The mixtus approach to automatic partial evaluation of full Prolog. In: Debray, S.K., Hermenegildo, M.V. (eds.) Proceedings of the 1990 North American Conference on Logic Programming, NACLP, October–November 1990, pp. 377–398. MIT Press (1990)
30. Weise, D., Conybeare, R., Ruf, E., Seligman, S.: Automatic online partial evaluation. In: Hughes, J. (ed.) FPCA 1991. LNCS, vol. 523, pp. 165–191. Springer, Heidelberg (1991)

An Abstraction Technique for Testing Decomposable Systems by Model Checking*

Paolo Arcaini[1], Angelo Gargantini[1], and Elvinia Riccobene[2]

[1] Dipartimento di Ingegneria, Università degli Studi di Bergamo, Italy
{paolo.arcaini,angelo.gargantini}@unibg.it
[2] Dipartimento di Informatica, Università degli Studi di Milano, Italy
elvinia.riccobene@unimi.it

Abstract. Test generation by model checking exploits the capability of model checkers to return counterexamples upon property violations. The approach suffers from the *state explosion problem* of model checking. For property verification, different abstraction techniques have been proposed to tackle this problem. However, such techniques are not always suitable for test generation. In this paper we focus on Decomposable by Dependency Asynchronous Parallel (DDAP) systems, composed by several subsystems running in parallel and connected together in a way that the inputs of one subsystem are provided by another subsystem. We propose a test generation approach for DDAP systems based on a decompositional abstraction that considers one subsystem at a time. It builds tests for the single subsystems and combines them later in order to obtain a global system test. Such approach avoids the exponential increase of the test generation time and memory consumption. The approach is proved to be sound, but not complete.

1 Introduction

Test generation by model checking is a well-known technique that exploits the capability of model checkers to efficiently explore the state space and build a counterexample when a property is falsified by the model. One main problem is the "state explosion problem", i.e., the size of the system state space grows exponentially w.r.t. the number of variables and the size of their domains. Much of the research in model checking over the past 30 years has involved developing techniques for dealing with this problem in the context of property verification [8]. There exist several abstraction techniques (like counterexample guided abstraction [7]) that address this problem for property verification, but they are not suitable for test generation [19]. Indeed, they can guarantee validity of a property in the original model if the property is verified in the abstract model, but they may not guarantee to find the right counterexample if the property is false. Other classical abstractions (like slicing [21] or reduction techniques like *finite focus* [1] that soundly reduces a state machine) reduce the original specification to a smaller one for which it may be easier to find the desired tests;

---

* This work is partially supported by GenData 2020, a MIUR PRIN 2010-11 project.

M. Seidl and N. Tillmann (Eds.): TAP 2014, LNCS 8570, pp. 36–52, 2014.

however, they may miss parts of the system specification that are necessary for building the tests.

The approach presented here can be viewed in the context of those abstraction techniques for test generation that, following the "divide and conquer" principle, are based on system [2,3] or property [16] decomposition. Since model checkers suffer exponentially from the size of the system, decomposition brings an exponential gain and allows to test large systems.

In this paper we focus on systems that can be decomposed in two (or more) subsystems that run asynchronously in parallel but such that (part of) the inputs of one subsystem are provided by another subsystem. For such systems, we propose a test generation approach based on model checking, exploiting the decomposition by dependency abstraction. The approach consists in generating the tests for the single subsystems and combining them later, in order to build a test for the whole system. The generation is performed by considering the dependency relation, starting from the "most" dependent subsystem, to the independent subsystem. Such approach permits to exponentially reduce the test generation time and the memory consumption with respect to the basic approach that builds a test for the whole system.

Section 2 provides some background on Kripke structures with inputs, on their representation in the model checker NuSMV. Test case generation by model checking is also briefly recalled in this section. Section 3 introduces DDAP systems, i.e., systems having two components in a dependency relation, and Section 4 proposes a test generation approach for them. Section 5 extends the approach to n-DDAP systems, i.e., systems having more than two components. Preliminary experiments are presented in Section 6. Section 7 reviews some related literature, and Section 8 concludes the paper.

2   Background

We here report some basic concepts regarding the formal structure and the test generation approach by model checking that represent the fundamentals of the theory of DDAP systems, developed in Sections 3, 4, and 5.

2.1   Kripke Structures

In this paper we use Kripke structures with inputs [15], that can be conveniently used to represent reactive systems.

Definition 1 (Kripke Structure with Inputs). *A* Kripke structure with inputs *is a 6-tuple* $M = \langle S, S^0, IN, OUT, T, \mathcal{L} \rangle$ *where*

- *S is a set of states;*
- *$(S^0 \subseteq S) \neq \emptyset$ is the set of initial states;*
- *IN and OUT are disjoint sets of atomic propositions;*
- *$T \subseteq S \times \mathcal{P}(IN) \times S$ is the transition relation; given a state s and the applied inputs I, the structure moves to a state s', such that $(s, I, s') \in T$.*
- *$\mathcal{L} : S \rightarrow \mathcal{P}(OUT)$ is the proposition labeling function.*

Definition 2 (Input Sequence). *An* input sequence *for a Kripke structure with inputs is a (possibly infinite) sequence of inputs* $I_0, \ldots, I_n, \ldots$ *with* $I_i \in \mathcal{P}(IN)$.

Definition 3 (Trace). *Given an input sequence* $I_0, \ldots, I_n, \ldots$, *a* trace *for a Kripke structure with inputs is a sequence* $s_0, I_0, s_1, \ldots, s_n, I_n, s_{n+1} \ldots$ *such that* $s_0 \in S^0$ *and* $(s_i, I_i, s_{i+1}) \in T$.

Definition 4 (Test). *A* test *for a Kripke structure with inputs is a finite trace* $s_0, I_0, s_1, \ldots, s_{n-1}, I_{n-1}, s_n$.

We define the set of atomic propositions as $AP = IN \cup OUT$ and CTL/LTL formulae are defined over AP.

Kripke structures with inputs differ from classical Kripke structures because the inputs are explicitly not part of the state and cannot be modified by the machine. However, since for every Kripke structure K with inputs there is a corresponding Kripke structure K' without inputs [5], all the model checking techniques can be still applied.

2.2 Encoding Kripke Structures with Inputs in NuSMV

NuSMV [6] is a well-known tool that performs symbolic model checking. It allows the representation of synchronous and asynchronous finite state systems, and the analysis of specifications expressed in *Computation Tree Logic* (CTL) and *Linear Temporal Logic* (LTL). A NuSMV specification describes the behavior of a Finite State Machine (FSM) in terms of a "possible next state" relation between states that are determined by the values of variables. A variable type can be Boolean, integer defined over intervals or sets, or an enumeration of symbolic constants. A *state* of the model is an assignment of values to variables.

There are two kinds of variables: *state* variables, declared in the section **VAR**, and *input* variables, declared in the section **IVAR**. The value of state variables can be determined in the **ASSIGN** section in the following way:

ASSIGN var := simple_expression *-- simple assignment*
ASSIGN init(var) := simple_expression *-- init value*
ASSIGN next(var) := next_expression *-- next value*

A simple assignment determines the value of variable *var* in the current state, the instruction **init** permits to determine the initial value(s) of the variable, and the instruction **next** is used to determine the variable value(s) in the next state(s).

Input variables represent inputs of the system, and their value cannot be bound as done for state variables. They can only be used to determine the next value of state variables.

A **DEFINE** statement (**DEFINE** id := exp) can be used as a macro to syntactically replace an identifier *id* with the expression *expr*.

NuSMV offers another more declarative way of defining initial states and transition relations. Initial states can be defined by the keyword **INIT** followed by characteristic properties that must be satisfied by the variables values in the initial states. Transition relations can be expressed by constraints, through the keyword **TRANS**, on a set of *current state/next state* pairs.

Temporal properties are specified in the **LTLSPEC** (resp. **CTLSPEC**) section that contains the LTL (resp. CTL) properties to be verified.

NuSMV can be used to describe Kripke structures with inputs. The inputs are modeled as input variables (**IVAR**), and the outputs as state variables (**VAR**) or definitions (**DEFINE**).

In this paper we use NuSMV, but the approach is general and applicable to any model checker.

2.3   Model-Based Test Generation by Model Checking

In model based testing [14,20], the specification describing the expected behavior of the system is used to generate tests that exhibit some desired system behaviors (*testing goals*). Test goals can be formally represented by test predicates.

Definition 5 (Test Predicate). *A test predicate is a formula over the model, and determines if a particular testing goal is reached.*

A classical technique for model-based test generation exploits the capability of model checkers to produce counterexamples [10,12]. If a test predicate can be expressed as a CTL/LTL formula over the model states, then a test suite *covering* the test goals corresponding to a desired coverage criterion can be generated as follows.

1. The test predicates set $\{tp_1, \ldots, tp_n\}$ is derived from the specification according to the desired testing goals. Test predicate structure depends on the particular desired coverage criteria [11].
2. For each test predicate tp_i, the *trap property* $\neg tp_i$ is verified. If the model checker proves that the trap property is false (tp_i is *feasible*), then the returned counterexample shows how to cover tp_i. We call the counterexample *witness*, and we translate it to a test. If the model checker explores the whole state space without finding any violation of the trap property, then the test predicate is said *unfeasible* and it is ignored. In the worst case, the model checker terminates without exploring the whole state space and without finding a violation of the trap property (i.e., without producing any counterexample), usually because of the state explosion problem. In this case the user does not know if either the trap property is true (i.e., the test is unfeasible), or it is false (i.e., there exists a sequence that reaches the goal).

Note that the specification is used also to produce a test oracle to assess the correctness of the implementation.

Example 1. Consider as example a simple system in which there is a statement like **if** C **then** .... A possible test goal, requiring that the condition is covered by at least a test, can be formalized by the LTL test predicate **F**(C), requiring

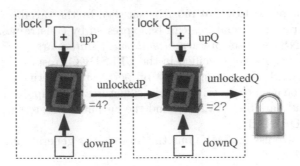

Fig. 1. DDAP system – *SafeLock*

that C is eventually true. If the model checker finds a counterexample for the trap property !$\mathbf{F}$(C), such counterexample leads the system to a state where C is true and, therefore, it is the desired test.

3   DDAP Systems

In this paper we focus on Decomposable by Dependency Asynchronous Parallel (DDAP) systems. A DDAP system is composed of two subsystems, running asynchronously in parallel, such that (part of) the inputs of the dependent subsystem are provided by the other subsystem which runs independently. Formally, DDAP systems are defined as follows.

Definition 6 (Dependency). *Given two Kripke structures with inputs* $P = \langle S_P, S_P^0, IN_P, OUT_P, T_P, \mathcal{L}_P \rangle$ *and* $Q = \langle S_Q, S_Q^0, IN_Q, OUT_Q, T_Q, \mathcal{L}_Q \rangle$, *Q depends on* P *if* $OUT_P \cap IN_Q \neq \emptyset$.

Definition 7 (DDAP System). *A DDAP system* $\langle P, Q \rangle$ *is a system having two components* P, Q *satisfying the following properties:*

- $P = \langle S_P, S_P^0, IN_P, OUT_P, T_P, \mathcal{L}_P \rangle$ *and* $Q = \langle S_Q, S_Q^0, IN_Q, OUT_Q, T_Q, \mathcal{L}_Q \rangle$ *are two Kripke structure with inputs;*
- *Q depends on* P, *but* P *does not depend on* Q;
- *only one system at a time is active (interleaving asynchronous parallelism).*

We call $D = OUT_P \cap IN_Q$ the *dependency set* of the DDAP system.

Example 2. Fig. 1 shows an example of DDAP system (called *SafeLock*). The safe lock system is composed by two locks, P and Q, which work in sequence. Both locks have two buttons (upP and downP, upQ and downQ) that change the digit of the lock. Lock P becomes *unlocked* (i.e., unlockedP = *true*) only if the digit is equal to the stored correct value (in the example, the value 4). Lock Q becomes *unlocked* (i.e., unlockedQ = *true*) only if the digit is equal to the stored correct value (in the example, the value 2) and if P is unlocked. So the safe lock is unlocked when Q is unlocked.

Lock P has as inputs $IN_P = \{\texttt{upP}, \texttt{downP}\}$ and as output $OUT_P = \{\texttt{digitP0},$
$\ldots, \texttt{digitP9}, \texttt{unlockedP}\}$. It has ten different states $(s_0^p, \ldots, s_9^p)$, distinguished by
the value of the digit; $\mathcal{L}_P(s_4^p) = \{\texttt{digitP4}, \texttt{unlockedP}\}$ and $\mathcal{L}_P(s_i^p) = \{\texttt{digitP}i\}$
for $i = 0, \ldots, 3, 5, \ldots 9$.

Lock Q has as inputs $IN_Q = \{\texttt{upQ}, \texttt{downQ}, \texttt{unlockedP}\}$ and as output $OUT_Q = \{\texttt{digitQ0}, \ldots, \texttt{digitQ9}, \texttt{unlockedQ}\}$. It has eleven different states $(s_0^q, \ldots, s_9^q,$
and $\tilde{s}_2^q)$, distinguished by the value of the digit and of $\texttt{unlockedQ}$; $\mathcal{L}_Q(\tilde{s}_2^q) = \{\texttt{digitQ2}, \texttt{unlockedQ}\}$, and $\mathcal{L}_Q(s_i^q) = \{\texttt{digitQ}i\}$ for $i = 0, \ldots, 9$.

The output $\texttt{unlockedP}$ of lock P is connected to the corresponding input of
lock Q, i.e., the dependency set is $D = \{\texttt{unlockedP}\}$.

Definition 8 (DDAP Input Sequence). *The* input set *of a DDAP system*
$K = \langle P, Q \rangle$ *is the set* $IN_K = IN_P \cup (IN_Q \setminus D)$. *An* input sequence *for the DDAP*
K *is a sequence* $J_0, \ldots, J_n$ *such that* $J_i \in \mathcal{P}(IN_K)$.

We define the concept of a trace of a DDAP system, reflecting the fact that
only one component makes a move at each step, and that, when the dependent
component moves, it reads some of its inputs from the outputs of the independent
component.

Definition 9 (DDAP Trace). *Given an input sequence* $J_0, \ldots, J_n, \ldots$ *for a*
DDAP system $\langle P, Q \rangle$, *a* trace *is the sequence* $(p_0, q_0), J_0, (p_1, q_1), \ldots, (p_n, q_n),$
$J_n, (p_{n+1}, q_{n+1}), \ldots$ *such that:*
[(1)]
1. $p_0 \in S_P^0$ *and* $q_0 \in S_Q^0$;
2. $((p_i, J_i \cap IN_P, p_{i+1}) \in T_P \wedge q_i = q_{i+1}) \oplus ((q_i, (J_i \cap IN_Q) \cup (\mathcal{L}_P(p_i) \cap D), q_{i+1}) \in T_Q \wedge p_i = p_{i+1})$.

Requirement (2) specifies that either the component P moves from p_i to p_{i+1}
and Q remains still in state $q_i = q_{i+1}$, or component Q moves from q_i to q_{i+1}
and P remains still in state $p_i = p_{i+1}$. When Q moves, it reads some of its inputs
from the outputs of P (i.e., $\mathcal{L}_P(p_i) \cap D$).

Example 3. For the safe lock system *SafeLock*, the input set is $IN_{SafeLock} = \{\texttt{upP},$
$\texttt{downP}, \texttt{upQ}, \texttt{downQ}\}$. Assuming that the both locks are initialized to 0, a possible
trace leading to the state in which the global lock is unlocked is: $(s_0^p, s_0^q), \{\texttt{upP}\},$
$(s_1^p, s_0^q), \{\texttt{upP}\}, (s_2^p, s_0^q), \{\texttt{upP}\}, (s_3^p, s_0^q), \{\texttt{upP}\}, (s_4^p, s_0^q), \{\texttt{upQ}\}, (s_4^p, s_1^q), \{\texttt{upQ}\},$
$(s_4^p, \tilde{s}_2^q)$.

Note that DDAP systems can be extended to systems with more that two
subsystems, as shown in Section 5.

3.1 Encoding DDAP Systems in NuSMV

NuSMV permits to split a model in different modules and run several module
instances in the *main* module. Modules instances can be run in a synchronous
or asynchronous way. Asynchronous modules instances are created through the

```
MODULE lockP                        MODULE lockQ
DEFINE keyP := 4;                   DEFINE keyQ := 2;
IVAR -- INP                         IVAR -- INQ
   upP: boolean;                       upQ: boolean;
   downP: boolean;                      downQ: boolean;
VAR -- OUTP                            unlockedP: boolean; -- D = OUTP ∩ INQ
   digitP: 0 .. 9;                  VAR -- OUTQ
DEFINE -- OUTP                         digitQ: 0 .. 9;
   unlockedP := digitP = keyP;-- D = OUTP ∩ INQ  DEFINE -- OUTQ
ASSIGN                                 unlockedQ := digitQ = keyQ & unlockedP;
   init(digitP) := 0;               ASSIGN
   next(digitP) :=                     init(digitQ) := 0;
   case                                next(digitQ) :=
      upP & !downP: (digitP + 1) mod 10;   case
      downP & !upP: (digitP + 9) mod 10;      upQ & !downQ: (digitQ + 1) mod 10;
      TRUE: digitP;                           downQ & !upQ: (digitQ + 9) mod 10;
   esac;                                      TRUE: digitQ;
                                           esac;
```

Code 1. Lock P **Code 2.** Lock Q

```
MODULE main
VAR
   procP: process lockP;
   procQ: process lockQ;
TRANS procP.unlockedP = procQ.unlockedP;
```

Code 3. DDAP system *SafeLock*

keyword **process**; at each step, one process is nondeterministically chosen and executed, while the other processes do not run and so do not change their state.

A DDAP system can be easily encoded in NuSMV. Subsystems P and Q are defined as two NuSMV modules, as described in Section 2.2, and asynchronously instantiated in the main module (as processes procP and procQ), so that only one subsystem is executed at a time. The connection between P outputs and Q inputs is established by a TRANS declaration in which each output x of P belonging to the dependency set (i.e., $x \in OUT_P \cap IN_Q$) is linked with the corresponding input of Q (i.e., procP.x = procQ.x). In the sequel, we refer to this global model as *whole model*.

Example 4. We have encoded the running case study *SafeLock* in NuSMV. Codes 1 and 2 show the NuSMV modules for locks P and Q; Code 3 shows the main module that asynchronously executes the two locks and connects the output unlockedP of P with the corresponding input of Q.

4   Test Generation for DDAP Systems

In this section we present a novel technique for test generation by model checking for DDAP systems. The technique introduces an abstraction that exploits the dependency among the subsystems.

Definition 10 (DDAP Test). *A* test *for a DDAP system* $\langle P, Q \rangle$ *is a finite trace* $(p_0, q_0), J_0, (p_1, q_1), \ldots, (p_{n-1}, q_{n-1}), J_{n-1}, (p_n, q_n)$.

```
-> State: 1.1 <-                    -> Input: 1.3 <-                    -> Input: 1.7 <-
  procP.upP = FALSE                   _process_selector_ = procP          _process_selector_ = procQ
  procP.downP = FALSE                 running = FALSE                     procQ.running = TRUE
  procP.digitP = 0                    procP.running = TRUE                procP.running = FALSE
  procP.unlockedP = FALSE           -> State: 1.3 <-                    -> State: 1.7 <-
  procQ.upQ = FALSE                   procP.digitP = 1                    procQ.digitQ = 1
  procQ.downQ = FALSE               -> Input: 1.4 <-                    -> Input: 1.8 <-
  procQ.unlockedP = FALSE           -> State: 1.4 <-                    -> State: 1.8 <-
  procQ.digitQ = 0                    procP.digitP = 2                    procP.upP = FALSE
  procQ.unlockedQ = FALSE           -> Input: 1.5 <-                     procP.downP = FALSE
  procP.keyP = 4                    -> State: 1.5 <-                     procQ.upQ = FALSE
  procQ.keyQ = 2trap                  procP.digitP = 3                    procQ.digitQ = 2
-> Input: 1.2 <-                    -> Input: 1.6 <-                     procQ.unlockedQ = TRUE
  _process_selector_ = main        -> State: 1.6 <-
  running = TRUE                      procP.downP = TRUE
  procQ.running = FALSE               procP.digitP = 4
  procP.running = FALSE               procP.unlockedP = TRUE
-> State: 1.2 <-                      procQ.upQ = TRUE
  procP.upP = TRUE                    procQ.unlockedP = TRUE
```

Fig. 2. Witness for the test predicate $\mathbf{F}(\mathtt{procQ.unlockedQ})$

Definition 11 (Soundness). *A test generation method for DDAP systems is sound if each produced sequence is a test for the DDAP.*

If a DDAP system is specified as a *whole model* (as described in Section 3.1), the technique presented in Section 2.3 can be used to generate tests for the DDAP. Let us call this technique M_{whole}.

Definition 12 (Completeness). *A test generation method M for DDAP systems is complete if M generates a test suite covering all the feasible test predicates of the whole model.*

Theorem 1. M_{whole} *is sound and complete.*

Example 5. Consider the DDAP system *SafeLock* shown in Codes 1, 2, and 3. A test predicate for the system (using M_{whole}) is $\mathbf{F}(\mathtt{procQ.unlockedQ})$, requiring that lock Q can become unlocked. In order to find a test for covering the test predicate, we check the trap property $!\mathbf{F}(\mathtt{procQ.unlockedQ})$, saying that Q never becomes unlocked. Since the test predicate is feasible, the trap property is violated and the returned counterexample is a witness for the test predicate. The counterexample is shown in Fig. 2; we can see that, in the last state of the sequence, the test predicate is covered because $\mathtt{procQ.unlockedQ}$ becomes true.

4.1 Decomposition by Dependency Abstraction

Given a test predicate *tp* over a DDAP system $\langle P, Q \rangle$, if *tp* contains only labels of P, one can apply the cone of influence (COI) abstraction technique [9], by not considering Q, and generating a test only for P. If the test predicate *tp* contains only labels of Q, instead, the application of COI is not effective, since it cannot simplify the model: indeed, P provides input values to Q and so both P and Q

Algorithm 1. Test generation algorithm M_{DD}

Require: Two specifications P and Q
Require: A test predicate tpQ for Q
Ensure: A test for the DDAP system
1:   $testQ \leftarrow \texttt{getWitness}(tpQ)$
2:   **if** $testQ \neq \texttt{UNFEASIBLE}$ **then**
3:     $inputSeq \leftarrow \texttt{getInputSeq}(testQ, P)$
4:     $rcP \leftarrow \texttt{getLTL}(inputSeq)$
5:     $testP \leftarrow \texttt{getWitness}(rcP)$
6:     **if** $testP \neq \texttt{UNFEASIBLE}$ **then**
7:       **return** $\texttt{merge}(testP, testQ)$
8:     **else**
9:       **return** UNKNOWN   ▷ It is unknown if the test predicate is feasible
10:    **end if**
11: **else**
12:    **return** UNFEASIBLE   ▷ The test predicate is unfeasible
13: **end if**

---

must be considered. A basic approach is to generate a test using M_{whole} that, however, may suffer from the state space explosion problem.

We propose an abstraction that exploits (un)dependency between inputs and outputs to decompose the complete system; the proposed test generation approach consists in generating two tests, one over Q and one P, and merging them later. Alg. 1 shows the test generation algorithm M_{DD} we propose.

Given a test predicate tpQ for Q, if tpQ is feasible, we compute its witness (line 1 in Alg. 1) by asking the model checker for a counterexample for the trap property $\neg tpQ$. The counterexample is a trace of Q

$$testQ = q_0, IQ_0, \ldots, q_m$$

where $q_0 \in S_Q^0$, and $IQ_j \subseteq IN_Q$ is the set of inputs of Q applied at state q_j to obtain state q_{j+1}, $j = 0, \ldots, m-1$. We identify the inputs coming from machine P (those of the dependency set) as $IQ_j \cap D$.

We split the sequence $testQ$ in subsequences σ_i, $i = 0, \ldots, n$, such that atomic propositions of the dependency set remain unchanged:

$$testQ = q_0, \sigma_0, \sigma_1, \ldots, \sigma_n$$

$$= q_0, \underbrace{\overbrace{IQ_0, q_1, \ldots, q_{k_1}}^{\sigma_0}}_{D_0}, \underbrace{\overbrace{IQ_{k_1}, q_{k_1+1}, \ldots, q_{k_2}}^{\sigma_1}}_{D_1}, \ldots,$$

$$\underbrace{\overbrace{IQ_{k_i}, q_{k_i+1}, \ldots, IQ_{k_{i+1}-1}, q_{k_{i+1}}}^{\sigma_i}}_{D_i}, \ldots, \underbrace{\overbrace{IQ_{k_n}, q_{k_n+1}, \ldots, q_m}^{\sigma_n}}_{D_n}$$

where $n < m$ and $0 = k_0 < \ldots < k_n < m$, and, for each σ_i, D_i is the set of inputs of the dependency set that are applied all over σ_i, i.e., $\forall j = k_i, \ldots, k_{i+1} - 1: IQ_j \cap D = D_i$.

Given the sequence $D_0, \ldots, D_n$ (called *inputSeq* in Alg. 1), we build a reachability condition rcP over P as LTL formula (line 4 in Alg. 1), requiring that $n + 1$ subsequent states (not necessarily contiguous) exist, in which P produces the output values D_i requested by Q to start the computation σ_i. It holds

$$rcP = \mathbf{F}\left(\bigwedge_{d_0 \in D_0} d_0 \wedge \mathbf{F}\left(\ldots \mathbf{F}\left(\bigwedge_{d_{n-1} \in D_{n-1}} d_{n-1} \wedge \mathbf{F}\left(\bigwedge_{d_n \in D_n} d_n\right)\right)\ldots\right)\right)$$

If rcP is feasible, we compute its witness as counterexample for the trap property $\neg rcP$ (line 5 in Alg. 1)

$$testP = p_0, IP_0, \ldots, p_t$$

P produces the output values D_i in the $n + 1$ states $p_{h_1}, p_{h_2}, \ldots, p_{h_n}, p_t$. We split the sequence $testP$ after states $p_0, p_{h_1}, p_{h_2}, \ldots, p_{h_n}$, obtaining the following computation segments

$$testP = p_0, \delta_0, \delta_1, \ldots, \delta_n$$

$$= p_0, \overbrace{IP_0, p_1, \ldots, p_{h_1}}^{\delta_0}, \overbrace{IP_{h_1}, p_{h_1+1}, \ldots, p_{h_2}}^{\delta_1}, \ldots,$$
$$\underbrace{}_{D_0} \quad \underbrace{}_{D_1}$$

$$\overbrace{IP_{h_i}, p_{h_i+1}, \ldots, IP_{h_{i+1}-1}, p_{h_{i+1}}}^{\delta_i}, \ldots, \overbrace{IP_{h_n}, p_{h_n+1}, \ldots, p_t}^{\delta_n}$$
$$\underbrace{}_{D_i} \quad \underbrace{}_{D_n}$$

with $0 = h_0 < h_1 < \ldots < h_n < t$, and where $p_0 \in S_P^0$ and $IP_j \subseteq IN_P$ is the set of inputs of P applied at state p_j to obtain state p_{j+1}. In the last state $p_{h_{i+1}}$ of a subsequence δ_i, P produces the output values D_i necessary to Q for beginning the subsequence σ_i, i.e., $\mathcal{L}_P(p_{h_{i+1}}) \cap D = D_i$.

The test for the DDAP system can be built, as described below, using information coming from $testP$ and $testQ$ (line 7 in Alg. 1).

Let $\langle \delta_i \circ q \rangle$ indicate the sequence $IP_{h_i}, (p_{h_i+1}, q), \ldots, (p_{h_{i+1}}, q)$ of the DDAP system in which P executes δ_i and Q keeps still at state q.

Let $\langle \sigma_i \circ p \rangle$ indicate the sequence $IQ_{k_i} \setminus D, (p, q_{k_i+1}), \ldots, (p, q_{k_{i+1}})$ of the DDAP system in which Q executes σ_i and P keeps still at state p.

A test for the DDAP system is the sequence

$$testPQ = (p_0, q_0), \langle \delta_0 \circ q_0 \rangle, \langle \sigma_0 \circ p_{h_1} \rangle, \langle \delta_1 \circ q_{k_1} \rangle, \ldots,$$
$$\langle \sigma_{i-1} \circ p_{h_i} \rangle, \langle \delta_i \circ q_{k_i} \rangle, \langle \sigma_i \circ p_{h_{i+1}} \rangle, \ldots, \langle \delta_n \circ q_{k_n} \rangle, \langle \sigma_n \circ p_t \rangle$$

Example 6. In this example we show how to apply the decomposition by dependency abstraction to the safe lock system *SafeLock* presented in Example 2, for generating the test that covers the test predicate $\mathbf{F}(\texttt{unlockedQ})$ in component Q. The test built for Q is

$$testQ = s_0^q, \overbrace{\{\texttt{up}_\mathsf{Q}, \texttt{unlockedP}\}, s_1^q, \{\texttt{up}_\mathsf{Q}, \texttt{unlockedP}\}, \tilde{s}_2^q}^{\sigma_0}$$
$$\underbrace{\hspace{6cm}}_{D_0 = \{\texttt{unlockedP}\}}$$

The corresponding reachability condition on P is

$$rcP = \mathbf{F} \, (\texttt{unlockedP})$$

The test built for P is

$$testP = s_0^p, \overbrace{\{\texttt{up}_\texttt{P}\}, s_1^p, \{\texttt{up}_\texttt{P}\}, s_2^p, \{\texttt{up}_\texttt{P}\}, s_3^p, \{\texttt{up}_\texttt{P}\}, s_4^p}^{\delta_0}$$
$$\underbrace{}_{D_0 = \{\texttt{unlockedP}\}}$$

The test for the DDAP system is

$$testPQ = (s_0^p, s_0^q), \overbrace{\{\texttt{up}_\texttt{P}\}, (s_1^p, s_0^q), \{\texttt{up}_\texttt{P}\}, (s_2^p, s_0^q), \{\texttt{up}_\texttt{P}\}, (s_3^p, s_0^q), \{\texttt{up}_\texttt{P}\}, (s_4^p, s_0^q),}^{\langle \delta_0 \circ s_0^q \rangle}$$
$$\underbrace{\{\texttt{up}_\texttt{Q}\}, (s_4^p, s_1^q), \{\texttt{up}_\texttt{Q}\}, (s_4^p, \tilde{s}_2^q)}_{\langle \sigma_0 \circ s_4^p \rangle}$$

Theorem 2 (Soundness). *The test generation method M_{DD} is sound.*

Proof. Proving the soundness of the proposed technique M_{DD} corresponds to prove that $testPQ$ is a test for the DDAP system.

$testP$ is a valid trace for P because $\forall j = 0, \ldots, t-1$: $(p_j, IP_j, p_{j+1}) \in T_P$.
$testQ$ is a valid trace for Q because $\forall j = 0, \ldots, m-1$: $(q_j, IQ_j, q_{j+1}) \in T_Q$.
In Def. 9, (1) holds since $p_0 \in S_P^0$ and $q_0 \in S_Q^0$ (by def. of $testP$ and $testQ$).
In Def. 9, (2) holds for all the transitions of $testPQ$:

- for the initial transition $((p_0, q_0), IP_0, (p_1, q_0))$, because $(p_0, IP_0, p_1) \in T_P$;
- for the subsequent transitions $((p, q), I, (p', q'))$, since one of the following cases occurs:
  - if the transition is in a $\langle \delta_i \circ q_{k_i} \rangle$, then $(p, I, p') \in T_P \wedge q = q' = q_{k_i}$;
  - if the transition is in a $\langle \sigma_i \circ p_{h_{i+1}} \rangle$, then $(q, I \cup D_i, q') \in T_Q \wedge \mathcal{L}_P(p_{h_{i+1}}) \cap D = D_i \wedge p = p' = p_{h_{i+1}}$;
  - if the transition moves from $\langle \delta_i \circ q_{k_i} \rangle$ to $\langle \sigma_i \circ p_{h_{i+1}} \rangle$ (with $i = 0, \ldots, n$), then $(q, I \cup D_i, q') \in T_Q \wedge p = p' = p_{h_{i+1}}$, with $I = IQ_{k_i} \setminus D_i$, $q = q_{k_i}$, and $q' = q_{k_i+1}$;
  - if the transition moves from $\langle \sigma_{i-1} \circ p_{h_i} \rangle$ to $\langle \delta_i \circ q_{k_i} \rangle$ (with $i = 1, \ldots, n$), then $(p, I, p') \in T_P \wedge q = q' = q_{k_i}$, with $I = IP_{h_i}$, $p = p_{h_i}$, and $p' = p_{h_i+1}$.

Proposition 1 (Incompleteness). *The method M_{DD} is not complete.*

Proof. A test predicate in Q may be covered by more than one test; the model checking approach, however, returns only one test. It is easy to build a DDAP system for which, given a test predicate tpQ for Q, there exist two tests, $testQ$ and $testQ'$, for covering tpQ in Q, and such that P can provide the values required by $testQ'$, but not the values required by $testQ$. If the model checker returns $testQ$, the test predicate is not covered with M_{DD} (Alg. 1 returns UNKNOWN), although it can be covered using M_{whole}.

MODULE P	MODULE Q	MODULE main
VAR $-- OUT_P$	IVAR $-- IN_Q$	VAR
x: 1 .. 4; $-- D$	x: 1 .. 4; $-- D$	procP: **process** P;
ASSIGN	DEFINE	procQ: **process** Q;
x := {2, 4};	y := (x + 1) **mod** 3;	TRANS procP.x = procQ.x;

Code 4. Example of DDAP system for proving that M_{DD} is not complete

Let us consider the DDAP system shown in Code 4. In order to cover the test predicate $\mathbf{F}(\mathbf{y} = 2)$ in Q, M_{DD} can require by P either value 1 or value 4 for the input variable x. If the required value is 1, M_{DD} can not find a test on P to provide 1 as value for x, since x can only assume values 2 and 4 in P; so M_{DD} returns UNKNOWN. However, the test predicate can be covered with M_{whole} (which finds a witness for the corresponding test predicate $\mathbf{F}(\mathbf{procQ.y} = 2)$), and could be covered using M_{DD} as well, if Q would request 4 as input value for x.

5   Generalization to DDAP Systems with n Components

DDAP systems (see Def. 7) can be extended to systems with more than two components.

Definition 13 (n-DDAP System). *An n-DDAP system is a system having n components $C_1, \ldots, C_n$ (with $n \geq 2$) satisfying the following properties:*

- $C_i = \langle S_{C_i}, S_{C_i}^0, IN_{C_i}, OUT_{C_i}, T_{C_i}, \mathcal{L}_{C_i} \rangle$ *is a Kripke structure with inputs;*
- C_i *depends only on C_{i-1}, for each $i = 2, \ldots, n$; C_1 does not depend on any other component;*
- *only one system at a time is active (interleaving asynchronous parallelism).*

We can adapt the test generation approach presented in Alg. 1 for dealing with n-DDAP systems. Alg. 2 shows the modified algorithm M_{DD}^n. Given a test predicate for a component C_i, the algorithm builds a test for C_i (line 1). Then, if the test predicate is feasible, for each previous component C_j it computes the reachability condition that specifies the values that C_j must pass to C_{j+1} (lines 5 and 6). If a test satisfying the reachability condition can be built for C_j, such test is merged with the previous tests generated so far for components $C_{j+1}, \ldots, C_i$ (line 9). If for a component C_j the test cannot be built, M_{DD}^n returns the UNKNOWN result, otherwise, at the end, it returns a test for the n-DDAP system.

6   Initial Experiment

We run all the experiments on a Linux machine, Intel(R) Core(TM) i7 CPU, 4 GB RAM. We have developed NuSMV models in the NuSeen framework[1] which provides an interface to the NuSMV model checker [6] and to a model advisor for NuSMV specifications [4].

---

[1] https://code.google.com/a/eclipselabs.org/p/nuseen/

Algorithm 2. Test generation algorithm M_{DD}^n for n-DDAP systems

---

Require: An n-DDAP system $\{C_1, \ldots, C_n\}$
Require: A test predicate tp for a C_i
Ensure: A test for the n-DDAP system
 1: $componentTest \leftarrow$ getWitness(tp)
 2: $systemTest \leftarrow componentTest$
 3: **if** $componentTest \neq$ UNFEASIBLE **then**
 4:     **for** $j = i - 1, \ldots, 1$ **do**
 5:         $inputSeq \leftarrow$ getInputSeq($componentTest, C_j$)
 6:         $rc \leftarrow$ getLTL($inputSeq$)
 7:         $componentTest \leftarrow$ getWitness(rc)
 8:         **if** $componentTest \neq$ UNFEASIBLE **then**
 9:             $systemTest \leftarrow$ merge($componentTest, systemTest$)
10:         **else**
11:             **return** UNKNOWN   ▷ It is unknown if the test predicate is feasible
12:         **end if**
13:     **end for**
14: **else**
15:     **return** UNFEASIBLE   ▷ The test predicate is unfeasible
16: **end if**
17: **return** $systemTest$

We have experimented our approach on the n-DDAP system n-*SafeLock*, an extension of the DDAP system *SafeLock* described in Example 2. n-*SafeLock* is composed of n locks $L_1, \ldots, L_n$, such that each lock L_i is unlocked if it contains the correct digit and (except for L_1) if the previous lock is unlocked. We have applied the basic technique M_{whole} and the proposed technique M_{DD}^n (see Alg. 2) on different instances of n-*SafeLock*, using an increasing number of locks n. For each experiment, we have always tried to cover the test predicate $\mathbf{F}(\texttt{unlockedLn})$ over the last lock L_n; all the test predicates are feasible. M_{whole} has find a test for each test predicate (as expected from Thm. 1); also M_{DD}^n has always obtained a test for the whole system (no UNKNOWN result).

Fig. 3 shows the experimental results. Fig. 3a shows the memory consumption (in terms of number of BBD nodes allocated) of the test generation using M_{whole} and using M_{DD}^n; we can see that, using M_{whole}, the required memory grows exponentially, whereas, using M_{DD}^n, it grows linearly. Fig. 3b shows the time taken by the two test generation methods (using a logarithmic); the required time grows exponentially using M_{whole}, whereas it grows linearly using M_{DD}^n. Note that M_{whole} calls the model checker only once, while M_{DD}^n does it n times. For small values of n, when the instantiation time constitutes the main part of the execution time, M_{whole} outperforms M_{DD}^n.

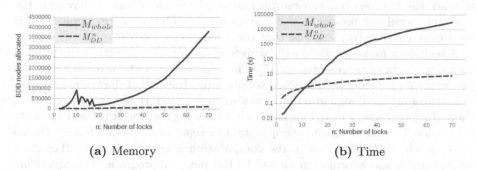

(a) Memory   (b) Time

Fig. 3. Experiment results

7   Related Work

In [2] we have proposed a test generation technique for *sequential nets* of Abstract State Machines (ASMs), which represent systems constituted by a set of ASMs such that only one ASM is active at a time. Given a net of ASMs, a test suite for every ASM in the net is built, and then the tests are combined in order to obtain a test suite for the entire system. Apart from the different notation, that technique shares with M_{DD} the fact that the generation of the tests is performed for the single subsystems that are subsequently combined. However, that technique only supports sequential systems, whereas M_{DD} supports interleaving asynchronous systems.

The technique presented in [2] has been extended in [3] for handling the passing of information between subsystems, in a similar way as done in M_{DD} with the dependency set. However, since the subsystems run in sequence, the information between two subsystems P and Q can only be passed by P to Q at the end of a P run in order to start a Q run; in M_{DD}, instead, P can pass information to Q several times in different states of their traces.

With respect to [2,3], the technique proposed here has required to handle, as test predicates, LTL temporal formulae. Moreover, tests are no more built by concatenating the tests for the single components, but by merging them.

Since our approach is based on model checking, we mainly relate to abstraction techniques for formal verification. The *cone of influence* (COI) technique [9] reduces the size of the transition graph by removing from the model the variables that do not influence the variables in the property one wants to check. In [18] COI is used to reduce the state space of *fFSM* models, a variant of Harel's Statecharts; models that could not be verified before, have been verified successfully after its application. The *data abstraction* technique [9], instead, consists in creating a mapping between the data values and a small set of abstract data values; the mapping, extended to states and transitions, usually reduces the state space, but it may not preserve properties. In [7] a technique to iteratively refine an abstract model is presented. The technique assures that, if a property is true in the abstract model, so it is in the initial model; if it is false in the abstract model, instead, the *spurious* counterexample may be the result of some behavior in the abstract model not present in the original model. The counterexample itself is used to refine the abstraction so that the *wrong* behavior is eliminated.

A technique for sequential *modular* decomposition for property verification of complex programs is presented in [17]. The approach consists in partitioning the program into sequentially composed subprograms (instead of the typical solution of partitioning the design into units running in parallel). Based on this partition, the authors present a model checking algorithm for software that arrives at its conclusion by examining each subprogram in separation. They identify *ending states* in the component where the computation is continued in another component and some information passed to the next subprogram. The algorithm then tries to formally prove the property in each component finding the necessary assumptions about the initial (entering) states of the component. The algorithm proceeds backwards until it finds that the property is true in every sub-component starting from any initial state of the system. Since the goal is formal verification, the algorithm must guarantee that the property holds in *any* state, while in our approach, since we want to find only a counterexample, we only need to find a path leading to interesting states.

An approach performing test generation by decomposing sequential *programs*, called SMART, is presented in [13]. It proposes a sequential decomposition technique: given a program calling several functions inside it, these called functions are tested in isolation and complete tests are composed only at the end. The main difference with our approach is that tests for sub-functions are not real tests but they are expressed as *summaries* using input preconditions and output postconditions, and then re-used when testing higher-level functions. The main advantage is that SMART is both sound and complete compared to monolithic test generation (like M_{whole}), while our approach is only sound. A disadvantage is that SMART must maintain the summaries and it can solve them only at the end. Sometimes constraints on some inputs can not be expressed (for instance a `hash` function) and sometimes all the collected constraints are very hard to solve, leaving some issues still open.

8   Conclusions

We have proposed a test generation approach by model checking for Decomposable by Dependency Asynchronous Parallel (DDAP) systems, i.e., systems composed by several subsystems connected together in a way that (part of) the inputs of one subsystem are provided by another subsystem. The approach is based on a decompositional abstraction: It builds tests for the single subsystems and combines them later in order to obtain a global system test. Such approach permits to mitigate the state explosion problem of model checking. The method has been proved to be sound but not complete.

As future work, we plan to apply the proposed technique M_{DD} to more complex systems, possibly leading to UNKNOWN results. This would require to improve M_{DD} to achieve its completeness, on the base of the following intuition. When

Alg. 1 returns the UNKNOWN result, it means that the value requested by test $testQ$ cannot be provided by P. In this case, the technique could ask for another test $testQ'$ for Q, and check if now the values requested by $testQ'$ can be provided by P; such procedure should be iterated until a test for the whole system is returned or no new test on Q can be found.

The approach M_{DD} is suitable for building tests for test predicates defined over AP_Q, i.e., the labels of only Q (or of only a component in an n–DDAP system). As future work, we plan to extend the technique for handling *general* test predicates built over all the labels of the system, i.e., over $AP_P \cup AP_Q$.

A further improvement could be dealing with systems in which one component may depend on several components. In this case, the dependency relation would be represented by an acyclic graph.

References

1. Ammann, P., Black, P.: Abstracting formal specifications to generate software tests via model checking. In: Proceedings of the 18th Digital Avionics Systems Conference, vol. 2, pp. 10.A.6-1–10.A.6-10 (1999)
2. Arcaini, P., Bolis, F., Gargantini, A.: Test Generation for Sequential Nets of Abstract State Machines. In: Derrick, J., Fitzgerald, J., Gnesi, S., Khurshid, S., Leuschel, M., Reeves, S., Riccobene, E. (eds.) ABZ 2012. LNCS, vol. 7316, pp. 36–50. Springer, Heidelberg (2012)
3. Arcaini, P., Gargantini, A.: Test Generation for Sequential Nets of Abstract State Machines with Information Passing. Science of Computer Programming (2014)
4. Arcaini, P., Gargantini, A., Riccobene, E.: A model advisor for NuSMV specifications. Innovations in Systems and Software Engineering 7(2), 97–107 (2011)
5. Browne, M.C.: An improved algorithm for the automatic verification of finite state systems using temporal logic. In: Proceedings, Symposium on Logic in Computer Science (LICS), Cambridge, Massachusetts, USA, June 16-18, pp. 260–266. IEEE Computer Society (1986)
6. Cimatti, A., Clarke, E., Giunchiglia, E., Giunchiglia, F., Pistore, M., Roveri, M., Sebastiani, R., Tacchella, A.: NuSMV Version 2: An OpenSource Tool for Symbolic Model Checking. In: Brinksma, E., Larsen, K.G. (eds.) CAV 2002. LNCS, vol. 2404, pp. 359–364. Springer, Heidelberg (2002)
7. Clarke, E., Grumberg, O., Jha, S., Lu, Y., Veith, H.: Counterexample-guided abstraction refinement for symbolic model checking. J. ACM 50, 752–794 (2003)
8. Clarke, E.M., Klieber, W., Nováček, M., Zuliani, P.: Model checking and the state explosion problem. In: Meyer, B., Nordio, M. (eds.) LASER 2011. LNCS, vol. 7682, pp. 1–30. Springer, Heidelberg (2012)
9. Clarke, E.M., Grumberg, O., Peled, D.A.: Model Checking. MIT Press (1999)
10. Fraser, G., Gargantini, A.: An evaluation of model checkers for specification based test case generation. In: ICST 2009, Denver, Colorado, USA, April 1-4, pp. 41–50. IEEE Computer Society (2009)
11. Fraser, G., Wotawa, F., Ammann, P.E.: Testing with model checkers: a survey. Software Testing, Verification and Reliability 19(3), 215–261 (2009)
12. Gargantini, A., Heitmeyer, C.L.: Using model checking to generate tests from requirements specifications. In: Wang, J., Lemoine, M. (eds.) ESEC 1999 and ESEC-FSE 1999. LNCS, vol. 1687, pp. 146–162. Springer, Heidelberg (1999)

13. Godefroid, P.: Compositional dynamic test generation. In: Proceedings of the 34th Annual ACM SIGPLAN-SIGACT Symposium on Principles of Programming Languages, POPL 2007, pp. 47–54. ACM, New York (2007)
14. Hierons, R., Derrick, J.: Editorial: special issue on specification-based testing. Software Testing, Verification and Reliability 10(4), 201–202 (2000)
15. Josko, B.: A context dependent equivalence relation between kripke structures. In: Clarke, E., Kurshan, R. (eds.) CAV 1990. LNCS, vol. 531, pp. 204–213. Springer, Heidelberg (1991)
16. Koo, H.-M., Mishra, P.: Functional test generation using design and property decomposition techniques. ACM Trans. Embed. Comput. Syst. 8(4), 32:1–32:33 (2009)
17. Laster, K., Grumberg, O.: Modular model checking of software. In: Steffen, B. (ed.) TACAS 1998. LNCS, vol. 1384, pp. 20–35. Springer, Heidelberg (1998)
18. Park, S., Kwon, G.: Avoidance of State Explosion Using Dependency Analysis in Model Checking Control Flow Model. In: Gavrilova, M.L., Gervasi, O., Kumar, V., Tan, C.J.K., Taniar, D., Laganá, A., Mun, Y., Choo, H. (eds.) ICCSA 2006. LNCS, vol. 3984, pp. 905–911. Springer, Heidelberg (2006)
19. Prenninger, W., Pretschner, A.: Abstractions for Model-Based Testing. Electron. Notes Theor. Comput. Sci. 116, 59–71 (2005)
20. Utting, M., Legeard, B.: Practical Model-Based Testing: A Tools Approach. Morgan-Kaufmann (2006)
21. Xu, B., Qian, J., Zhang, X., Wu, Z., Chen, L.: A brief survey of program slicing. SIGSOFT Softw. Eng. Notes 30(2), 1–36 (2005)

An All-in-One Toolkit
for Automated White-Box Testing*

Sébastien Bardin, Omar Chebaro, Mickaël Delahaye, and Nikolai Kosmatov

CEA, LIST, Gif-sur-Yvette, F-91191, France
first.name@cea.fr

Abstract. Automated white-box testing is a major issue in software engineering. Over the years, several tools have been proposed for supporting distinct parts of the testing process. Yet, these tools are mostly separated and most of them support only a fixed and restricted subset of testing criteria. We describe in this paper FRAMA-C/LTEST, a generic and integrated toolkit for automated white-box testing of C programs. LTEST provides a unified support of many different testing criteria as well as an easy integration of new criteria. Moreover, it is designed around three basic services (test coverage estimation, automatic test generation, detection of uncoverable objectives) covering most major aspects of white-box testing and taking benefit from a combination of static and dynamic analyses. Services can cooperate through a shared coverage database. Preliminary experiments demonstrate the possibilities and advantages of such cooperations.

1 Introduction

Automated white-box testing is a major issue in software engineering. Along the years, several tools have been proposed for supporting distinct parts of the testing process, such as test replay, coverage estimation or automatic test generation. Yet, these tools are mostly separated, and most of them support only a fixed and restricted subset of existing testing criteria.

Our main goals are (1) to provide tool support for most steps of the white-box testing process, and (2) to support a large range of coverage criteria and to offer flexible ways of adding new ones. We propose FRAMA-C/LTEST, a *generic* and *integrated* toolkit for automated white-box testing of C programs. It is generic in the sense that it supports a broad class of coverage criteria in a unified way, and integrated in the sense that it covers most major aspects of white-box testing. FRAMA-C/LTEST is implemented on top of the FRAMA-C verification platform [4] and relies on a combination of test generation and static analysis. More precisely:

- LTEST provides three basic services for test automation: coverage estimation, automatic test generation (ATG) and detection of uncoverable test objectives. Moreover, several coverage criteria are already supported, and adding new ones is straightforward. We achieved this by building the tool upon label coverage [2], a specification mechanism allowing to manage many existing criteria in a unified way.

---

* Work partially funded by EU FP7 (project STANCE, grant 317753) and French ANR (project BINSEC, grant ANR-12-INSE-0002).

M. Seidl and N. Tillmann (Eds.): TAP 2014, LNCS 8570, pp. 53–60, 2014.

- The toolkit is designed around four basic modules (program annotation, coverage estimation, ATG and detection of uncoverable labels) that advantageously combine static and dynamic analysis techniques and communicate through a shared database of coverage information. This modular architecture allows for flexible interactions between modules and gives opportunities for dedicated optimisations.
- We provide a summary of preliminary results demonstrating the benefits of our hybrid analysis approach, typical use-case scenarios and gains of our optimisations.

The paper is organized as follows. Section 2 provides necessary background on labels. An overview of the LTEST platform is given in Section 3, including a description of the provided services, a typical use-case and implementation details. Section 4 presents a summary of experiments. Finally, related work is discussed in Section 5 and Section 6 concludes the paper.

2   Labels

Label coverage [2] provides a convenient and powerful specification mechanism for coverage criteria. *Labels* are predicates attached to program instructions. A program with labels is called an *annotated program*. A label is covered if a test execution reaches it and satisfies the predicate. Labels can faithfully emulate many standard coverage criteria, from decision or condition coverage to a substantial subset of weak mutations, allowing us to manage all of them in a unified way. Basically, for each test objective a new label is added to the program under test, such that covering the label in the annotated program is equivalent to covering the test objective in the program under test. The automatic insertion of adequate labels for a given coverage criterion is performed by a so-called *labelling function*. Several examples are presented in Fig. 1.

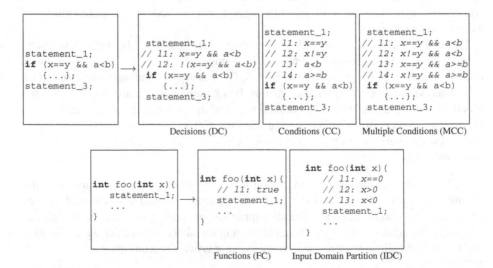

Fig. 1. Simulating standard coverage criteria with labels

Dynamic Symbolic Execution (DSE) [7,11] is a popular approach to automatic test generation, based on path exploration. We showed in previous work [2] how to extend DSE for handling labels with only very small overhead, while prior instrumentation-based approaches incur a blow-up of the search space [9]. We denote by DSE* this modified version of DSE.

3   Overview of the Platform

3.1   From the User Perspective

LTEST comes as a series of FRAMA-C plugins [4]. The toolkit offers the following main services:

Uncoverability Detection: the service detects uncoverable test objectives, i.e. those objectives which cannot be covered by any test datum. The information is primarily used by other modules, but it can also be exported for external use.

Coverage Estimation: the service replays a given test suite and reports its coverage. Coverage is given as a whole (all test objectives taken into account) and per criterion. Moreover, uncoverable or uncovered test objectives are reported.

ATG: the service produces a test suite which can be replayed for coverage estimation. In case a test suite has already been replayed, the ATG service will try to complete the achieved coverage rather than to start from scratch.

The platform currently supports the following test criteria [1,2]: decision coverage (DC), function coverage (FC), condition coverage (CC), multiple-condition coverage (MCC), weak mutation (WM, operators AOR, ROR, COR, ABS) and input domain partition (IDC). Moreover, coverage criteria can be combined together, test objectives can be restricted to certain procedures of the program under test and it is possible to add hand-written test objectives.

3.2   A Typical Use-Case

To illustrate the usage of the platform, let us consider a toy example. The function quadrant of Fig. 2 takes as inputs the coordinates of two points $P_1 = (x_1, y_1)$ and $P_2 = (x_2, y_2)$ on the plane and checks if they belong to the same quadrant.

Suppose we run LTEST first to generate labels for this function and choose the MCC coverage criterion [1]. Here, 16 labels will be added by the tool before each if statement, that is, 64 labels in total. For instance, the labels with the following conditions are added just before line 6 of Fig. 2:

$$x_1 \diamond 0 \ \wedge \ x_2 \diamond 0 \ \wedge \ y_1 \bullet 0 \ \wedge \ y_2 \bullet 0, \quad \text{where } \diamond \in \{\leq, >\}, \bullet \in \{\geq, <\}.$$

Next, we run the ATG service based on DSE*. It covers 58 of the 64 labels after exploring 409 (partial) program paths. The remaining 6 labels are indeed uncoverable. For example, the label $\psi = x_1 > 0 \ \wedge \ x_2 > 0 \ \wedge \ y_1 \geq 0 \ \wedge \ y_2 \geq 0$ added before the statement of line 6 is uncoverable since the condition ψ is weaker than the condition

```
1  // Checks if input points (x1,y1) and (x2,y2) lie in the same quadrant
2  // of the plane. Returns the quadrant number if so, otherwise returns 0.
3  int quadrant (int x1, int y1, int x2, int y2){
4    if(x1 >= 0 && x2 >= 0 && y1 >= 0 && y2 >= 0)
5      return 1;                              // (+,+): quadrant 1
6    if(x1 <= 0 && x2 <= 0 && y1 >= 0 && y2 >= 0)
7      return 2;                              // (-,+): quadrant 2
8    if(x1 <= 0 && x2 <= 0 && y1 <= 0 && y2 <= 0)
9      return 3;                              // (-,-): quadrant 3
10   if(x1 >= 0 && x2 >= 0 && y1 <= 0 && y2 <= 0)
11     return 4;                              // (+,-): quadrant 4
12   return 0;                                // not in the same quadrant
13 }
```

Fig. 2. Function quadrant

of the first if statement followed by a return (cf lines 4–5 in Fig. 2), so ψ cannot be satisfied at this program point. Similarly, two uncoverable labels are generated for line 8 and three for line 10, each of them being unsatisfiable because of the preceding if and return statements. Note that, here, using a standard DSE approach with a direct instrumentation instead of DSE* [2] would lead to exploring 3938 program paths.

To avoid wasting time trying to cover uncoverable labels, we can first run the uncoverability detection service based on static analysis, successfully marking the six uncoverable labels. The ATG service will now ignore them, exploring only 284 program paths (instead of 409) while still covering the same 58 labels.

3.3 Inside LTEST

The toolkit is designed around the notions of labels and annotated programs, and structured in four modules: LANNOTATE, LREPLAY, LUNCOV and LGENTEST. Modules can interact through shared information comprising the annotated program and a database mapping each label to its current status, namely: *covered*, *uncoverable*, *unknown* (i.e. neither covered nor proven uncoverable). LANNOTATE acts as a front-end: it annotates the program with labels according to the chosen criteria and creates the status database. The other modules provide user-level services. They can update label statuses and in some cases take advantage of them. Compared to the description given in Sec. 2, labels are equipped with a unique identifier used by the database and a "category" tag allowing their classification according to coverage criteria. Finally, besides annotated programs which are our core language and the primary input for DSE*, we use two closely related classes of instrumented programs for uncoverability detection (Fig. 3(b)) and test replay (Fig. 3(c)).

The whole architecture is depicted in Fig. 4. We give hereafter a few clues about the technologies behind each module.

LANNOTATE: The module implements the idea of labelling functions [2] and can be seen as a mapping

$$(\text{program}, \text{set of criteria}) \mapsto (\text{annotated program}, \text{status database}).$$

Given a C program and a set of supported criteria (listed in Sec. 3.1), LANNOTATE automatically computes a program annotated with the labels corresponding to the selected criteria. It also initializes the status database that can be used by other LTEST services.

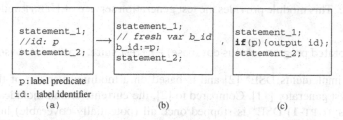

p : label predicate
id : label identifier

(a)   (b)   (c)

Fig. 3. An annotated program (a), its instrumentations for LUNCOV (b) and LREPLAY (c)

LANNOTATE contains an annotation function per criterion. The module relies on the FRAMA-C kernel services for program transformation [4], based themselves on the CIL library. More precisely, each annotation function takes as input the program's abstract syntax tree (AST), inserts the required labels for the target criterion, and outputs a new AST containing the labels. In addition to already supported criteria, users can extend the module by writing their own annotation functions. LANNOTATE provides facilities to easily insert labels into an AST and to collect all inserted labels into the shared status database. Note that annotated programs can be exported for external use.

LUNCOV: This module acts as a mapping

(annotated program, status database) ↦ status database.

Given an annotated program and its status database, LUNCOV runs static analysis to identify uncoverable labels and marks them as uncoverable in the database. A label can be uncoverable for example when it has an unreachable location (dead code) or an unsatisfiable condition.

The implementation of LUNCOV strongly relies on the value analysis plugin (VALUE) of FRAMA-C [4]. VALUE computes (an overapproximation of) the set of possible values of variables at each program point through abstract interpretation. Given an annotated program, we launch VALUE on the instrumented version depicted in Fig. 3(b): if VALUE reports that a "label variable" cannot be true, then the associated label is uncoverable. For example, in Fig. 3(b), if b_id cannot be true before statement_2, then either the execution cannot reach statement_2 or the predicate p cannot be satisfied. In both cases, it follows that label id in the original annotated program of Fig. 3(a) is uncoverable.

LREPLAY: The interface of this module can be seen as a mapping

(annotated program, test suite, status database) ↦ status database.

Given an annotated program and an existing test suite, the module runs each test on the instrumented version of Fig. 3(c) and inspects output traces in order to update label statuses in the status database. In addition, it computes coverage statistics for the given test suite.

LGENTEST: This module provides the test generation service of LTEST and performs the mapping

(annotated program, status database) ↦ (test suite, status database).

LGENTEST implements DSE* [2] and is based on a modified version of the PATH-CRAWLER test generator [11]. Compared to [2], the current version includes two new optimisations: (OPT-1) DSE* is stopped once all (potentially coverable) labels have been covered, and (OPT-2) already-covered labels (e.g. by another test suite) and un-coverable labels are ignored by DSE*. In this way, test generation effectively benefits from static analysis results computed by LUNCOV (cf Sec. 3.2 & 4).

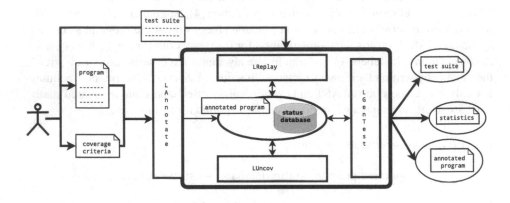

Fig. 4. Overview of LTEST Architecture

3.4 Implementation Details

The LTEST toolkit is built on top of the FRAMA-C verification platform for C pro-grams [4] (open source, LGPL). We took advantage of the plugin-based architecture of FRAMA-C as much as possible, reusing existing analyses of interest for our needs. The FRAMA-C kernel, LANNOTATE, LGENTEST and LUNCOV modules are written in OCaml. The LGENTEST module is based on a modified version of PATHCRAWLER [11], which is written in ECLiPSe/Prolog. The LTEST code is open source (LGPL), except the LGENTEST module, and available online.[1]

4 Experiments

Experiments[1]were conducted to evaluate the interest of the proposed combination of test generation with static analysis and the new optimizations of DSE* in LGENTEST.

---

[1] Source code, benchmark programs and a detailed description of experiments are available online at http://micdel.fr/ltest.html

We consider the same annotated benchmark programs and the same three coverage criteria (CC, MCC and WM) as in [2]. These are standard benchmark programs from the literature, coming from the Siemens test suite, the Verisec benchmark and MediaBench. Their sizes range from a few dozen to a few hundred lines of codes.

We compare the following variants of LGENTEST: the DSE* technique as described in [2], DSE*+s that includes in addition the stopping criterion (OPT-1, Sec. 3.3), and DSE*+u+s that exploits in addition uncoverable labels detected through a preliminary pass of LUNCOV (OPT-2, Sec. 3.3).

Our results are very promising. First, experiments confirm the interest of the stopping criterion. When full coverage is reached, test generation becomes in average 2.95× faster, and up to 600× faster on some examples. Second, LUNCOV is indeed able to detect several uncoverable objectives, and marks as uncoverable up to 35% of labels in some examples. This yields an improvement of reported coverage ratios by discarding uncoverable objectives. Coverage ratios can thus reach in some cases 100% of coverable objectives. Moreover, by combining the knowledge of statically-detected uncoverable objectives and the stopping criterion, test generation on programs with uncoverable objectives becomes in average 1.36× faster, the speedup going up to 11.52×. Note that the detection of uncoverable objectives takes a reasonable amount of time on our benchmark programs (12% of the total computation time in average, up to 30% on a few cases where test generation terminates quickly, but less than 3% when test generation takes more than 10s). Finally, these experiments underline the real synergy between the two optimisations: the stopping criterion is efficient as long as everything is coverable, while static analysis improves the performances of test generation by removing some uncoverable objectives.

5 Related Work

Many different automatic testing tools are available, from test suite coverage estimation and test replay to automatic test generation. Yet, these tools are usually limited to few services and to few coverage criteria. On the opposite, we aim at providing an integrated and generic toolbox for automated white-box testing.

Most DSE tools support only the basic decision coverage criterion, sometimes enhanced with some implicit "run-time error" coverage criterion (see [2] for a more detailed discussion). An interesting exception is APEX [9], which targets the .NET platform. It operates by adding additional predicates to path conditions during DSE, whereas LTEST annotates the code with predicates. Our approach is less ATG-centric since predicates can be reused outside test generation. In particular, we can use static analysis in order to detect uncoverable labels or measure the (weak) mutation score of a third party's test suite. In addition, LTEST's ATG service implements DSE* [2] dedicated to labels, drastically limiting the overhead observed for example with APEX.

The SANTE approach [3] combines static analysis and DSE in order to prove the absence or presence of run-time errors. The present work can be seen as an extension of SANTE, providing a larger choice of coverage criteria and a larger choice of services (test replay and completion), together with a more flexible combination scheme.

Several recent results have been obtained concerning the combinations of different formal methods inside a single tool [5,6]. FRAMA-C is primarily devoted to verification rather than testing: plugins collaborate in order to prove assertions written in the high-level language ACSL, cooperation is based on recording which assertions have been proved under which hypotheses [6]. The extensions SANTE and STADY [10] take advantage of dynamic analysis in order to disprove assertions as well. A similar combination has been studied using DAFNY and PEX [5]. While we also combine static and dynamic techniques, our goal is clearly the opposite: we target testing, and use static analysis for optimizing test generation and sharpening coverage measures.

6 Conclusion and Future Work

We propose FRAMA-C/LTEST, a generic and integrated toolkit for automated white-box testing of C programs implemented on top of the FRAMA-C verification platform and relying on a combination of test generation and static analysis.

LTEST can be used in black-box as a powerful testing tool. Yet, thanks to its modular architecture and open-source license, it can also be very useful as a basic building block for developing other advanced testing tools. In the future, we plan to explore additional cooperations with other FRAMA-C plugins and features. For example, we could take advantage of the expressive annotation language ACSL [4] for specifying richer test objectives.

References

1. Ammann, P., Offutt, A.J.: Introduction to software testing. Cambridge University Press (2008)
2. Bardin, S., Kosmatov, N., Cheynier, F.: Efficient Leveraging of Symbolic Execution to Advanced Coverage Criteria. In: ICST 2014. IEEE, Los Alamitos (2014)
3. Chebaro, O., Kosmatov, N., Giorgetti, A., Julliand, J.: Program slicing enhances a verification technique combining static and dynamic analysis. In: SAC 2012. ACM, New York (2012)
4. Cuoq, P., Kirchner, F., Kosmatov, N., Prevosto, V., Signoles, J., Yakobowski, B.: Frama-C - a software analysis perspective. In: Eleftherakis, G., Hinchey, M., Holcombe, M. (eds.) SEFM 2012. LNCS, vol. 7504, pp. 233–247. Springer, Heidelberg (2012)
5. Christakis, M., Müller, P., Wüstholz, V.: Collaborative verification and testing with explicit assumptions. In: Giannakopoulou, D., Méry, D. (eds.) FM 2012. LNCS, vol. 7436, pp. 132–146. Springer, Heidelberg (2012)
6. Correnson, L., Signoles, J.: Combining Analyses for C Program Verification. In: Stoelinga, M., Pinger, R. (eds.) FMICS 2012. LNCS, vol. 7437, pp. 108–130. Springer, Heidelberg (2012)
7. Godefroid, P., Klarlund, N., Sen, K.: DART: Directed Automated Random Testing. In: PLDI 2005. ACM, New York (2005)
8. Godefroid, P., Levin, M.Y., Molnar, D.: Automated Whitebox Fuzz Testing. In: NDSS 2008 (2008)
9. Jamrozik, K., Fraser, G., Tillman, N., de Halleux, J.: Generating Test Suites with Augmented Dynamic Symbolic Execution. In: Veanes, M., Viganò, L. (eds.) TAP 2013. LNCS, vol. 7942, pp. 152–167. Springer, Heidelberg (2013)
10. Petiot, G., Kosmatov, N., Giorgetti, A., Julliand, J.: How Test Generation Helps Software Specification and Deductive Verification in Frama-C. In: Seidl, M., Tillmann, N. (eds.) TAP 2014. LNCS, vol. 8570, pp. 204–211. Springer, Heidelberg (2014)
11. Williams, N., Marre, B., Mouy, P.: On-the-Fly Generation of K-Path Tests for C Functions. In: ASE 2004. IEEE, Los Alamitos (2004)

Behaviour Driven Development for Tests and Verification

Melanie Diepenbeck[1], Ulrich Kühne[1], Mathias Soeken[1,2], and Rolf Drechsler[1,2]

[1] Institute of Computer Science, University of Bremen, 28359 Bremen, Germany
[2] Cyber-Physical Systems, DFKI GmbH, 28359 Bremen, Germany
{diepenbeck,ulrichk,msoeken,drechsle}@informatik.uni-bremen.de

Abstract. The design of hardware systems is a challenging and error-prone task, where a signifcant portion of the effort is spent for testing and verification. Usually testing and verification are applied as a post-process to the implementation. Meanwhile, for the development of software, test-first approaches such as *test driven development* (TDD) have become increasingly important. In this paper, we propose a new design flow based on *behaviour driven development* (BDD), an extension of TDD, where acceptance tests written in natural language drive the implementation. We extend this idea by allowing the specification of properties in natural language and use them as a starting point in the design flow. The flow also includes an automatic generalisation of test cases to properties that are used for formal verification. In this way, testing and formal verification are combined in a seamless manner, while keeping the requirements — from which both tests and formal properties are derived — in a single consistent document. The approach has been implemented and evaluated on several examples to demonstrate the advantages of the proposed flow.

1 Introduction

In the design of hardware and software systems, testing and verification are often more labour and cost intensive than the implementation itself. The higher the quality standards — up to safety critical systems in cars, avionics, or medical equipment — the more time needs to be spent in writing good test benches or formal properties. In traditional hardware design flows, verification is often done at post-design time. This practice can result in long design cycles, since serious bugs discovered at this late stage might lead to major design changes or modifications of the specification. This is why it is desirable to start the validation as early as possible.

In the software domain, agile techniques have become quite popular, as a means to shorten the design cycles and achieve a more flexible flow, where changes can be integrated quickly. In *test driven design* (TDD), the tests are written first [1], which forces the designer to think about the requirements and interfaces before getting started with coding. *Behaviour driven development* (BDD) is an extension of TDD, where the tests are written in natural language [2]. In BDD, textual scenarios, which can easily be derived from the

M. Seidl and N. Tillmann (Eds.): TAP 2014, LNCS 8570, pp. 61–77, 2014.

requirements, provide a valuable link between the specification and the implementation. During the design process, the scenarios are ported step by step to executable tests. Writing tests and implementing the required code is interleaved, resulting in short design cycles. There have been some attempts to make use of agile techniques in the hardware domain [3], also with a focus on formal models and verification techniques [4, 5].

In the context of BDD, the natural language scenarios are usually used to describe acceptance tests, i.e. scenarios that test whether certain features are implemented according to the requirements. But, when applied to safety critical hardware designs, just testing is not enough. Since it is infeasible to cover the whole input and state space even of smaller hardware blocks by mere simulation, there remains a risk that subtle bugs will be missed. This is where formal methods come into play. Using automatic or semi-automatic proof techniques, high confidence can be reached in the correct functionality. In particular, SAT-based model checking techniques like [6–8] have been successfully applied to industrial scale hardware designs. However, their application is difficult and requires writing properties in dedicated languages such as the *property specification language* (PSL, [9]).

In this paper, we present for the first time a hardware design flow that completes the BDD method by complementing tests with formal verification techniques in a flexible and agile way. The methodology builds on the popular BDD tool *cucumber* [2]. We enhance the existing test driven flow by integrating formal verification, while keeping the natural language requirements in a single consistent document. As a first step to improve the design quality, test cases can be generalised automatically to PSL properties. This enables the use of model checking tools with no additional effort for the user. However, not all test cases can be generalised in this way. We add further flexibility by allowing to write requirements dedicated to formal verification only, that will be translated directly to PSL. This allows the use of more powerful constructs, which cannot easily be described by single test cases.

Overall, the contributions of this work are the following:

- Strengthening BDD for hardware design by automated test generalisation
- A seamless integration of tests and formal properties in a single human readable document
- The implementation within the popular BDD tool cucumber
- The experimental evaluation on several examples

The paper is structured as follows. First, the used property specification language and the basics of BDD are introduced in Sect. 2. The proposed BDD flow for hardware design and verification are presented in Sect. 3. Section 4 discusses advantages and limitations of our approach. Related work can be found in Sect. 5. The paper is concluded in Sect. 6.

2 Background

2.1 Property Specification Language

PSL has been adapted as IEEE standard 1850 in 2005 [9]. It is supported by many verification tools, both dynamic (simulative) and formal. PSL comes in different *flavors* for the hardware description languages VHDL, Verilog, and SystemVerilog, as well as for SystemC, a C++ library for hardware and system design.

The language is organised in *layers*, starting at the bottom with the Boolean layer, which consists of expressions from one of the flavor languages. On top of this, timing can be added in the temporal layer. Basically, PSL is a superset of *linear time logic* (LTL, [10]). Besides the standard operators such as `always`, `until`, and `next`[1], a convenient way to describe computations in PSL are *sequentially extended regular expressions* (SEREs). Like ordinary regular expressions, they allow for pattern matching and provide an easy way to express repetitions and concatenation, but focusing on temporal aspects. Finally, at the verification layer, directives are given to the verification tool, what to do with the stated properties. Here, we will only introduce a subset of this very rich standard. A good introduction to PSL for hardware verification can be found in [11].

Example 1. Consider the following simple PSL property:

```
property reset = always {rst; !rst} |-> pc == 0;
```

The operator `always` indicates that the following expression should be considered an invariant, which must hold at *every* single cycle in *any* computation. The invariant given by property `reset` is formed by the *overlapping suffix implication* operator '`|->`'. On the left hand side of the suffix implication, a SERE is formed, consisting of two cycles, where the signal `rst` is high in the first and low in the second cycle. The suffix implication has the following meaning: if the left hand side sequence occurs, then the right hand side must hold simultaneously to the last cycle of the sequence. Overall, the property `reset` states that after asserting and releasing signal `rst`, the signal `pc` must be set to zero. A slightly more complex property is stated below:

```
property release_req = always {{req; ack} | {req; rty}} |=> !req;
```

Here, the operator '`|=>`' is called *non-overlapping suffix implication*. The property holds if the right hand side holds in the cycle directly *after* the last cycle of the sequence on the left hand side. The left hand side SERE is a composition of two sequences, combined with the *non-length matching or* '`|`'. The left hand side matches if any of the two given sequences match. Overall, the property says that `req` should be released after it has been asserted and after either `ack` or `rty` has occurred.

Besides the operators in the above examples, we will use the *non-length matching and*, expressed by a single '`&`', which combines two sequences analogously to

---

[1] According, respectively, to G, U and X in LTL.

the non-length matching or. The built-in functions $\text{next}(\varphi)$ and $\text{prev}(\varphi)$ can be used to retrieve the value of an expression φ in the next or the previous cycle, respectively. The built-in function $\text{stable}(\varphi)$ is a shortcut for the expression $\varphi == \text{prev}(\varphi)$.

2.2 Running Examples

As a running example, a *first-in-first-out queue* (FIFO) and an *arithmetic-logic unit* (ALU) will be used. Figure 1 shows block diagrams of the designs under test. The FIFO is a synchronous circuit, driven by the clock signal clk. The single bit outputs empty and full give information on the fill status of the FIFO, while elems shows the exact number of elements currently in the queue. The oldest data element can be read from output dat_out. By asserting the input rst_n (active low), the FIFO is cleared. Elements are added and removed using the signals push and pop, respectively, where dat_in is used to present the data to be added to the queue. The actual design under test has a capacity of four elements.

The ALU in Fig. 1(b) computes 2-input logic and arithmetic functions. The type of function is selected via the five bit input func_i. The ALU implements 17 different functions, among them addition, shifting, multiplication and comparisons like equals or less. The single bit input signed_i indicates whether both the 32 bit data inputs are to be treated as signed or unsigned integers. The ALU is part of an open source hardware project.[2]

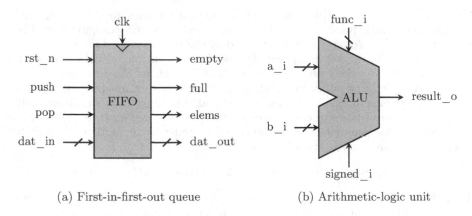

(a) First-in-first-out queue   (b) Arithmetic-logic unit

Fig. 1. Block diagrams of example circuits

2.3 Behaviour Driven Development

BDD extends the idea of TDD with natural language written user stories or acceptance tests, which are called *scenarios*. These are grouped by means of *features* and each scenario is described as a sequence of *sentences*.

---

[2] http://opencores.org/project,m1_core

Scenario Outline: *Pushing*
  When the FIFO is empty
  And I push <a>
  And I wait 1 cycle
  Then the output is <a>
  Examples:
    | a |
    | 1 |
    | 0 |
    | 127 |

(a) Scenario

```
When /^the FIFO is empty$/ do
  $assert( empty );
end

When /^I push (\d+)$/ do |arg|
  rst_n = 1;
  push = 1;
  pop  = 0;
  dat_in = arg;
end

Then /^the output is (\d+)$/ do |arg|
  $assert( dat_out == arg );
end
```

(b) Step definitions

Fig. 2. BDD scenario with step definitions

Example 2. Figure 2(a) shows an example scenario that describes how data is written (push operation) into the FIFO from the previous section. When an element is pushed to the empty queue, then it is the oldest element in the FIFO and therefore it can be read from the output.

In order to have a nicely readable text, the BDD flow suggest to use the keywords *Given, When,* and *Then,* that refer to test code containing assumptions, conditions, and assertions, respectively. Note that these keywords have no further semantic meaning in the BDD tool. The keyword *And* can be used to avoid repetition and one can also use * as a generic keyword to introduce a sentence. In fact, the keyword does not even have to match the keyword used in the step definitions. Consequently, *Then* sentences can e.g. also be used as *When* sentences.

To automatically execute a sentence in a scenario, one has to provide a *step definition* which is a 3-tuple consisting of a keyword, a regular expression, and test code. The BDD tool then essentially works as follows:

1. For each sentence in a scenario it is checked whether it is matched by a regular expression of a step definition. Step definitions are ordered and the first matching step definition is taken.
2. If necessary, values are extracted from the sentence using capture groups in the regular expression. Then, the test code is executed.

Since regular expressions are used in order to match a sentence to a step definition, there is no restriction on the natural language that is used to describe the scenarios (An exception is the approach that is presented in [12] and uses natural language processing techniques to extract structural information to create a formal model from a set of natural language scenarios). Optionally, it is possible to add special test code that is executed before and after each scenario. Every scenario is executed separately within its own test bench environment.

Example 2 (continued). For each sentence in the scenario the designer creates a step definition, as listed in Fig. 2(b). Since no implementation is available at this

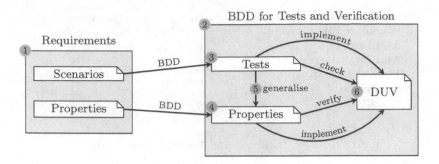

Fig. 3. Improved BDD flow

point, the designer only decides on the input and output signals of the FIFO module in the step definitions.

A predefined sentence "**And** I wait t cycles" handles timing where test code in succeeding sentences takes place t cycles after the sentence before this timing sentence.

This scenario can now be used for testing, however, step definitions cannot be run directly. Instead, they require a test bench that encloses the test code of all sentences of a scenario. This test bench can either be written by the designer or generated automatically from the design information given by the designed module.

In our examples we mainly use *scenario outlines* instead of scenarios. A scenario outline is a parameterised scenario which is enriched with an *examples table* that allows the specification of several test assignments given by each row in the table. The variables of a scenario outline, denoted e.g. with <a>, enable property generalisation, which will be shown in Sect. 3.1.

3   BDD for Tests and Verification

Based on the BDD flow that has been described in the previous section, the idea for the improved flow is introduced in this section. Our proposed flow is driven by tests and properties.

The first thing that is usually done in a BDD based approach is writing test cases in terms of scenarios to drive the implementation. This is a first step in verifying the *design under verification* (DUV), and helps in achieving a good design quality. Nevertheless, this is usually insufficient to completely verify the design, since the input and state space of non-trivial designs can hardly be covered by test runs. As a first improvement, it is possible to automatically *generalise* test cases to formal properties, thereby covering more potential bugs. However, some requirements cannot be easily stated as test cases. This holds especially for global properties like in the following example.

Example 3. Consider the FIFO example of Sect. 2.2 which has a capacity of four elements. In order to check this requirement of the FIFO, the designer needs to check two scenarios; (1) a scenario which checks if it is possible to insert at least four elements and (2) a scenario that checks that a fifth element cannot be inserted into the queue. Even then, possible bugs — like an underflow when popping from an empty queue — could be missed, which would violate this requirement.

Therefore, we propose to drive the implementation by both tests and properties, as shown on the left hand side of Fig. 3 (marked by 1), where requirements are described by scenarios and properties. For each sentence of each scenario and property, step definitions are defined to express the desired behaviour of a sentence using test code or PSL expressions. This code is then used to guide the implementation of the design (2). The properties and tests are used in all stages of the BDD approach to implement, test, and verify the DUV (3,4,6). By generalising tests to properties (5), the verification is strengthened. The generalisation even allows to reuse parts of a test scenario in a property.

In the remainder of this section it is described how test cases can be generalised, but also limitations are drawn. It is then shown how to overcome these limitations by writing properties in addition to scenarios to cover more requirements of the DUV.

3.1   From Tests to Generalised Properties

As described in Sect. 2.3, acceptance tests are used to create a circuit design using Verilog. The tests are created in a BDD manner, as shown in Fig. 3 and can be used to check the DUV.

Acceptance tests as illustrated in Example 2 usually consider only few selected test input data and never cover a scenario exhaustively. Such scenarios can be generalised in terms of a PSL property which covers the whole test input space. To obtain the PSL property, the structure of the scenario defined by the *Given-When-Then* keywords is mapped to an implication property. While the antecedent of the implication property is filled with the step definition code of all *When*-steps of a scenario, the consequent is filled with the step definition code of all *Then*-steps of scenario. In this way, the verification intent of the test scenario is captured in a PSL property. A property is generated as follows.

Algorithm P (*Property Generation*). Given a scenario and its step definitions, this algorithm generates a property for it.

P1. [Sorting step definitions.] The step definition code of every step of the scenario is mapped to the appropriate part of the property.

P2. [Resolve dependencies.] Since inputs and outputs need to be related, the parameters used to set the test input data inside the step definition must be replaced by the placeholder variable from the scenario.

P3. [Timing.] Timing information from all step definitions needs to be extracted. Every statement of the step definition code is assigned to one time step.

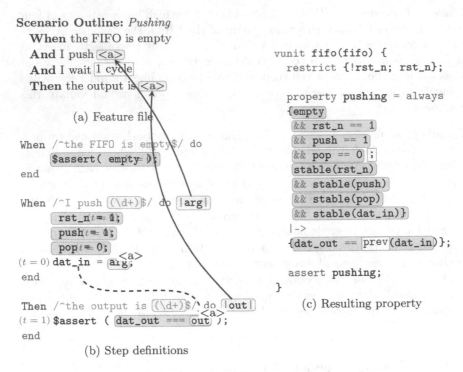

Scenario Outline: *Pushing*

When the FIFO is empty

And I push <a>

And I wait 1 cycle

Then the output is <a>

(a) Feature file

```
When /^the FIFO is empty$/ do
    $assert( empty );
end

When /^I push (\d+)$/ do |arg|
    rst_n t = 1;
    push t = 1;
    pop t = 0;
(t = 0) dat_in = arg;
end

Then /^the output is (\d+)$/ do |out|
(t = 1) $assert ( dat_out === out );
end
```

(b) Step definitions

```
vunit fifo(fifo) {
    restrict {!rst_n; rst_n};

    property pushing = always
    {empty
        && rst_n == 1
        && push == 1
        && pop == 0 ;
        stable(rst_n)
        && stable(push)
        && stable(pop)
        && stable(dat_in)}
    |->
    {dat_out == prev(dat_in)};

    assert pushing;
}
```

(c) Resulting property

Fig. 4. From a scenario to a generalised property

P4. [Test semantics.] In order to follow the same semantics as in the test, the property is extended by expressions that ensure the test semantics.

P5. [Assembling.] Assemble all statements of the antecedent and the consequent to SERE expression using the timing information of step P3 and the additional test expressions of step P4.

Figure 4 illustrates the briefly sketched algorithm P. All statements in Fig. 4(b) that have a grey background will be inserted into the appropriate part of the property, depending on whether the step is a *When* or *Then*-step, as described in step P1. The last statement of the second step definition is left out, because it only assigns test input data.

After that the dependencies between the inputs and the outputs are resolved. For this purpose, the implicit information of the *glue code* is used. The glue code is the part of the scenario and the step definitions that relates the input and output signals with placeholders such as <a>. Placeholders correspond to selected test input data. Since the same placeholder variables are used to target the same inputs and outputs in the scenario, it is possible to resolve the dependencies in the step code. In Fig. 4(b) the parameters **arg** and **out** are substituted by the placeholder <a>. This is indicated by the solid arrows that connect the parameters of the step definitions with the placeholder <a> in the scenario. Both mark the same input dat_in. For this reason, the parameter out can be replaced by the input dat_in in the last step definition, which is indicated by the dashed arrow.

For timing consideration each statement is annotated with a current time t. The timing of the statements can be seen in Fig. 4(b) on the left side of each statement. The predefined Timing sentence "**And** I wait t cycles" increments the current time step.

Before the complete property can be assembled, it is necessary to consider the test semantics first. While testing, the input signals are assigned imperatively. A new time step does not change the value of the signals unless explicitly specified. Since the imperative semantics of test code is not implicitly considered in properties for verification, these test semantics need to be ensured explicitly. For signals that do not change, a stable-expression is inserted to ensure the value of the signal stays the same. These statements can be seen in the resulting property in Fig. 4(c).

In the last step, the property is assembled using all gathered informations. The timing informations gathered in step P3 is used to assemble the SERE expression for the antecedent and consequent. This can be seen in Fig. 4(c) in the antecedent of property pushing where a ';' is added between the expressions of the first and the second time step. In the antecedent the second time step consists of all stable-assignments of all unchanged signals.

SEREs provide a concise and flexible way to express complex properties, in particular when compared to the initial approach in [13], which only allowed the translation of rather simple test cases. For instance, in this style, the generalisation of an if-then-else statement can be represented as follows:

{{{condition} & {if_assigns}} | {{!condition} & {else_assigns}}}

3.2   Limitation of Test Generalisation into Properties

The method to generalise properties as discussed in the previous section cannot be applied to all scenarios. Limitations of the approach are listed in the section, and two types of test cases that lead to invalid properties are illustrated.

Example 4. Consider the exemplary generalisation of the scenario for an addition operation of the ALU in Fig. 5. Figure 5(a) shows a valid scenario for this requirement. The step definitions for this scenario are given in Fig. 5(b). The first two step definitions set the inputs to the values from the examples table. When this test is generalised the design inputs a_i and b_i are detected as inputs that can have arbitrary values. The fourth step definition compares the result of the design output with the given value for <c> in the table. But the assertion of the design output result_o cannot be generalised since <c> cannot be mapped to anything in the design. That is because no input-output-relationship is known. This is shown in the property of Fig. 5(c) where arg is replaced by a question mark. Although <c> is the addition of <a> and <b>, the relation is never explicitly stated. Therefore this scenario can not be generalised and would be skipped.

Scenario Outline: *Adding*
  When I set the 1st operand to <a>
  And I set the 2nd operand to <b>
  And I want to add these
  Then the output should be <c>
  Examples:

a	b	c
10	15	25
20	15	35
-20	15	-5

(a) Feature file

```
① When /^I set the 1st operand to
        (\d+'b\d+)$/ do |arg|
      a_i = arg;
    end

② And /^I set the 2nd operand to
        (\d+'b\d+)$/ do |arg|
      b_i = arg;
    end

③ And /^I want to add these$/ do
      signed_i = 1;
      func_i = 4;
    end

④ Then /^the result should be
        (-?\d+)$/ do |arg|
      $assert( result_o === arg );
    end
```

(b) Step definitions

```
property addition_signed = always
    {signed_i==1 && func_i==4} |-> {result_o == ⑦ };
```

(c) Resulting property

Fig. 5. Missing input-output-relationship

The designer could make this scenario generalisable when she restates the last step to "**Then** the output should be the addition of **<a>** and **<b>**" and creates a complying step definition for it that explains the relation.

```
Then /^the result should be the sum of (-?\d+) and (-?\d+)$/
do |arg1, arg2|
    $assert( result_o === arg1 + arg2 );
end
```

There might also be test cases where generalisation does not yield a useful property. This is often the case when the relationship of the design *input* signals is relevant.

Example 5. Consider the relation operator '<' of the ALU module. A typical scenario for an acceptance reads as follows:

Scenario Outline: *less than*
  When I set the first operand to <a>
  And I set the second operand to <b>
  And I use the less-than operator
  Then the output should be true
  Examples:

(1)

a	b
10	15
400	512
-40	15

The property that is being generalised from this scenario and the corresponding step definitions is:

```
property less_than = always {signed_i==1 && func_i==13} |-> {result_o==1};
```

Although the property can be generalised it will fail when verifying it against the implementation. The relationship of the inputs `a_i` and `b_i` cannot be derived from the test case. A specific counter example for this property is that the design input `a_i` is set to 7, while `b_i` is set to 0. Therefore `a_i` (respectively `<a>`) is greater than `b_i` (respectively `<b>`). Again, this relationship has only been stated implicitly in the examples table. This is why the property will fail when considering arbitrary values of `<a>` and `<b>`.

In this case, the user needs to make the relationship explicit by adding it as an assumption. This can be done using *Given*-sentences. In the above example, the designer can fix the property by adding the sentence "**Given** `<a>` is less than `<b>`" to the beginning of the scenario. This *Given*-sentence is then translated to a global assumption, using an `assume` directive in PSL:

```
property is_less_than = always {a_i < b_i};
assume is_less_than;
```

The refactoring of scenarios can lead to a better code inspection and therefore improves the design understanding. In general, it is easy to rephrase the scenarios in order to apply property generalisation. But it may also be desirable to treat a scenario as a normal test case. We offer this possibility by annotating a scenario with a tag indicating it must not be generalised.

3.3 Specifying Properties

As motivated in the previous section, the property generalisation approach has its limitations. However, when disabling property generalisation for certain scenarios, an exhaustive consideration of the input space is no longer guaranteed. As an alternative, we extended the features to contain standalone properties next to scenarios. They work like scenarios with the difference that step definitions do not contain test code but PSL code to build the property. Consequently, properties are checked using an automatic formal verification tool and not executed as part of a test bench. On the level of the natural language requirements, there is no difference between plain properties and test cases.

A natural language property can be specified in two different ways: (1) as an implication property similar to the generated properties given by the *Given-When-Then*-structure or (2) as an invariant property without using the provided structure.

Specifying Natural Language Implication Properties. In the following we illustrate how to specify natural language implication properties. The structuring of this type of properties is very similar to the specification of scenarios.

Property: *Incrementing*
When the FIFO is not empty
And I push an element
And I wait 1 cycle
Then the number of elements has increased

(a) Property

```
When /^the FIFO is          When /^I push an element$/ do     Then /^the number of elements
    not empty$/ do          Verilog::add_antecedent do            has increased$/ do
Verilog::add_antecedent do      rst_n == 1 && push == 1       Verilog::add_consequent do
  !empty                        && pop == 0                       elems == prev(elems) + 1
end                         end                               end
end                         end                               end
```

(b) Step definitions

Fig. 6. Implication property

Example 6. Figure 6(a) shows how to write an implication property that states that the number of elements of a FIFO is increased whenever an element is pushed. The property looks very similar to a scenario which is used for testing, but instead of writing test code, the desired behaviour is expressed with PSL code. The step definitions in PSL are given in Fig. 6(b).

The PSL property code is written in a Verilog flavour. To build the property, the designer specifies for which part of the property, i.e. antecedent, consequent, or assume, the given PSL code is written. For each part an API command is provided.

Although this information could in principle be generated from the appropriate keywords (*When* as antecedents, *Then* as consequents, and *Given* as assumes), it is not generated automatically, so that properties can be written more flexible. In some cases those keywords are not suitable at all as described in the following section.

Specifying Natural Language Invariant Properties. When an implication structure is not needed to express a property, the usual *When* and *Then* keyword may be superfluous.

Example 7. As an example for a simple invariant, this property fixes the maximum amount of elements that can be stored in the FIFO.

Property: *Invariant*   (2)
 * The number of elements in the FIFO is at most 4.

The following step definition contains the PSL code for the property, stating that the number of elements shown at output `elems` will at most be 4:

```
Then /^the number of elements in the FIFO is at most 4\.$/ do
Verilog::add_antecedent do
  elems <= 4
end
end
```

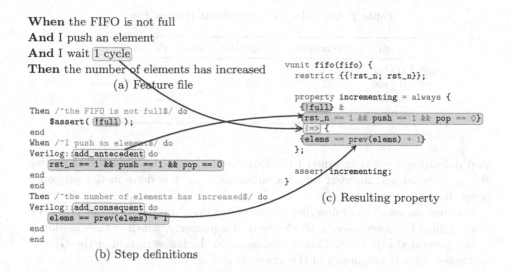

When the FIFO is not full
And I push an element
And I wait 1 cycle
Then the number of elements has increased

(a) Feature file

```
Then /^the FIFO is not full$/ do
    $assert( !full );
end
When /^I push an element$/ do
Verilog: add_antecedent do
    rst_n == 1 && push == 1 && pop == 0
end
end
Then /^the number of elements has increased$/ do
Verilog: add_consequent do
    elems == prev(elems) + 1
end
end
```

(b) Step definitions

```
vunit fifo(fifo) {
    restrict {{!rst_n; rst_n}};

property incrementing = always {
    {!full} &
    {rst_n == 1 && push == 1 && pop == 0}
} |=> {
    {elems == prev(elems) + 1}
};

assert incrementing;
}
```

(c) Resulting property

Fig. 7. Implementation

In this case it may seem that a comment to a PSL property would also suffice to describe the property, but the difference is that the natural language description also serves as a specification. Therefore the invariant property is an important part of the feature description of the design.

Assembling the Property. The property code in the step definitions needs to be assembled to a correct property in PSL syntax in order to be checked against the implementation. Similar to the property generalisation, the PSL code from the antecedent parts and the consequent parts of the step definitions are mapped to the antecedent and the consequent of the resulting property, as can be seen in Fig. 7.

The PSL code of each step is joined for the antecedent and consequent block, respectively. If the property code of the antecedent (respectively consequent) occurs in the same time step, they are assembled as parallel sequences using the *non-length matching and '&'* operator. Steps in consecutive cycles are treated using the concatenation operator ';' between the statements as it is done in the generalisation.

In the property in Fig. 7, the timing is explicitly stated by one of the steps that separates the antecedent and consequent blocks. Using the non-overlapping suffix implication operator '|=>' in the generated property, it is expressed that the consequent is expected to hold one cylce after the last cycle of the antecedent.

The first step definition in the example in Fig. 7 is particularly interesting, since it is written in Verilog test code. This example shows that it is additionally possible to reuse sentences that are used in acceptance tests. To add this test code to the resulting property it is necessary to generalise the statement. The

Table 1. Examples used to evaluate the new flow

Design	#Scenarios	#Properties	#Gen. Properties
FIFO	7	4	5
m1_alu	22	19	8
counter	1	4	1
hamming	6	5	2

step definition code is assumed to belong to the antecedent block due to the *When* keyword and inserted into the antecedent as it is done in the property generalisation.

Because *assume*-blocks describe global restrictions, an independent property is assembled for every *assume*-block given in a property, which is then assumed in the generated PSL code. This is analogous to the transcription of the *Given*-sentences. This is not shown in the example in Fig. 7.

4   Discussion

In this section we discuss the new flow which has been implemented on top of the *cucumber* tool in Ruby. We use WoLFram [14] as the underlying model checker. Our approach was applied to several examples which are listed in Table 1. The table states the number of specified scenarios and properties that have been used to drive the implementation in the first two columns. The third column states the number of properties that could be generalised from the specified scenarios. Every functionality of each example is verified using properties that have either been written or been generalised from the specified scenarios.

In the following we discuss the advantages that arise with the new proposed flow by referring to some of the examples on which we applied our approach. The first point to be noticed is the previously explained limitation of the property generalisation which is described in Sect. 3.2. In the proposed approach of [13] the generalised properties were the only possibility to formally verify the design. Therefore, it was sometimes necessary to rephrase the scenario or add a new step in order to create a valid property. While this is generally easy, it is rather uncommon when defining tests. In this case, the direct mapping from a scenario to a property is a convenient alternative.

In Fig. 8 the specification of scenarios and properties for the logical AND operation of the ALU example can be compared. It is apparent that stating the requirements in a scenario is more long-winded than the specification of the requirement as a property. This shows an advantage of this approach since requirements can be described more concisely which improves the discussion with stakeholders. This could be observed while specifying tests for the 17 functions of the ALU.

Scenario Outline: *and operation*
  When I set the first input to <a>
  And I set the second input to <b>
  And I use the AND operation
  Then the result is the logical
        AND of <a> and <b>
Examples:

a	b
2'b11	2'b00
2'b01	2'b10
2'b00	2'b00
2'b11	2'b01

Property *and operation*
  When I want to and two operands
  Then the result is the logical AND

Fig. 8. Scenarios vs. Properties

Also some requirements cannot be easily stated just using scenarios. Consider the invariant from the previous section that stated that the FIFO can only contain at most 4 entries.

Property: *Invariant*
  * the number of elements in the FIFO is at most 4

In order state this invariant as acceptance tests, the designer would need to write several scenarios. At least one that states that the FIFO *can* contain 4 elements and another one that states that the FIFO will not take a fifth element after four elements have been inserted. This is very laborious and not very concise. This observation has an important implication on the original idea of BDD; defining properties as "acceptance tests" completes the aspect of behaviour driven development.

However, it is not just that scenarios and properties can be defined in the same document and then tests and verification is used separately. It is even possible to use steps from scenarios that were only designed for testing in the specification of properties. The significance of this became very evident while applying the approach on the examples of Table 1. While implementing the FIFO one third of the step definitions in properties were reused from test scenarios. Even complete properties were defined using only steps from scenarios, but instead of resulting in executable test code creating a valid provable property.

5   Related Work

A first step in this direction has been presented in [13]. But this approach is one-sided since it only supports a test-based approach that generalises properties. Our new approach additionally supports a property-based BDD which goes hand in hand with the previously presented test-based BDD approach. It is also enhanced by a more advanced property generalisation that supports a more complex test bench design. Both tests and verification are the main driver for the implemented design.

Baumeister proposed an approach of a generalisation of tests to a formal specification in [15]. His work considers Java as target language where the specification is checked using generated JML. The drawback is that the approach does not facilitate an automatic generalisation of tests. In [16] a property driven development approach is presented where a UML model is developed together with a specification and tests in a TDD manner and OCL constraints are being added to the UML models while generalising test cases. But this approach is not implemented.

Agile techniques for hardware design are heavily discussed in several blog post [17]. One of the most promising approaches that was presented is SVUnit [3], which is a unit test framework created for SystemVerilog that enables TDD for circuit design.

The combination of formal techniques and agile design has been considered in [4]. There, Henzinger et al. propose a paradigm called "extreme model checking", where a model checker is used in an incremental fashion during the development of software programs. Another approach is called "extreme formal modeling" [18]. In contrast to our work, a formal model is derived first, which can then be used as a reference in the implementation process. The technique has also been applied to hardware [5].

6   Conclusions

We proposed a new BDD based flow that combines testing and verification in a seamless manner using natural language tests and properties as starting point for the design. For this purpose we introduced a new element for defining properties in natural language and supported the assembling of PSL code to valid properties that can be used for verification. This approach helps designers to write properties by starting from natural language. Our new flow supports the idea of *completeness driven development* (CDD) [19] by also defining properties as a starting point.

Further research will explore how to generate tests from properties written in BDD style. This can be useful to speed up regression tests during the design, when the formal verification of global properties would take too long. Future work will extend the specification language for properties to make scenarios and properties more expressive and to help the designer in writing properties more easily, especially if he or she is not a verification engineer.

Acknowledgments. This work was supported by the German Research Foundation (DFG) within the Reinhart Koselleck project DR 287/23-1 and by the Graduate School SyDe, funded by the German Excellence Initiative within the University of Bremen's institutional strategy.

References

1. Beck, K.: Test Driven Development. By Example. Addison-Wesley Longman, Amsterdam (2003)
2. Wynne, M., Hellesøy, A.: The Cucumber Book: Behaviour-Driven Development for Testers and Developers. The Pragmatic Bookshelf (January 2012)
3. Morris, B., Saxe, R.: svunit: Bringing Test Driven Design Into Functional Verification. In: SNUG (2009)
4. Henzinger, T.A., Jhala, R., Majumdar, R., Sanvido, M.A.A.: Extreme model checking. In: Dershowitz, N. (ed.) Verification: Theory and Practice. LNCS, vol. 2772, pp. 332–358. Springer, Heidelberg (2004)
5. Suhaib, S., Mathaikutty, D., Shukla, S., Berner, D.: Extreme formal modeling (XFM) for hardware models. In: Fifth International Workshop on Microprocessor Test and Verification, MTV 2004, pp. 30–35 (2004)
6. Biere, A., Cimatti, A., Clarke, E.M., Zhu, Y.: Symbolic Model Checking without BDDs. In: Cleaveland, W.R. (ed.) TACAS 1999. LNCS, vol. 1579, pp. 193–207. Springer, Heidelberg (1999)
7. Sheeran, M., Singh, S., Stålmarck, G.: Checking safety properties using induction and a SAT-solver. In: Johnson, S.D., Hunt Jr., W.A. (eds.) FMCAD 2000. LNCS, vol. 1954, pp. 108–125. Springer, Heidelberg (2000)
8. Bradley, A.R.: SAT-based model checking without unrolling. In: Jhala, R., Schmidt, D. (eds.) VMCAI 2011. LNCS, vol. 6538, pp. 70–87. Springer, Heidelberg (2011)
9. Accellera: Accellera property specification language reference manual, version 1.1 (2005), http://www.pslsugar.org
10. Pnueli, A.: The temporal logic of programs. In: FOCS, pp. 46–57. IEEE Computer Society (1977)
11. Eisner, C., Fisman, D.: A Practical Introduction to PSL. Integrated Circuits and Systems. Springer, Secaucus (2006)
12. Soeken, M., Wille, R., Drechsler, R.: Assisted behavior driven development using natural language processing. In: Furia, C.A., Nanz, S. (eds.) TOOLS 2012. LNCS, vol. 7304, pp. 269–287. Springer, Heidelberg (2012)
13. Diepenbeck, M., Soeken, M., Grosse, D., Drechsler, R.: Behavior driven development for circuit design and verification. In: Int'l Workshop on High Level Design Validation and Test Workshop (HLDVT), pp. 9–16 (November 2012)
14. Sülflow, A., Kühne, U., Fey, G., Grosse, D., Drechsler, R.: WoLFram – A word level framework for formal verification. In: Proceedings of the IEEE/IFIP International Symposium on Rapid System Prototyping, RSP 2009, pp. 11–17. IEEE (2009)
15. Baumeister, H.: Combining formal specifications with test driven development. In: Zannier, C., Erdogmus, H., Lindstrom, L. (eds.) XP/Agile Universe 2004. LNCS, vol. 3134, pp. 1–12. Springer, Heidelberg (2004)
16. Baumeister, H., Knapp, A., Wirsing, M.: Property-driven development. In: Proceedings of the Second International Conference on Software Engineering and Formal Methods, SEFM 2004, pp. 96–102. IEEE (2004)
17. Johnson, N., Morris, B.: AgileSoC (2012), http://www.agilesoc.com/
18. Suhaib, S.M., Mathaikutty, D.A., Shukla, S.K., Berner, D.: XFM: an incremental methodology for developing formal models. ACM Trans. Des. Autom. Electron. Syst. 10(4), 589–609 (2005)
19. Drechsler, R., Diepenbeck, M., Große, D., Kühne, U., Le, H.M., Seiter, J., Soeken, M., Wille, R.: Completeness-driven development. In: Ehrig, H., Engels, G., Kreowski, H.-J., Rozenberg, G. (eds.) ICGT 2012. LNCS, vol. 7562, pp. 38–50. Springer, Heidelberg (2012)

Quality Assurance in MBE Back and Forth

Sebastian Gabmeyer

Institute of Software Technology and Interactive Systems
Vienna University of Technology, Vienna, Austria
gabmeyer@big.tuwien.ac.at

Abstract. The maturing of model-based engineering (MBE) has led to
an increased interest and demand on the verification of MBE artifacts.
Numerous verification approaches have been proposed in the past and, in
fact, due to their diversity it is sometimes difficult to determine whether a
suitable approach for the verification task at hand exists. In the first part
of this tutorial, we thus present a classification for verification approaches
of MBE artifacts that allows us to categorize approaches, among others,
according to their intended verification goal and the capabilities of their
verification engine. Based thereon, we briefly overview the landscape of
existing verification approaches. In the second part, we iteratively build
and verify the behavioral correctness of a small software system with our
OCL-based model checker MocOCL.

1 Introduction

Software models and model transformations are the core development artifacts in
model-based engineering (MBE) [7,8]. Following the MBE paradigm, programs
are specified in terms of software models and the executable code and other deliv-
erables are generated through successive applications of model transformations.
Therefore, the correctness of the software models and the model transformations
correlates directly with the correctness of the generated artifacts. Hence, errors
made in the former most likely propagate to the latter. As a consequence, recent
years have seen an impressive rise of verification approaches that aim to prevent the propagation of defects from the modeling to the code layer by verifying
the system directly at the modeling layer. In fact, the diversity of the proposed
approaches, which stems from, e.g., the different verification scenarios that the
approaches support and the capabilities of their underlying verification engines,
make it hard to overview existing verification approaches.

In the first part of this tutorial we will thus review the state-of-the-art of verification approaches for MBE artifacts and present a classification that will help us
to categorize and compare these approaches [4,5]. We will focus, but not limit,
our presentation to formal verification techniques and, wherever appropriate,
highlight connections and possible applications to testing-based approaches. In
particular, we will survey model checking and theorem proving-based approaches
that

– check whether a set of models provides a consistent view onto the system,

M. Seidl and N. Tillmann (Eds.): TAP 2014, LNCS 8570, pp. 78–81, 2014.

- verify whether a transformation performs a semantically consistent conversion from the source to the target model, or
- assert whether the behavior of a model satisfies its specification.

Contrasting this theoretic presentation, the second part of the tutorial demonstrates an iterative, model-based development process that builds the implementation and specification of a small software system hand in hand. At the end of each iteration we assess the system's behavioral correctness by verifying that its implementation satisfies the specification. The software system's implementation consists of a MOF-conforming structural description and a set of model transformations that capture the system's behavior. The specification is formulated in cOCL [2], an extension that augments OCL [6] with temporal operators based on Computation Tree Logic (CTL) [3]. The verification is then conducted with MocOCL, a model checker for cOCL specifications [2].

2   Outline of the Tutorial

After motivating the need and usefulness of formal verification techniques in model-based engineering, we start with an introduction to the two predominant verification techniques, model checking and (interactive) theorem proving. Next, we analyze common verification tasks in MBE. These tasks can be categorized according to their *verification goal*. We will subsequently identify three such verification goals, namely *consistency checking*, *translation correctness*, and *behavioral correctness*. The identification of these goals leads naturally to a classification scheme for verification approaches. In the following, we amend this classification by additional categories. In particular, we refine the classification to distinguish approaches according to the input format of the problem description, that is, the type of software models they can verify. Further refinements of our classification allow us to categorize approaches according to the their verification technique, where we distinguish between model checking and theorem proving-based approaches. Final elaborations on the classification list different specification languages, that various approaches use to formulate/phrase verification properties, and formal encodings, which are generated from the inputted problem description and subsequently analyzed by the underlying verification engine. In this way, we develop a feature model that allows us to identify and compare suitable approaches for a given verification task quickly. Moreover, after categorizing existing approaches according to this feature-based classification we point out possible future research direction that have not or only partly been investigated according to our classification.

In the second part of the tutorial we present the explicit-state model checker MocOCL and show how it can be used to eliminate bugs in MBE artifacts. After a short discussion of its features, we will define structure and behavior of our running example. The system's static structure is captured by an Ecore model and its behavior is defined by model transformations. We will then formulate the cOCL specification and verify with MocOCL whether the modeled system satisfies this specification. The interpretation of the verification results will unveil, at first, that the specification is incorrect, and, after refining the specification, we notice that a bug in our implementation causes erroneous behavior. We fix the implementation and deem our model correct with respect to its specification after a final verification run.

3   cOCL and MocOCL

Among the insights that we derive during the discussion of existing verification approaches we also conclude that the majority of the presented approaches translates the models under verification into some lower level representation that corresponds to the input format of the underlying verification engine. For example, if the verification engine SPIN is used, the models are converted into PROMELA code. From a practical perspective, this requires to translate back the results produced by the verification engine to the modeling layer, and, from a theoretical perspective, it is necessary to verify whether the translation from model to low-level representation and back is indeed correct in order to trust the produced results. These considerations motivated the work on cOCL and MocOCL that allow us to verify the software system directly at the modeling layer; thus, translations between models and their verification representations are avoided.

In the following we introduce the concrete syntax of cOCL and discuss the verification workflow of our model checker MocOCL.

cOCL. The cOCL language extends OCL by five temporal operators, *Next*, *Globally*, *Eventually*, *Until*, and *Unless*, that must be preceded by a path quantifier, either *Always* or *Exists*. The semantics of these operators follow those defined for the branching-time logic CTL [3]. Expressions formulated with cOCL evaluate to Boolean values and must adhere to the following syntax definition:

$$(\textit{Always} \mid \textit{Exists})(\textit{Next } \varphi \mid \textit{Globally } \varphi \mid \textit{Eventually } \varphi \mid \varphi \textit{ Until } \psi \mid \varphi \textit{ Unless } \psi)$$

where φ, ψ are either Boolean OCL expressions or cOCL expressions. An OCL invariant can only assert properties of single states, whereas a cOCL expression allows us to formulate assertions over a sequence, or *path*, of system states. Consider, for example, the Dining Philosophers problem. We formulate the following cOCL expression to check whether it is possible that we finally reach a state from which a path starts where one of the philosophers is always *hungry*:

```
philosphers →
        exists( p | Exists Eventually Exists Globally p.status = St :: hungry)
```

If this property is found to hold, it shows that there exists at least one philosopher that starves forever. Further, we can check safety properties and assert with the following expression that the number of forks remains constant:

```
let initialNumForks = forks → size() in
                Always Globally forks → size() = initialNumForks
```

MoCOCL. The model checker MoCOCL verifies cOCL expressions. For this purpose, the modeler provides an Ecore (meta)model that defines the static structure of the system, a set of graph transformations that define the system's behavior, an initial model, and a cOCL expression as input. Starting with the initial model MoCOCL applies the graph transformations iteratively to incrementally derive new states represented by graphs. At each iteration it evaluates the cOCL expression and, if the evaluation fails, produces a counter-examples. Otherwise, MoCOCL continues its state space exploration until it either (*a*) concludes that the expression holds for the given system or (*b*) runs out of memory. In all but the last case, MoCOCL reports back the *cause* of the verification that explains why the cOCL expression evaluated successfully or why it failed.

Currently, MoCOCL uses HENSHIN [1] to apply graph transformations to Ecore models during the state space exploration. Moreover, it extends the OCL engine[1] integrated into Eclipse to evaluate cOCL expression over sequences of Ecore (instance) models. MoCOCL is available for download at http://modelevolution.org/prototypes/mococl.

References

1. Arendt, T., Biermann, E., Jurack, S., Krause, C., Taentzer, G.: Henshin: Advanced Concepts and Tools for In-Place EMF Model Transformations, pp. 121–135 (2010)
2. Bill, R., Gabmeyer, S., Kaufmann, P., Seidl, M.: OCL meets CTL: Towards CTL-Extended OCL Model Checking, pp. 13–22
3. Clarke, E.M., Emerson, E.A.: Design and Synthesis of Synchronization Skeletons Using Branching-Time Temporal Logic, pp. 52–71 (1981)
4. Gabmeyer, S., Brosch, P., Seidl, M.: A Classification of Model Checking-Based Verification Approaches for Software Models. In: Proceedings of the STAF Workshop on Verification of Model Transformations (VOLT 2013), pp. 1–7 (2013)
5. Gabmeyer, S., Kaufmann, P., Seidl, M.: A feature-based classification of formal verification techniques for software models. Tech. Rep. BIG-TR-2014-1, Institut für Softwaretechnik und Interaktive Systeme; Technische Universität Wien (2014), http://publik.tuwien.ac.at/files/PubDat_228585.pdf
6. OMG, O.M.G.: Object Constraint Language (OCL) V2.2. (February 2010), http://www.omg.org/spec/OCL/2.2/
7. Selic, B.: The Pragmatics of Model-driven Development. IEEE Software 20(5), 19–25 (2003)
8. Sendall, S., Kozaczynski, W.: Model transformation: The heart and soul of model-driven software development. IEEE Softw. 20(5), 42–45 (2003), http://dx.doi.org/10.1109/MS.2003.1231150

---

[1] http://projects.eclipse.org/projects/modeling.mdt.ocl

Visualizing Unbounded Symbolic Execution

Martin Hentschel, Reiner Hähnle, and Richard Bubel

TU Darmstadt, Dept. of Computer Science, Darmstadt, Germany
{hentschel,haehnle,bubel}@cs.tu-darmstadt.de

Abstract. We present an approach for representing and visualizing *all* possible symbolic execution paths of a program. This is achieved by integrating method contracts and loop invariants into a symbolic execution engine and rendering them visually in a suitable manner. We use the technique to create an omniscient visual symbolic state debugger for JAVA that can deal with unbounded loops and method calls.

1 Introduction

Symbolic execution [3,14] is a method to explore systematically *all* possible execution paths of a program for *all* possible input data. This property makes it into a powerful program analysis technique that is useful in a wide variety of application scenarios. Recently, symbolic execution enjoyed renewed interest and efficient implementations of symbolic execution engines for industrial programming languages are available (e.g., [2,4,5]). From its very inception, symbolic execution has been employed in two fundamentally different scenarios: (i) state exploration for the purpose of, for example, test case generation or debugging [14] and (ii) formal verification of programs against a functional property[3]. For the latter, program annotations in the form of loop invariants and method contracts, are necessary. Recent verification approaches use contract-based specification languages specific to the target language for this purpose, such as the Java Modeling Language (JML) [15] or SPEC# [1].

A main drawback of the second scenario is that meaningful contracts are often unavailable. But in fact also the first scenario cannot do without annotations in practice: loops with symbolic bounds and method calls quickly render symbolic execution infeasible or allow to explore only a fraction of all possible execution paths. As a remedy, compositional symbolic execution was proposed [10] where approximate contracts, so-called method summaries, are constructed on the fly.

In this paper we unify both strands of symbolic execution: our contribution is an approach for representing and visualizing *all* possible symbolic execution paths of a program. This is achieved by integrating method contracts and loop invariants into a symbolic execution engine and rendering them visually in a suitable manner. We use the technique in the context of computer-assisted debugging to deal with unbounded loops and method calls.

M. Seidl and N. Tillmann (Eds.): TAP 2014, LNCS 8570, pp. 82–98, 2014.

2 Symbolic Execution

Symbolic execution means to execute a program with symbolic values in lieu of concrete values. We explain symbolic execution by example: method sum() shown in Listing 1.1 takes an array a as argument and computes the sum of all of a's elements. If the passed reference a is **null**, an exception is thrown.

Listing 1.1. Sum of array elements

```
1  public static int sum(int[] a) throws Exception {
2    if (a == null) {
3      throw new Exception("Array is null.");
4    }
5    else {
6      int sum = 0;
7      for (int i = 0; i < a.length; i++) {
8        sum += a[i];
9      }
10     return sum;
11   }
12 }
```

For a JAVA method to be executed it must be called explicitly. For instance, the expression sum(**new int**[]{42}) invokes method sum() with a freshly created array of length one with content 42 as argument. This results in a single execution path: first line 2 is executed, i.e., the guard of the conditional is evaluated. The guard evaluates to **true**, so execution continues with lines 6–9, where the sum is computed. Execution finishes with the return statement in line 10. We note that concrete execution (i) requires fixture code to set up a specific state and to call the method of interest with specific arguments, and (ii) results (assuming a deterministic programming language) in a single execution path through the program.

Let us execute the same method symbolically, i.e., without a concrete argument, but a reference to a symbolic value a0 which can stand for any array object or **null**. The symbolic interpreter starts execution at line 2 and evaluates the guard of the conditional statement. As there is no information about the value of a0, one cannot rule out any of the two branches of the conditional statement. Consequently, the symbolic interpreter has to split execution into two continuations, (i) for the case where the condition a0 == **null** is true, and (ii) for its complement. These conditions are called *branch conditions*.

Symbolic execution on branch (i) continues with the **throw**-statement, while on branch (ii) it is concerned with the sum computation. We discuss branch (ii) in more detail: executing the next statement declares the local variable sum and initializes it with value 0. The symbolic state maintained by the interpreter looks then as follows:

$$a : a0 \ \{a0 \neq \textbf{null}\}$$
$$sum : 0$$

The left column lists all relevant (i.e., until now accessed) locations such as local variables, fields and array elements (here: a and sum), while the second column shows their symbolic value. (We consider concrete values as special cases of symbolic ones.) The third column lists possible constraints on symbolic values. These represent knowledge we have about a symbolic value either a priori from preconditions in specifications (see Section 3) or accumulated during symbolic execution from the branch conditions (here, we know a0 ≠ **null**).

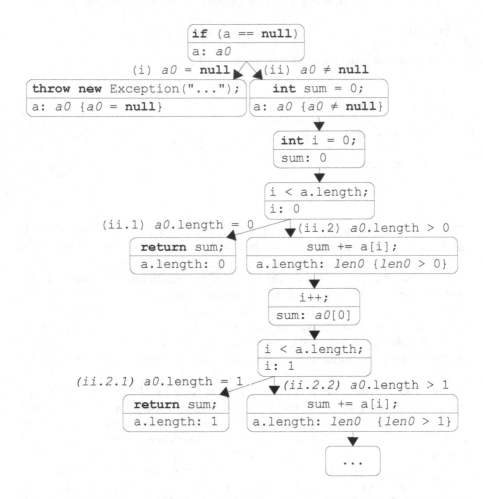

Fig. 1. Initial section of infinite symbolic execution tree of sum() from Listing 1.1

Now symbolic execution enters the loop. First the initializer of the counter i is executed. Then the loop guard i < a.length is tested, i.e., the interpreter attempts to determine whether 0 < a0.length holds. Clearly, the current symbolic state represents concrete states, where the condition is true, but also concrete states, where it is false. Hence, we obtain two new execution branches with branch conditions (ii.1) a0.length == 0 and (ii.2) a0.length > 0. Each execution path is determined by the conjunction of all branch conditions that occur on it. For a given path, this conjunction is called *path condition*.

In branch (ii.1) the loop exits and the **return** statement is executed. In branch (ii.2) the loop is entered and its body is executed. After execution of the loop body, the loop condition is evaluated again, causing further branching (with branch conditions (ii.2.1) a0.length == 1, (ii.2.2) a0.length > 1), etc.

The symbolic execution tree up to here is shown in Fig. 1. The top compartment of each node contains the statement to be executed *next* in the symbolic state shown in the optional bottom compartment. It lists the locations modified by its parent with name, symbolic value and optional constraints in braces. The complete symbolic state of a node consists of all variables defined in parent nodes with their most recent value and constraints. Branch conditions appear as annotations along the edges of branching nodes.

In contrast to concrete execution, symbolic execution does not require fixture code, but can start execution at any code position—newly encountered locations are initialized with a fresh symbolic value about which nothing is assumed. It generates a symbolic execution *tree* that represents *all* possible concrete execution paths (up to its depth): each symbolic execution path through the symbolic execution tree may represent infinitely many concrete executions and is determined by its path condition. Symbolic execution may not terminate in presence of loops, e.g., when iterating over data structures with unbounded symbolic length. In standard symbolic execution method calls are handled by inlining the method body of the callee. If multiple implementations for a method exist, symbolic execution creates one branch for each of them. Recursive methods exhibit the same problem as loops and can result in infinite symbolic execution trees.

The symbolic execution tree in Fig. 1 contains not all possible branches. For example, the one checking the array for being **null** during the access in line 8 is omitted, because it can be shown to be infeasible (its path condition is contradictory). Only feasible paths need to be explored.

3   Symbolic Execution with Specifications

We saw that symbolic execution of loops and recursive method calls leads to infinite symbolic execution trees. Our solution to this problem employs loop invariants and method contracts as known from program specification and verification. Method contracts do not only provide the means to render symbolic execution trees finite, but allow also to realize compositional symbolic execution. The necessity to have method contracts available is no principal limitation, because it is possible to use schematically generated, abstract contracts [12].

3.1   Symbolic Execution using Loop Invariants

Our solution uses similar techniques as in program verification to keep proof representations (proof trees) finite. To explain this better, we discuss briefly how loops are handled in program verification. For ease of presentation we consider only programs that contain local variables but no fields or arrays. For the same reason, we do not consider termination. A full presentation is in [2].

Finite representation of all possible loop executions can be achieved either by induction or by loop invariants. We focus on the latter approach which is technically somewhat simpler: assume we prove that if a program is started in a state satisfying property P then in its final state property Q holds. In Hoare-style notation this is usually written as "$\{P\}$ **while** (b) { body } rest; $\{Q\}$".

A loop invariant I is a property that is satisfied on entering a loop and is preserved throughout the execution of the loop, i.e., it has to hold at the beginning and the end of each loop iteration. We give the loop invariant rule in Hoare notation:

$$\text{loopInv} \ \frac{\begin{array}{ll} \vdash P \to I & (\textit{init}) \\ \{I \wedge \text{b}\} \text{ body } \{I\} & (\textit{preserves}) \\ \{I \wedge \neg\text{b}\} \text{ rest } \{Q\} & (\textit{use}) \end{array}}{\{P\} \textbf{ while } (\text{b}) \ \{ \text{ body } \} \text{ rest; } \{Q\}}$$

Here, $\vdash \phi$ is a first-order problem to be discharged by an first-order reasoning. The rule is applied bottom to top and splits a proof into three subgoals, where (*use*) marks the exit from the loop. The established invariant I is then used to prove the program rest following the loop.

Note that precondition P in the conclusion cannot be used to prove the (*preserves*) and (*use*) subgoals, because the execution of body might change the value of locations in P. This means that those parts of P that are not affected by body must be encoded into the invariant, which is clearly inefficient. For this reason, we track the set of locations that are modifiable in the loop body with a so-called *assignable* (or *modifies*) clause mod. In this case, P can be used to prove (*preserves*) and (*use*) provided that we execute the program in a state where we wiped out all knowledge about locations occurring in mod. This can be achieved by a kind of skolemization. Details and the generalization to fields and arrays are in [2].

Definition 1 (Loop Specification). *The pair $L = (I, mod)$ with I being a first-order formula and mod a set of locations is called a* loop specification.

The Java Modeling Language (JML) [15] is a popular specification language for JAVA programs that we use in the following to demonstrate our approach. Listing 1.2 shows a loop specification for the loop from Listing 1.1 in JML:

The loop invariant limits the range of i and stipulates that sum is equal to the sum of all array elements visited so far. The assignable clause lists all locations changed by the loop: the local variables i and sum.

We use loop specifications to finitely represent loop execution within symbolic execution trees. Assume we have a symbolic execution path p whose leaf n_l refers to a code position with a loop statement l as the next statement to be executed. Let $L = (I, mod)$ be the loop specification for loop l. Then, instead of unwinding

Listing 1.2. Loop invariant for loop in Listing 1.1

```
1 /*@ loop_invariant i >= 0 && i <= a.length &&
2 @                     sum == (\sum int j; 0<=j && j<i; a[j]);
3 @ assignable sum, i;
4 @*/
5 for (int i = 0; i < a.length; i++) { ... }
```

the loop, we create two new symbolic execution branches with root nodes n_{it} and n_{exit}. The subtree rooted at n_{it} represents the symbolic execution of an arbitrary loop iteration and n_{it} refers to the first statement of the loop body to be executed next, while n_{exit} represents the execution of the program after exiting the loop.

The corresponding branch conditions are $I \wedge$ b and $I \wedge \neg$b where I is the loop invariant as given by the loop specification L and b is the loop guard. The assignable clause of the loop specification is used to compute the symbolic states for the nodes n_{it} and n_{exit}. These symbolic states coincide with the state of n_l on all locations which are not contained in *mod* while the symbolic value of all locations contained in *mod* are replaced by fresh symbolic values. Note that there might exist already constraints on the fresh symbolic values. These constraints stem from the loop invariant and the branch condition.

The resulting symbolic execution tree for the array sum computation using the loop specification from Listing 1.2 is shown in Fig. 2. The values of the local variables i and sum in the assignable clause have been replaced by fresh symbolic values i0, sum0 and i1, sum1. The constraints shown in the bottom compartment of the nodes directly after the loop node are obtained using the branch condition.

Where do loop specifications come from? They can either be inferred automatically by various tools or simply provided by the user. In the latter case, the provided loop specification might be wrong or insufficient: one can always supply the trivial invariant **true**. We can construct the symbolic execution tree regardless of whether the invariant and assignable clause are provable, but if not, then we mark the corresponding node accordingly. Whether it is acceptable to consider a possibly incorrect symbolic execution tree or not is a decision to be made by the application using the tree.

3.2 Symbolic Execution Using Contracts

Next we look at using method contracts as an alternative to method inlining in symbolic execution. This has three major advantages: (i) symbolic execution becomes compositional and more robust against implementation changes, (ii) it becomes possible to create a finite symbolic execution tree for recursively defined methods with unbounded recursion depth; and, (iii) the size of the symbolic execution tree stays manageable compared to inlining.

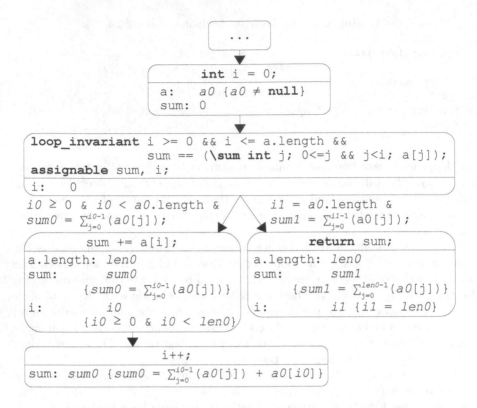

Fig. 2. Finite symbolic execution tree of sum() using loop invariant in Listing 1.2

We use the notion of a *method contract* (or simply contract) in the sense of the *design by contract* specification paradigm [17].

Definition 2 (Method Contract). *A method contract $C_m := (R, E, mod)$ of a method m consists of a precondition formula R, a postcondition formula E, and an assignable clause mod containing the locations modifiable by m.*

An implementation of a method m *satisfies* its contract if it guarantees that whenever m is called in a state satisfying R then E holds in the final state and it changes at most those locations contained in *mod*. There can be more than one method contract for a method.

JML permits to specify method contracts as structured JAVA comments. Listing 1.3 shows the contract for sum(). It consists of two specification cases (separated by **also**). The normal behavior case has a precondition (keyword **requires**), a postcondition (**ensures**), and an assignable clause (**assignable**). A method satisfies the normal behavior specification case if it satisfies the contract and terminates normally without throwing an uncaught exception. The exceptional specification case consists of a precondition, an exceptional postcondition (**signals**), and an assignable clause. A method satisfies the exceptional specification case if, when called in a state that satisfies the precondition, an exception is thrown and in the exit state the exceptional postcondition holds. Both specification cases can be encoded in terms of a single method contract. The details depend on the formalism used and are out of scope of this paper.

Listing 1.3. Specification of method sum()

```
1  /*@ normal_behavior
2  @ requires a != null;
3  @ ensures \result == (\sum int i; 0<=i && i<a.length; a[i]);
4  @ assignable \nothing;
5  @ also
6  @ exceptional_behavior
7  @ requires a == null;
8  @ signals (Exception e) true;
9  @ assignable \nothing;
10 @*/
11 public static int sum(/*@ nullable @*/ int[] a) throws Exception {...}
```

A method contract can be used instead of method inlining to represent a method invocation within a symbolic execution tree. We borrow the idea once again from program verification. The method contract application proof rule looks as follows (simplified for presentation purposes, e.g., ignoring null pointer exceptions and assignable clause):

$$\mathsf{mcApp}_{C_m} \frac{\vdash P \to R \qquad \{E\}\mathtt{rest};\{Q\}}{\{P\}o.m(\bar{v});\mathtt{rest};\{Q\}}$$

Here, the method contract is $C_m := (R, E, \_)$. The first subgoal establishes that before the invocation of m() on object o the precondition holds. In the second subgoal we assume that the postcondition holds and continue execution of the remaining program rest following the method invocation.

In symbolic execution tree construction, method contracts can be used instead of inlining as follows: let n_{before} denote a node with an invocation of method m as the statement to be executed next. Similar as in loop specification, we generate a node n_{after}, which represents the symbolic state directly after the invoked method returns and before the next statement is executed. The edge between n_{before} and n_{after} is labeled with the precondition R of method m. The assignable clause and postcondition are used to update the symbolic state in n_{after} similar as in the use case of loop invariant specification. All locations contained in the assignable clause are given a fresh symbolic value. Constraints on their values stem from the postcondition of the method contract.

We do not check whether the implementation of a method satisfies its contract. This is a task that has to be performed independently using program verification or other means. In this sense a symbolic execution tree is only correct relative to the correctness of the used contracts. We do, however, check whether the precondition of a method is satisfied at invocation time. If this check fails the invocation node is flagged. Another alternative would be to *generate* correct partial specifications by compositional symbolic execution and insert them.

The node representing the applied contract may have several children, if there are several exclusive specification cases. In this case, the branch condition of each child refers to the precondition of the corresponding specification case.

Method contracts provide also a solution with respect to branching induced by dynamic dispatch. In case of method inlining we have to branch over all possible method implementations as we can in general not determine the exact dynamic type of the callee. However, if Liskov's principle [16] is satisfied (JML enforces it by specification inheritance), branching can be avoided by using the method contract of the callee's static type.

Listing 1.4. Average of array elements

```
1 public static int average(int[] a) throws Exception {
2    try {
3        int sum = sum(a);
4        return sum / a.length;
5    }
6    catch (Exception e) {
7        throw new Exception("Can't␣compute␣average.");
8    }
9 }
```

We extend our previous example by the method average() shown in Listing 1.4, which computes the average of all array values by invoking sum(). The initial segment of the resulting symbolic execution tree in which the method specification from Listing 1.3 is applied is shown in Fig. 3.

The first statement in the **try**-clause declares sum and calls sum(), which is handled in the next node by using its contract. Since nothing is known about parameter a, execution splits into two branches. The left branch continues symbolic execution when the method terminates normally, while the right branch continues execution in case that an uncaught exception has been thrown during method execution. We stop symbolic execution just before the return statement in the left branch and before the throw statement in the right.

4   Application and Visualization

One important application of symbolic execution using specifications, is program understanding in the context of debugging. Interestingly, using symbolic execution to help debugging programs has been already suggested in one of the earliest papers on the subject [14].

Based on symbolic execution with specifications, as described in Sect. 3, we built an Eclipse extension called Symbolic Execution Debugger (SED) (available at www.key-project.org/eclipse/SED) that extends the Eclipse debug platform by symbolic execution and by visualization capabilities. SED is a complete

```
int sum = sum(a);
a: a0
```

```
normal_behavior
requires a != null;
ensures \result == (\sum int i;
                        0<=i && i<a.length; a[i]);
assignable \nothing;
also
exceptional_behavior
requires a == null;
signals (Exception e) true;
assignable \nothing;
```

$a0 \neq null$ $a0 = null$

```
return sum / a.length;
a:              a0
                {a0 ≠ null}
a.length:   len0
sum:            sum0
    {sum0 = Σ_{i=0}^{len0-1}(a0[i])}
```

```
throw new Exception("...");
a:  a0
        {a0 = null}
e:  e0
        {e0 instanceof Exception}
```

Fig. 3. Partial symbolic execution tree of method average() using contract of sum()

rewrite with extended functionality of an earlier tool [11], which (i) lacked the capability to use specifications, i.e., it could not represent unbounded loops and recursive method calls; (ii) provided an inferior visualization and state inspection compared to the approach presented in this paper.

SED works for nearly full sequential JAVA and realizes a symbolic execution engine based on the KeY verification system [2].

A major advantage of SED over standard interactive debuggers is that any method or (block of) statements can be executed directly without setting up a fixture. Being based on symbolic execution, SED lets the user debug simultaneously all feasible execution paths. One can focus on a path of interest and control symbolic execution by the usual navigation functions of debuggers, such as step into/step over or breakpoints. The symbolic execution tree is built up and visualized incrementally, its layout is done automatically. Users can inspect the symbolic state and symbolic call stack of any node as well as its path condition.

To be feasible, debugging needs to focus on a specific part of the code, such as a method, rather on an execution path trough the whole application [20]. To obtain a quick overview over a single method is possible thanks to the finite and usually compact symbolic execution trees that use specifications, which represent all possible execution paths. If all paths match the expected behavior, the user of SED can continue to systematically inspect called methods, where a method contract was applied during symbolic execution, or the callers. In combination with verification, failed proofs point directly to a possibly buggy method.

In the visualization we use icons and flags to underscore the semantics of different symbolic execution tree nodes. *Start* nodes mark the beginning of a symbolic execution run and represent the initial state in which the program fragment (any method or any block of statements) is executed. *Statement* nodes mark a symbolically executed statement and represent the state in which it is executed. There are several subtypes of statement nodes for conditional statements, loop statements, etc. In general, these cause branching. *Branch condition* nodes are used whenever execution splits to visualize the branch condition under which a path is taken. *Normal termination* and *exceptional termination* nodes indicate that a path terminates normally/exceptionally with an uncaught exception. *Method call* nodes are used to mark the entrance point to an invoked method if the method call is treated by inlining. In case of overwritten methods, branch condition nodes immediately prior to the method invocation represent the dynamic dispatch. *Method return* nodes indicate that an inlined method body has been executed completely. These nodes may contain return values. *Loop invariant* nodes show the used loop specification (according to Def. 1). A flag on these nodes indicates whether the loop invariant is initially satisfied or not. *Loop body termination* nodes are used in the loop invariant (*preserves*) branch of used loop specifications to indicate that execution stops. A flag on such nodes indicates whether the invariant still holds or not. *Method contract* nodes represent an applied method contract (according to Def. 2). A flag on the node indicates whether the precondition of the applied contract is fulfilled or not. An optional second flag shows whether the caller object can be `null`.

Listing 1.5 shows the buggy method `indexOf()`, which returns the first index of an object in the given array accepted by the filter and `-1` if no element is accepted. Objects are selected by method `accept()` of the `Filter` interface.

The corresponding symbolic execution tree is shown in Figure 4. As precondition `array != null && filter != null && \invariant_for(filter)` was assumed. The start node at the root defines the program fragment to execute, here a call to `indexOf()`, which is handled by inlining as shown by the following method call node. The method body is then symbolically executed and the next two statement nodes declare local variables `acceptedIndex` and `i`. At loop entry, the user decided to apply the loop specification to continue symbolic execution. Notice that the loop invariant is too weak for verification but powerful enough for debugging: *even obvious loop invariants are often helpful for debugging!*

After applying the loop invariant, two branch condition nodes increase readability. They are labeled *Body Preserves Invariant* and *Use Case*. In the Body Preserves Invariant branch the filter is queried whether it accepts the current array element. This splits execution since the array index can be outside of the array bound. In the left branch the array index is in bound and we handle the call of method `accept()` by applying its contract. This allows to continue execution without considering all available implementations of `Filter`. If the comparison result is true `acceptedIndex` is set to the value of `i` and execution stops after the loop body is completely executed. The crossed icon in the loop termination node indicates that the loop invariant is not preserved. The reason is that termination

Listing 1.5. Search in array

```java
public class Arrays {
    public static int indexOf(Object[] array, Filter filter) {
        int acceptedIndex = -1;
        int i = 0;
        /*@ loop_invariant i >= 0 && i <= array.length;
          @ decreasing array.length - i;
          @ assignable \strictly_nothing;
          @*/
        while (acceptedIndex < 0 && i <= array.length) {
            if (filter.accept(array[i])) {
                acceptedIndex = i;
            }
            else {
                i++;
            }
        }
        return i;
    }

    public static interface Filter {
        /*@ normal_behavior
          @ requires true;
          @ ensures true;
          @ assignable \strictly_nothing;
          @*/
        public boolean accept(/*@ nullable @*/ Object object);
    }
}
```

of the loop cannot be shown (the variant is not strictly monotonuosly decreasing). Otherwise if the comparison result is false, execution stops after merely increasing i. In the case when the current array index is not in bound, execution terminates with an uncaught exception. This is not an expected behavior and directly indicates that the loop guard is buggy.

This bug is also reflected in the branch condition for the Use Case. Inspecting the branch condition reveals that the statements after the loop are only executed, if acceptedIndex is non-negative, i.e., if no element is accepted, the return statement at the end is never reached.

In case an element has been accepted the return statement is executed and the value of variable i is returned as the method's result[1]. This indicates a second bug, because the value of acceptedIndex is the expected return value. Finally, the use case branch terminates normally.

---

[1] If multiple return values were possible, the method return node would show all of them, together with the condition when each is valid.

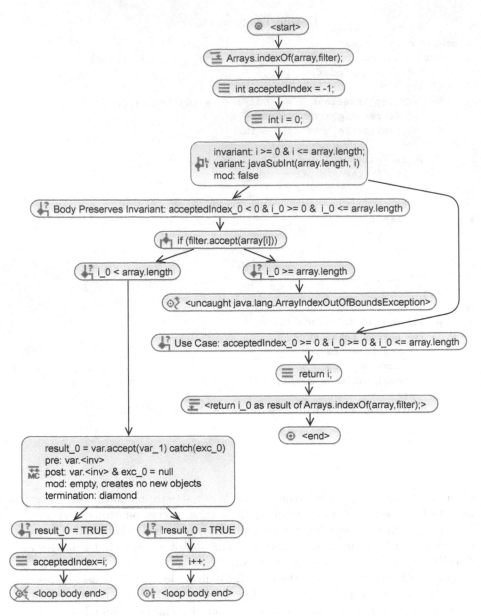

Fig. 4. Visualized symbolic execution tree of indexOf() in the SED (slightly beautified)

In this example no flags were raised for the loop invariant and method contract nodes. This means that the applied invariant was initially valid; likewise, the precondition of the applied method contract was fulfilled.

Fig. 5 shows the correct program code (fixed loop and return statement) together with the visualized symbolic execution tree produced by SED. We can immediately see, that (i) the `ArrayIndexOutOfBoundException` is no longer shown, (ii) the loop invariant can now be proven to be preserved, and, (iii) the returned result is the expected one, namely, the value of variable `acceptedIndex`.

```
1 while (acceptedIndex < 0 &&
2        i < array.length) {
3    if (filter.accept(array[i])) {
4       acceptedIndex = i;
5    }
6    i++;
7 }
8 return acceptedIndex;
```

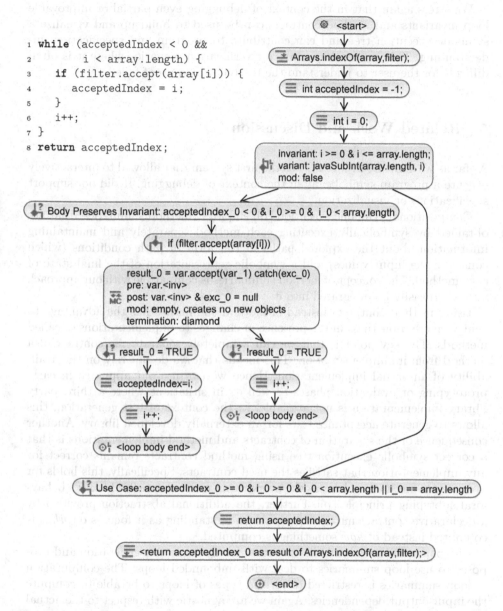

Fig. 5. Symbolic execution tree of the *correct* version of `indexOf()` (slightly beautified)

Thanks to the use of specifications we obtained a finite and compact symbolic execution tree that nevertheless represents the full program behavior. The developer can use this tree to verify that the program behavior matches her expectations.

We stress again that in the context of debugging even partial or unprovable loop invariants and method contracts can be used to build up and visualize a symbolic execution tree and can contribute to program and specification understanding. This is even important for verification scenarios where it is often difficult for the user to understand the reasons why a proof failed.

5   Related Work and Discussion

As far as we know EFFIGY [14] was the first system that allowed to interactively execute a program symbolically in the context of debugging. It did not support specifications or visualization.

Compositional symbolic execution [19] employs "method summaries" that are obtained by symbolically executing each method separately and maintaining information about the explored paths in the form of path conditions (which constrain the input values) and a symbolic representation of the final state of each method. The concept of method summaries is compatible with our approach and could easily be integrated into it.

Using method contracts instead of method summaries has the advantage to achieve more robustness in the presence of changes to implementations of called methods. The key point is that we can completely separate the contract of a method from its implementation. This means that we do not rely on the availability of an actual implementation. Hence we can use our approach in early prototyping or evaluation phases as well as in situations where a third party library implementation is not available. In the context of test generation, this allows to generate acceptance tests for an externally developed library. Another consequence of the separation of contracts and method implementations is that a correct symbolic execution tree using method contracts remains correct for any implementation that satisfies the used contracts. Specifically, this holds for overwritten methods as long as the overwriting method satisfies Liskov's behavioral subtyping principle [16]. Further, the additional abstraction provided by a declarative contract nurtures program understanding as it focuses on *what* is computed instead of *how* something is computed.

The paper [10] uses symbolic execution for dynamic test generation and proposes to use loop summaries to deal with unbounded loops. The computation of loop summaries is restricted to certain types of loops to be able to compute the input-output dependencies. Again we are agnostic with respect to the actual loop invariant generation method and not limited to a specific loop inference approach. Even though our approach is presented in a static symbolic execution setting, we expect it to be applicable also to dynamic symbolic execution strategies as presented in [5,13].

Behavior trees [6] are an abstract visual notation to specify the behavior of software systems. They are derived from a detailed requirements analysis rather than from source code and they do not represent symbolic states.

There is clearly a relation between symbolic execution trees and code representations used traditionally in static analysis, such as control flow graphs and program dependence graphs [18]. A main difference is that the latter do not contain symbolic state information (except indirectly, in the form of path conditions).

6   Conclusion and Future Work

We extended symbolic execution by the use of specifications to ensure that the resulting symbolic execution trees are finite even in presence of loops and recursive methods. The use of method contracts also makes execution more robust against implementation changes and allows symbolic execution even if the concrete implementation is not (yet) available. We applied our approach successfully in the context of debugging and presented a meaningful visualization of symbolic execution trees.

The support of JML contracts in SED means that any contract or loop invariant generation tool which outputs JML can be used to annotate the analyzed programs. Our approach to symbolic execution with specifications and to visualization could be implemented also for other languages than Java/JML, for example, Code Contracts [9].

An interesting class of programs for our approach are algorithms that are difficult to specify in a declarative manner, such as voting or incomplete optimization algorithms. A compact, visual representation of their behavior, such as it can be produced with SED, could be a useful description.

The SED could also be the basis of a tool that makes code inspections [8] more efficient and to increase the defect discovery rate. Another application scenario we plan to investigate in the future is to extend the test generation in KeY [7] to symbolic execution trees with specifications. One problem to be solved is that path conditions are no longer necessarily quantifier-free formulas which might impair the computation of test input values.

It would be interesting to formalize the relation between symbolic execution with specifications, control flow graphs, and program dependence graphs. As the underlying construction algorithms are rather different, it is likely that synergies can be gained from their combination.

We plan to use the visualization of a symbolic execution tree as an alternative graphical user interface for the KeY verification system [2]. The visualization capabilities and a debugger-like interface will flatten the learning curve to use a verification system. A thorough evaluation of our approach and its application to real world JAVA programs is in its planning stage.

References

1. Barnett, M., Leino, K.R.M., Schulte, W.: The spec# programming system: An overview. In: Barthe, G., Burdy, L., Huisman, M., Lanet, J.-L., Muntean, T. (eds.) CASSIS 2004. LNCS, vol. 3362, pp. 49–69. Springer, Heidelberg (2005)
2. Beckert, B., Hähnle, R., Schmitt, P.: Verification of Object-Oriented Software. LNCS, vol. 4334. Springer (2007)
3. Burstall, R.M.: Program proving as hand simulation with a little induction. In: Information Processing 1974, pp. 308–312. Elsevier/North-Holland (1974)
4. Cadar, C., Dunbar, D., Engler, D.R.: KLEE: unassisted and automatic generation of high-coverage tests for complex systems programs. In: Draves, R., van Renesse, R. (eds.) 8th USENIX Symp. on Operating Systems Design and Implementation, OSDI. USENIX Association, San Diego (2008)
5. De Halleux, J., Tillmann, N.: Parameterized unit testing with Pex. In: Beckert, B., Hähnle, R. (eds.) TAP 2008. LNCS, vol. 4966, pp. 171–181. Springer, Heidelberg (2008)
6. Dromey, R.G.: From requirements to design: Formalizing the key steps. In: 1st Intl. Conf. on Software Engineering and Formal Methods, SEFM. IEEE Computer Society, Brisbane (2003)
7. Engel, C., Hähnle, R.: Generating unit tests from formal proofs. In: Gurevich, Y., Meyer, B. (eds.) TAP 2007. LNCS, vol. 4454, pp. 169–188. Springer, Heidelberg (2007)
8. Fagan, M.E.: Design and code inspections to reduce errors in program development. IBM Systems Journal 15(3), 182–211 (1976)
9. Fähndrich, M., Barnett, M., Logozzo, F.: Code Contracts, http://research.microsoft.com/en-us/projects/contracts
10. Godefroid, P.: Compositional dynamic test generation. In: POPL, pp. 47–54 (2007)
11. Hähnle, R., Baum, M., Bubel, R., Rothe, M.: A visual interactive debugger based on symbolic execution. In: ASE, pp. 143–146 (2010)
12. Hähnle, R., Schaefer, I., Bubel, R.: Reuse in Software Verification by Abstract Method Calls. In: Bonacina, M.P. (ed.) CADE 2013. LNCS, vol. 7898, pp. 300–314. Springer, Heidelberg (2013)
13. Jamrozik, K., Fraser, G., Tillmann, N., Halleux, J.D.: Augmented dynamic symbolic execution. In: ASE, pp. 254–257. ACM (September 2012)
14. King, J.C.: Symbolic Execution and Program Testing. Communications of the ACM 19(7), 385–394 (1976)
15. Leavens, G.T., Poll, E., Clifton, C., Cheon, Y., Ruby, C., Cok, D., Müller, P., Kiniry, J., Chalin, P., Zimmerman, D.M.: JML Reference Manual (September 2009)
16. Liskov, B., Wing, J.M.: A behavioral notion of subtyping. ACM Trans. Program. Lang. Syst. 16(6), 1811–1841 (1994)
17. Meyer, B.: Applying "design by contract". IEEE Computer 25(10), 40–51 (1992)
18. Ottenstein, K.J., Ottenstein, L.M.: The program dependence graph in a software development environment. In: Riddle, W.E., Henderson, P.B. (eds.) Proc. of the ACM SIGSOFT/SIGPLAN Software Engineering Symposium on Practical Software Development Environments, pp. 177–184. ACM (1984)
19. Vanoverberghe, D., Piessens, F.: Theoretical Aspects of Compositional Symbolic Execution. In: Giannakopoulou, D., Orejas, F. (eds.) FASE 2011. LNCS, vol. 6603, pp. 247–261. Springer, Heidelberg (2011)
20. Zeller, A.: Why Programs Fail: A Guide to Systematic Debugging, 2nd edn. Elsevier (2009)

Filmstripping and Unrolling:
A Comparison of Verification Approaches
for UML and OCL Behavioral Models*

Frank Hilken, Philipp Niemann, Martin Gogolla, and Robert Wille

University of Bremen, Computer Science Department
D-28359 Bremen, Germany
{fhilken,pniemann,gogolla,rwille}@informatik.uni-bremen.de

Abstract. Guaranteeing the essential properties of a system early in
the design process is an important as well as challenging task. Modeling languages such as the UML allow for a formal description of structure and behavior by employing OCL class invariants and operation
pre- and postconditions. This enables the verification of a system description prior to implementation. For this purpose, first approaches
have recently been put forward. In particular, solutions relying on the
deductive power of constraint solvers are promising. Here, complementary approaches of how to formulate and transform respective UML and
OCL verification tasks into corresponding solver tasks have been proposed. However, the resulting methods have not yet been compared to
each other. In this contribution, we consider two verification approaches
for UML and OCL behavioral models and compare their methods and
the respective workflows with each other. By this, a better understanding of the advantages and disadvantages of these verification methods is
achieved.

1 Introduction

The *Unified Modeling Language* (UML) has been widely accepted as the standard
language for modeling and documentation of software systems. UML allows for
an initial description of a system at a high level of abstraction, i.e. before precise
implementation steps are performed. For this purpose, UML employs appropriate description means which hide implementation details while being expressive
enough to formally describe the structure and behavior of a complex system.
Additionally, the *Object Constraint Language* (OCL) can be applied to refine
a UML model with textual constraints describing further properties e.g. of the
respective components or defining pre- and postconditions of their operations.

The resulting models may be composed of numerous different components
with various relations, dependencies, or constraints and usually lead to non-
trivial descriptions where errors can easily arise. Hence, guaranteeing that the

---

* This work was partially funded by the German Research Foundation (DFG) under
grants GO 454/19-1 and WI 3401/5-1 as well as within the Reinhart Koselleck project
DR 287/23-1.

M. Seidl and N. Tillmann (Eds.): TAP 2014, LNCS 8570, pp. 99–116, 2014.

resulting descriptions are plausible and consistent is an important as well as challenging task. This motivated the development of approaches for the validation and verification of UML/OCL models.

In this contribution, we focus on the verification of behavioral models, i.e. descriptions employing operations whose functionality is provided by OCL pre- and postconditions. Due to the formal nature of the corresponding UML/OCL components, automatic reasoning engines can be utilized in order to check whether certain properties do or do not hold. In particular, solutions relying on the deductive power of constraint solvers such as Kodkod or for *SAT Modulo Theory* (SMT) have been shown to be promising [17,23]. Here, two complementary approaches of how to formulate and transform respective UML and OCL verification tasks into corresponding solver tasks have been proposed, namely

- a solution which transforms the given problem into a so called *filmstrip model* [14], i.e. an equivalent UML/OCL description in which all behavioral model elements and the verification task are represented by static descriptions and, afterwards, are checked for interesting properties, and
- a solution which *unrolls* the dynamic behavior resulting in a skeleton for all possible system states while constraints and the verification task are directly formulated by means of an SMT theory to be solved by a corresponding solving engine [23].

Both approaches represent proper solutions which address the respective UML and OCL verification tasks. However, while certain differences between both approaches are evident at a first glance (e.g. the use of relational logic versus the use of an SMT engine), a detailed comparison of them has not been conducted yet.

In this contribution, we conduct such a comparison. More precisely, we contrast the workflows of both verification approaches to each other and provide a step-by-step description of the respective steps for each of them. Using a recently proposed UML/OCL model representing the *dining philosophers* problem (taken from [4]), the application of both approaches is illustrated. By this, an in-depth understanding of respective benefits and drawbacks of these complementary verification approaches is provided. This enables a better comprehension of their potential and possible application scenarios.

The remainder of this contribution is structured as follows: Section 2 provides an overview of the workflows of both verification approaches including their respective workflow steps. Afterwards, each step is described and illustrated in more detail in Section 3 using the model of the *dining philosophers* problem. Based on that, a discussion on the benefits and drawbacks of the approaches is provided in Section 4 before related work is considered and conclusions are drawn in Section 5 and Section 6, respectively.

2   Conceptual Workflows

Before the considered verification approaches are described in detail, this section briefly reviews their conceptual workflows. For this purpose, the major steps are

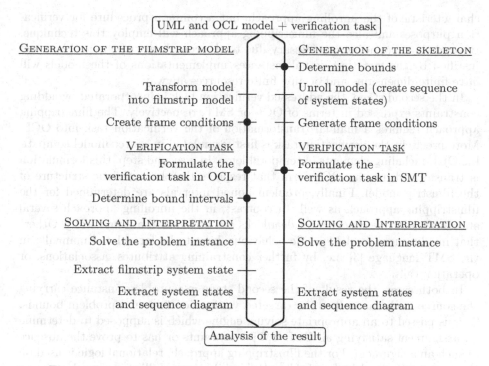

Fig. 1. Conceptual workflows of filmstripping (left) and unrolling (right)

illustrated in Fig. 1. Steps that require manual interaction are indicated by a bullet in order to distinguish them from steps that are performed automatically.

Both approaches take as input a UML model description enriched by OCL constraints together with a verification task which is to be performed on the model. Possible verification tasks comprise e.g. checking for deadlocks, verifying executability of operations, reachability of particular system states, or may address other behavioral aspects of the model.

First, the given UML/OCL model is extended in order to support the consideration of behavioral aspects. For the filmstripping approach, this includes an automatic transformation of the source model into the corresponding *filmstrip model* [14] followed by a manual creation of *frame conditions*, i.e. additional OCL constraints to limit the effects of the operation call to the relevant changes. For the unrolling approach, behavioral aspects are supported by automatically *unrolling* the model, i.e. creating an empty *skeleton* of system states (containing objects, their attributes and associations) for a certain number of observation points as well as operation calls connecting consecutive states. In contrast to the filmstripping approach, a (restricted set of) frame conditions is automatically generated. In order to create a skeleton of appropriate size, problem bounds (e.g. the number of observation points, the number of objects to be instantiated, or the range for primitive data types like integers to be considered) need to be fixed manually at this early stage. Note that bounding is not a special characteristic of the unrolling approach, but a common procedure for verification purposes and also the filmstripping approach will employ this technique. Beyond that, bounding is necessary due to the complexity of the problem and justified by the fact that actual instances/implementations of the models will have finite dimensions and occupy finite resources anyway.

In the second stage, the addressed verification task is incorporated by adding constraints expressed in terms of OCL or SMT, respectively. The filmstripping approach requires a manual transformation of the verification task into OCL. More precisely, the verification task is first formulated in source model compatible OCL including elements of temporal logic. In a second step, this formulation is transformed into an OCL form that respects the characteristic structure of the filmstrip model. Finally, problem bound intervals are determined for the filmstripping approach as well. In contrast, in the unrolling approach several standard tasks like checking for deadlocks can be handled automatically. Others that involve more model-specific behaviour, have to be formulated manually in the SMT language [3], i.e. by further constraining attributes, associations, or operation calls.

In both cases, the result of the second stage is a problem instance carrying the source model as well as the targeted verification task and problem bounds. This is passed to an appropriate solving engine which is supposed to determine an assignment satisfying all OCL/SMT constraints or has to prove the absence of such an assignment. For the filmstripping approach, relational logic is used on the basis of Kodkod [26] and Alloy [16], while the unrolling approach employs an SMT solver (like Boolector [6] or Z3 [9]). As a last step, both approaches translate the assignment retrieved from the solver back to the model context. The filmstripping approach provides an instance of the filmstrip model which contains all necessary information of the system states. Source model compatible object and sequence diagrams can be extracted if needed. Due to the different layer of abstraction, the unrolling approach extracts a sequence of system states (one for each observation point) and additionally creates a sequence diagram in order to provide the same information as contained in a (single) system state of the filmstrip model. Using this representation, the developer can analyze the result and draw conclusions with respect to the given verification task.

3   Comparison of the Verification Approaches

For a better comparison of the verification processes, they are exemplified using the same UML and OCL model (*dining philosophers*) and verification task (finding a deadlock) as a running example. We begin with the model definition and afterwards explain the approaches in detail separately.

3.1   Running Example Model Definition

The classic *dining philosophers* problem serves as an example to compare the verification approaches. The UML and OCL model is derived from [4] and

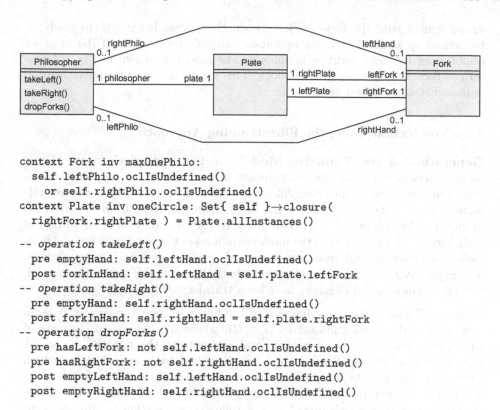

```
context Fork inv maxOnePhilo:
  self.leftPhilo.oclIsUndefined()
    or self.rightPhilo.oclIsUndefined()
context Plate inv oneCircle: Set{ self }→closure(
  rightFork.rightPlate ) = Plate.allInstances()

-- operation takeLeft()
  pre emptyHand: self.leftHand.oclIsUndefined()
  post forkInHand: self.leftHand = self.plate.leftFork
-- operation takeRight()
  pre emptyHand: self.rightHand.oclIsUndefined()
  post forkInHand: self.rightHand = self.plate.rightFork
-- operation dropForks()
  pre hasLeftFork: not self.leftHand.oclIsUndefined()
  pre hasRightFork: not self.rightHand.oclIsUndefined()
  post emptyLeftHand: self.leftHand.oclIsUndefined()
  post emptyRightHand: self.rightHand.oclIsUndefined()
```

Fig. 2. The dining philosophers model

slightly simplified. The well known problem of the forks, being shared by two philosophers each, has not changed. The model definition is shown in Fig. 2. A philosopher is connected to exactly one plate, which should not change during an execution period. Each plate has a left fork and a right fork, where two adjacent plates share one fork in between them, i.e. the left fork of one plate is the right fork of another plate. Lastly the philosopher is connected with the forks to model the picking up and dropping of forks.

The model embodies two additional constraints that cannot be expressed in UML. These requirements are specified as OCL invariants and shown at the bottom of Fig. 2. The first invariant Fork::maxOnePhilo enforces the important rule that a fork may only be used by a single philosopher at a time. The second invariant Plate::oneCircle assures a single circle of plates and forks. Otherwise the philosophers can split up into small groups that each have their own set of plates and forks.

The model dynamics are specified as pre- and postconditions for the three operations of the model, namely takeLeft(), takeRight() and dropForks(). The operations takeLeft() and takeRight() make the philosopher pick up the left fork – or right fork, respectively – if it is not already picked up. The operation dropForks() puts the forks back between the plates, leaving them ready to be picked up again. The latter operation can only be invoked, if the involved philosopher has both forks in his hands. The model as shown in Fig. 2 has a serious flaw, in fact leads to a deadlock. This can be detected using verification approaches as described next.

3.2   Verification Using the Filmstripping Approach

Generation of the Filmstrip Model. To find a deadlock in the *dining philosophers* model using the filmstripping approach, the first step is to transform the source model into the philosopher filmstrip model [14]. For easier reference, we call the source model the *application model* and our transformed model the *filmstrip model*. The result of the transformation is another UML and OCL model, which represents the model dynamics of the application model with classes, associations and invariants instead of operation pre- and postconditions. The expressiveness of the filmstrip model is the same as the application model, but all dynamic model elements have been transformed into static ones.

Example. Consider the class diagram of the filmstrip model in Fig. 3. It is an extension of the application model (Fig. 2), where the behavioral elements of the application model became structural elements in the filmstrip model. A system state of the application model is described by a Snapshot, to which every object of a state is linked, and several snapshots can be connected to a filmstrip with operation call objects (OpC) between each of them. Aside of this filmstrip connection, each object gets a reflexive association to link different representation of the same object along the snapshots. The three operations of the application model become concrete classes extending the base operation call class. The operation pre- and postconditions are transformed into invariants and corresponding OCL constraints ensure the correct representation of the model dynamics.

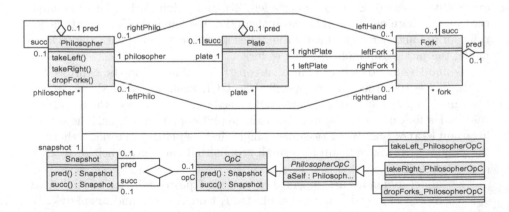

Fig. 3. Philosopher filmstrip model class diagram

```
context dropForks_PhilosopherOpC inv noForkChangeExcept:
  let except = aSelf in
  pred().philosopher→forAll( p | p <> except implies
     ( p.leftHand.succ = p.succ.leftHand
         and p.rightHand.succ = p.succ.rightHand ))
context Snapshot inv sameCountPhilosopher:
  not succ().oclIsUndefined() implies philosopher→size() =
     succ().philosopher→size()
context OpC inv predBecomesSucc:
  self.pred().philosopher→forAll( p |
     self.succ().philosopher→includes( p.succ ) )
```

Fig. 4. Example frame conditions for the dining philosophers filmstrip model

The next step in the verification process is the creation of frame conditions. The OCL invariant noForkChangeExcept, in Fig. 4, forces links between philosophers and forks to persist during the dropForks() operation call, except for the one philosopher, on which the operation is invoked. This philosopher shall drop the forks onto the table, i.e. the links between the philosopher and the forks are removed. Due to the assignment of the invariant to the specific operation call class, it is possible to specify different behavior for different operation calls, e.g. the same invariant for the operation takeLeft() allows changes for the specified exceptions' left hand only and all other links persist. Similar invariants are created for the other associations, to keep their links between operation calls.

In the philosophers example there are two more invariant types, also shown in Fig. 4, that are added to the model. One constrains the number of objects to be the same in every snapshot, i.e. no new philosopher joins the system, once it is running. An example for this constraint is represented by the invariant sameCountPhilosopher. The second condition enforces a link between all objects of successive snapshots, to prevent object destruction and creation, i.e. no philosopher gets exchanged with a new one. The invariant predBecomesSucc illustrates such constraint for the philosopher objects. These two conditions are added for every class of the application model. These extra constraints are not necessarily required for the verification, since the filmstrip model can handle object creation and destruction, but they simplify the formulation of the verification task for the application model, because they remove a lot of side effects. If an application model specifically handles object creation and destruction, these constraints do not need to be added.

Verification Task. The next step towards the verification of the system is the transformation of the verification task into OCL. A wide variety of verification tasks can be expressed in OCL due to the capabilities of the filmstrip model. Special properties for a defined state can be expressed as an OCL invariant, e.g. to define an initial state for the system. Temporal requirements for the model can also be expressed as invariants, e.g. using one of the temporal OCL proposals [21,27,10]. Given that an application model state sequence is captured

```
context Snapshot inv initialState:
  let firstSnapshot = Snapshot.allInstances()→select( s |
      s.pred().oclIsUndefined() ) in
  firstSnapshot.philosopher→forAll( ph | ph.leftHand = null and
      ph.rightHand = null )
context Snapshot inv deadlock:
  Snapshot.allInstances()→exists( s |
    not s.philosopher→exists( ph |
-- takeLeft preconditions and invariants
      (ph.leftHand.oclIsUndefined() and
          ph.plate.rightFork.leftPhilo.oclIsUndefined())
-- takeRight preconditions and invariants
      or (ph.rightHand.oclIsUndefined() and
          ph.plate.leftFork.rightPhilo.oclIsUndefined())
-- dropForks preconditions and invariants
      or (ph.leftHand.oclIsUndefined() and
          ph.rightHand.oclIsUndefined()) ) )
```

Fig. 5. Formulation of the verification task

by a single filmstrip model state, it is possible to verify tasks expressed in terms
of LTL formulas.

Example. The OCL invariants to describe the verification task for the filmstrip
model are shown in Fig. 5. The invariant `initialState` asserts that the system
starts in a state where no philosopher has picked up a fork yet. The deadlock
verification task is expressed in the OCL invariant `deadlock`. It defines a state
for a snapshot, where no more operations can be invoked. This is done by looking
at all possible preconditions of the model operations and ensure, that none of
those are valid in the snapshot. Additionally the invocation of the operation may
not interfere with an invariant, once the operation call is finished, thus invariants
interfering with the postconditions are added as well. The individual parts for
the three operations from the application model are marked in the constraint.
Other properties like the number of philosophers are left open and will be chosen
by the solver.

The result of this verification task not only describes the condition whether
the system contains a deadlock or not, but also the final state, in which the
system came to hold and the whole sequence of operation invocations that lead
there from the initial state. In the case that there is no deadlock in the system,
there exists no valid system state for the prepared model and the solver yields
`unsatisfiable`.

The last preparation for the model is to determine the problem bound intervals, i.e. the minimum and maximum quantities of objects for each class and
association. Especially by addressing the classes from the filmstrip model, it is
possible to define how many and which operation invocations are allowed. For
the dining philosopher example, the number of operation invocations is limited

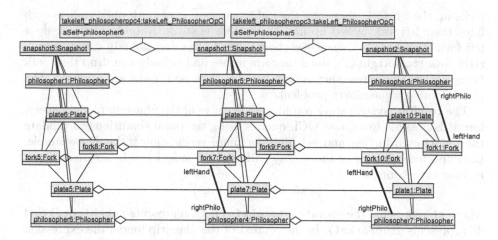

Fig. 6. Object diagram of the found solution for the philosopher verification task

to 4 and the number of application class objects is limited to 10. The lower bounds are set to 0. Note, however, that these bounds limit the system state of the filmstrip model instead of a system state in the application model, i.e. they allow for a maximum of 10 objects per class split among the snapshots of the filmstrip model. To affect the distribution per snapshot, OCL constraints can be used. The chosen configuration gives no hints for the verification engine, i.e. it is unknown whether a deadlock exists in the system and the validation tool shall try every possible combination.

Solving and Interpretation. Now the problem description is complete and the next step is to solve the problem instance. Since all behavioral aspects of the application model have been transformed and eliminated in the filmstrip model, it can be validated with techniques designed for structural analysis [2,7,20,12]. We solve the problem using relational logic utilizing our model validator [17]. The model validator uses Kodkod [26] to transform the model, which itself uses Alloy [16] to encode the problem. The resulting problem instance is then solved by one of the supported SAT solvers, e.g. Sat4j, MiniSat or Glucose, which yields either the bindings of the found solution, if the problem is satisfiable, or marks the problem as unsatisfiable otherwise.

Example. In our example the solver finds a solution for the problem. The model validator extracts the bindings and creates an object diagram from it. Figure 6 illustrates the solution, representing a system state of the filmstrip model. The elements on the left show a snapshot, which represents the initial state. No philosopher is linked with any fork in this state, as defined. At the top are the operation calls. The first operation call lets the lower philosopher pick up the left fork. The snapshot in the middle illustrates this property with a link between the philosopher and the fork, labelled (leftHand,rightPhilo). All other connections remain the same. For the second operation call, the upper philosopher picks up the left fork, shown by the right snapshot. Now both philosophers each have their left fork picked up and the system is stuck. Nobody can pick up a left fork (`takeLeft()`), since everybody already has one, nobody can pick up a right fork (`takeRight()`), since they are in use and nobody can drop their fork (`dropForks()`), because that is only possible once both forks are acquired. The classic *dining philosophers* problem.

The resulting system state contains all features of the filmstrip model. Therefore it is possible to express OCL queries using temporal conditions to validate the model even further and get hints for more verification tasks. For example, the expected behavior of the *dining philosophers* model can be expressed as a regular expression as

$$\big(\,(\,\texttt{tL}\ \ \texttt{tR}\ |\ \texttt{tR}\ \ \texttt{tL}\,)\ \ \texttt{dF}\,\big)^{*}$$

where `tL` represents the operation `takeLeft()`, `tR` represents `takeRight()` and `dF` represents `dropForks()`. In the context of the filmstrip model the expression can be transformed into an OCL query to find sequences of operation invocations in the system state, that match the pattern.

Finally, the object diagram of the filmstrip model can be transformed back to object and sequence diagrams of the application model. This is useful to track back errors in the application model revealed by performing the verification task on the filmstrip model.

3.3   Verification Using the Unrolling Approach

Generation of the Skeleton. In this section, we describe the unrolling approach in detail using the previously introduced *dining philosophers* model as a running example. The basic idea of the approach is to unroll the source model, thereby generating a skeleton, i.e. an initially empty sequence of system states [23]. Note that the maximum number of objects and states must be determined in advance in order to generate a skeleton of appropriate size.

Example. Figure 7 shows a skeleton generated for the *dining philosophers* model with two instances of each class per state. Objects of the same type are automatically enumerated which allows to immediately identify corresponding objects at different states (observation points) and to easily observe the lifeline of each object. Transitions between the states are made by operation calls ω_0, ω_1. Note that the number of objects and states must be determined in advance in order to generate a skeleton of appropriate size.

The purpose of the skeleton is to describe the dynamic behavior of the model at a level that can easily be transferred to a formulation suitable for SMT constraint solvers. In contrast to classical SAT solvers which expect the problem instance to be in *Conjunctive Normal Form (CNF)*, SMT solvers support higher-level theories which allows to formulate the problem instance at a higher level of abstraction thereby providing structural information that can accelerate the solving process. In our context, we especially make use of the theory of *Quantifier-Free Bit-Vectors (QF_BV)* logic which features bit-vectors of arbitrary length, comparisons like, e.g., $<$ or $\leq$, and other bit-vector operations [3].

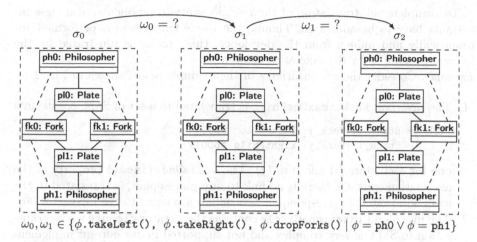

$$\omega_0, \omega_1 \in \{\phi.\texttt{takeLeft()}, \ \phi.\texttt{takeRight()}, \ \phi.\texttt{dropForks()} \mid \phi = \texttt{ph0} \vee \phi = \texttt{ph1}\}$$

Fig. 7. Skeleton consisting of a sequence of system states and connecting operations

Accordingly, object attributes and associations are translated to bit-vectors of appropriate length as illustrated by the following example.

Example. Consider the association $(\texttt{leftHand}, \texttt{rightPhilo})$ of the *philosophers* model (Fig. 2). In order to represent this in the skeleton we introduce bit-vector variables $\lambda_{\textsf{leftHand}}$, one for each `Philosopher` object. Since the target of this association is of type `Fork`, the bit-width is set to the maximum number of forks with the implicit semantics that the i-th bit of $\lambda_{\textsf{leftHand}}$ is set to 1 if and only if `Fork` i is part of the `leftHand` relation. Likewise, $\lambda_{\textsf{rightPhilo}}$ variables (one for each `Fork` object) are used for the other association end. This is illustrated by means of Fig. 8.

Finally, the cardinality constraint 0..1 for the association ends is translated to the constraint that at most one bit of the bit-vector is set to 1. Many SMT solvers natively support such cardinality constraints for bit-vectors. For others, transformation frameworks like metaSMT [15] can be used to automatically translate these constraints to a more explicit, solver compatible form.

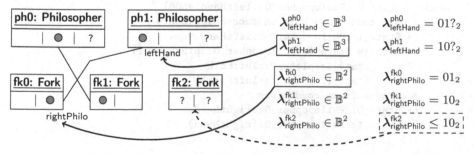

Fig. 8. Translating associations to λ-variables

To complete the translation of the model's static components, also class invariants have to be addressed. Though the whole translation is performed automatically and hidden from the developer, this process is illustrated by the following example for the sake of completeness.

Example. Consider the two invariants of the example model shown in Fig. 2.

1. The invariant Fork::maxOnePhilo is translated to a set of SMT constraints

   ```
   (OR (= State_i::Fork_j::leftPhilo  #b00)
       (= State_i::Fork_j::rightPhilo #b00))
   ```

   one for each state (i) and fork (j). The oclIsUndefined() property of the association ends, i.e. there is no link to any philosopher, is translated to the assertion that the corresponding λ-variables are equal to the bit-vector 00_2.

2. The invariant Plate::oneCircle contains the iterator closure whose translation to SMT is very complex and not supported in our current implementation. For simplicity, we use the invariant

   ```
   inv noIsolatedPlate:   self.leftFork <> self.rightFork
   ```

   instead. This invariant can be easily translated to a set of SMT constraints as above and is equivalent to the original invariant for up to three plates, since it then suffices that none of the plates forms a "circle" on its own.

The last important step of generating the skeleton is to add transitions between the states, i.e. to translate operation calls. For this purpose, we introduce ω-variables (one per transition) that are further constrained in order to represent respective operation calls.

Example. Consider the transition from the initial state σ_0 to the following state σ_1. Since there are two philosophers and three operations per philosopher, there are six possible operations in total, resulting in a bit-width of $\lceil \log_2(6) \rceil = 3$ for the corresponding ω_0-variable. For each possible value of ω (corresponding to some operation call), we add an SMT constraint saying that if this particular

```
(=> (= omega_0 #b000)     ; representing ph0.takeLeft()
          ; pre-conditions hold in current state
    (AND (= State_0::Philosopher_0::leftHand #b00)
         ; post-conditions hold in succeeding state
         (= State_1::Philosopher_0::leftHand
            (ite (= State_1::Philosopher_0::plate #b01)
                 State_1::plate_0::leftFork
                 State_1::plate_1::leftFork))
         ; enforce frame conditions
         (= State_0::Philosopher_0::rightHand
            State_1::Philosopher_0::rightHand)
         ...
```

Fig. 9. SMT constraint representing a call to the ph0.takeLeft() operation

operation call is chosen for the state transition, we require that the corresponding pre- and postconditions hold in the pre- and post-state, respectively, and enforce frame conditions, e.g. which attributes and associations are allowed to be changed during an operation call and which shall not be altered. Figure 9 exemplarily shows the respective constraint for the takeLeft() operation invoked on philosopher ph0.

Remark. While pre- and postconditions are given by the source model, obtaining frame conditions is a non-trivial problem and can be an elaborate task. However, there is built-in functionality to generate frame conditions automatically under certain premises, e.g. fixing all variables that do not occur in postconditions. For more details on the whole translation process, we refer to [22].

Verification Task. The next step is to consider the targeted verification task. First of all, the skeleton can be passed to the solving engine directly in order to check *consistency* of the model, i.e. to answer the question whether or not there exists a sequence of operation calls starting from an arbitrary initial state and satisfying all invariants, pre- and postconditions. In most cases, however, the verification task has to be included by further constraining attributes, associations, or operation calls. The approach offers a wide range of possibilities for this purpose:

- The constraining can be done very fine granular by addressing single variables of the skeleton, e.g. enforce a certain operation to be called at least once or at a certain position by constraining the corresponding ω-variables.
- At a larger scale, partially or completely preassigned states, e.g. the initial or final state, can be loaded and automatically constrain the corresponding variables or additional invariants can be enforced for a selection of states.
- Beyond that, several standard tasks like checking for deadlocks can be handled automatically. For instance, a deadlock finder extends the skeleton by adding a helper state for each possible operation call. These states have the same structure as normal system states, but only have a single invariant that states that the respective operation may not be called since either the preconditions are not fulfilled or the postconditions would raise a conflict with some invariant.

Example. In our running example, the deadlock finding method can be employed in multiple ways. If the number of states is set to one, i.e. no dynamic behaviour, it can prove whether deadlock states exists at all. Increasing the number of states, also sequences of operation calls leading to a deadlock state can be determined. Alternatively, the extracted deadlock state can be fed in as the final state of a reachability problem. Clearly, this is most useful in combination with a preassigned initial state.

Solving and Interpretation. In the last stage of the approach, the problem instance is passed to an SMT solver, e.g. Boolector [6] or Z3 [9], which, in turn, either determines a satisfying assignment (SAT) or proves the absence of such an assignment (UNSAT). In the case of UNSAT, it is proven that the desired

```
// Generate skeleton
input    = loadModel( "DiningPhilosophers.ecore" )
bounds   = new Bounds( AllObjectsSameBounds(2),
                       FixedNumberOfStates(3) )
skeleton = generateSkeleton( input.model, bounds )

// Incorporate verification task
initialState = loadState( "PhilosophersInitial.xmi" )
skeleton.getState(0).assign( initialState )
instance = DeadlockFinder( skeleton )

// Solve the problem instance
solver = new SMT_Solver
sat = solver.solve( instance )
assertEquals( true, sat )

// Extract states and sequence diagram
extractStatesAsXMI( solver.solution )
printTransitions( solver.solution )
```

Fig. 10. Deadlock finding in the *dining philosophers* model (developer's perspective)

behaviour can not be achieved in the underlying model with respect to the specified problem bounds. In the case of SAT, a witness for the desired behaviour in form of object and sequence diagrams can be extracted automatically by translating the assignments of λ- and ω-variables (as demonstrated by Fig. 8).

Finally, the whole flow of the approach from the developer's perspective is illustrated by means of example code shown in Fig. 10. Our current implementation is written in Xtend/Closure and is fully integrated into Eclipse. We use Ecore as the input format for source models as well as XMI to in- and output system states. Note again that the whole translation process to SMT is performed automatically and hidden from the developer who does not need to write a single line of SMT code.

First, a skeleton is generated for the *dining philosophers* model with two philosophers/plates/forks each. Then the verification task, i.e. finding a deadlock that can be reached in three steps from a given initial state, is incorporated. Finally, the problem instance is passed to a solver and system states and transitions are extracted from the solution. Most parts of the code serve as template which can be reused for other problems or bounds. So far, problem bounds like the number of states or the number of objects per state have to be specified explicitly. However, we plan to support interval bounds in order to delegate the exact determination of bounds from the developer to the solving engine.

After setting up the instructions shown in Fig. 10, the problem considered here can be solved fully automatically.

4   Discussion of Comparison Criteria

After we have seen both verification approaches illustrated and applied to the same example, we now discuss their respective pros and cons. A comparison of core criteria (that are not necessarily disjoint) is summarized in Table 1.

The level of operation is a crucial difference between the approaches. The filmstripping approach mainly operates at the model level (UML/OCL) while the unrolling approach operates much closer to the solver level (SMT).

The procedure and applicability of the approaches is consequently quite different. Filmstripping essentially relies on manual interaction, particularly for the formulation of frame conditions and the verification task. However, these are to be formulated in UML/OCL which can be expected to be the designer's expertise. This allows for a higher flexibility and more universal applicability. In contrast, the unrolling approach is highly automated (automatic generation of frame conditions, predefined verification tasks) at the expense of a somewhat more restricted applicability. More precisely, some features of OCL are currently not supported.

Frame conditions are formulated manually for the filmstripping approach in due consideration of the structure of the derived filmstrip model. Therefore, they are problem-specific and thus compatible to the input model. In contrast, for the unrolling approach the frame conditions are generated automatically following a given set of rules, which may not be adequate for every given model.

Verification task To formulate the verification task, the engineer might need to understand the basics of the approaches. For the filmstripping approach, this is the structure of the filmstrip model which have to be enriched by additional OCL constraints. In contrast, the unrolling approach requires the verification task specified by means of SMT constraints which require a deeper understanding of SMT. This can not always be expected from the designer. However, for common verification tasks, such as reachability and deadlock detection, predefined automatic checks can be conducted which require no further expertise at all.

Table 1. Overview of important comparison criteria for the verification approaches

Criterion	Filmstripping	Unrolling
Level of operation	model level (UML/OCL)	solver level (SMT)
Procedure	essential manual interaction, thus more flexible	Highly automated, but less flexible
Applicability	Universal	Restricted
Frame conditions	Explicit formulation for model	Generated from set of rules
Verification task	Formulation in OCL (templates possible)	Formulation in SMT (some predefined)
Search bounds	Intervals	Fixed
Validation on result	OCL queries on filmstrip state	Not directly possible
Runtime	Good solving time	Optimized solving time
Solving engine	Relational logic (Kodkod)	SMT solver

Search bounds are provided as intervals for the filmstripping approach. This makes the determination easier, e.g. when the exact problem bounds are unknown, but has a negative impact on solving times. Changing the bounds also does not affect the other steps of the verification task. In contrast, the unrolling approach is currently based on fixed bounds. In the case that the initial bounds are not sufficient, new bounds have to be determined and individual constraints may have to be adapted to these new bounds.

Validation on result In the filmstripping approach, the extracted filmstrip state contains all behavioral features and can be directly accessed by OCL queries, allowing for further validation on the result. For the unrolling approach, the extracted diagrams are split into several object and sequence diagrams that are not directly accessible by OCL queries.

Runtimes Previous results for static model aspects [24] indicate a structural advantage (in terms of *runtimes*) of solver-driven approaches against model-driven approaches. This is in accordance with what we observed for the verification of behavioral aspects in this study (though a detailed analysis is left for future work), even if the higher manual interaction for the filmstripping is ignored.

Solving engine The filmstripping approach uses relational logic to solve problem instances. In this field currently only one solving engine is available. Using SMT in the unrolling approach allows to choose from a wide variety of solvers.

Performance In general, the performance of both approaches highly depends on the complexity of the input model and the desired verification task and, thus, is hard to compare. Moreover, there is no standard metric for the complexity of OCL or SMT constraints. Consequently, the effort for manual creation of frame conditions (in the filmstripping approach) and manual incorporation of verification tasks (in both approaches) cannot be measured precisely.

Overall, the unrolling approach promises fast results for a set of common, predefined verification tasks and input models that are compatible with the automatic generation of frame conditions (like, but clearly not limited to the considered *dining philosophers* model). For rather complex models, e.g. containing sophisticated side effects in the OCL constraints, or very dedicated verification tasks, the more flexible filmstripping approach is likely to be the better choice, at the price of substantial manual interaction.

5   Related Work

Besides from the approaches already mentioned, the two discussed methods have connections to related papers. In a previous contribution [13] we have identified verification tasks like consistency and independence of invariants in UML and OCL models and established a benchmark. The running example in this paper (*dining philosphers*) would be another candidate for the benchmark. In contrast to testing methods, there are a number of works applying interactive theorem proving techniques for UML and OCL, like for example the works based on

PVS [18], the KeY approach [1], and the combination of testing and proving based on Isabelle and HOL/OCL [5]. A classification of model checkers with respect to verification tasks can be found in [11].

(Semi)-automatic proving approaches for UML class properties have been put forward on the basis of description logics [19], on the basis of relational logic and pure Alloy [2] using a subset of OCL, and in [25] focussing on model inconsistencies by employing Kodkod, the programming interface of Alloy.

Verification of OCL operation contracts have been studied on the basis CSP solvers in [8]. The unrolling approach tackled in this paper was presented in [23] and the filmstripping approach in [14].

6   Conclusion and Future Work

In this contribution, we provided a comparison of the filmstripping approach to the unrolling approach – two recently proposed solutions aiming for the verification of behavioral models given in UML/OCL. Both approaches allow to check the functional correctness of a system description prior to its implementation. However, the fashion in which they formulate and eventually solve the respective verification tasks is significantly different. Our comparison discussed the main differences and, by this, provided a better understanding of the advantages and disadvantages of these verification methods. Future work will focus on the analysis and extension of these verification approaches with respect to scalability, i.e. the support of larger and more complex models, as well as applicability, i.e. the support of further descriptions means and verification tasks.

References

1. Ahrendt, W., Beckert, B., Hähnle, R., Schmitt, P.H.: KeY: A Formal Method for Object-Oriented Systems. In: Bonsangue, M.M., Johnsen, E.B. (eds.) FMOODS 2007. LNCS, vol. 4468, pp. 32–43. Springer, Heidelberg (2007)
2. Anastasakis, K., Bordbar, B., Georg, G., Ray, I.: On Challenges of Model Transformation from UML to Alloy. Software and System Modeling 9(1), 69–86 (2010)
3. Barrett, C., Stump, A., Tinelli, C.: The Satisfiability Modulo Theories Library (SMT-LIB) (2010), www.SMT-LIB.org
4. Bill, R., Gabmeyer, S., Kaufmann, P., Seidl, M.: OCL meets CTL: Towards CTL-Extended OCL Model Checking. In: Proceedings of the MODELS 2013 OCL Workshop. vol. 1092, pp. 13–22 (2013)
5. Brucker, A.D., Wolff, B.: Semantics, calculi, and analysis for object-oriented specifications. Acta Inf. 46(4), 255–284 (2009)
6. Brummayer, R., Biere, A.: Boolector: An Efficient SMT Solver for Bit-Vectors and Arrays. In: Kowalewski, S., Philippou, A. (eds.) TACAS 2009. LNCS, vol. 5505, pp. 174–177. Springer, Heidelberg (2009)
7. Cabot, J., Clarisó, R., Riera, D.: UMLtoCSP: A Tool for the Formal Verification of UML/OCL Models using Constraint Programming. In: Stirewalt, R.E.K., Egyed, A., Fischer, B. (eds.) ASE 2007, pp. 547–548. ACM (2007)
8. Cabot, J., Clarisó, R., Riera, D.: Verifying UML/OCL Operation Contracts. In: Leuschel, M., Wehrheim, H. (eds.) IFM 2009. LNCS, vol. 5423, pp. 40–55. Springer, Heidelberg (2009)

9. De Moura, L., Bjørner, N.: Z3: An Efficient SMT Solver. In: Ramakrishnan, C.R., Rehof, J. (eds.) TACAS 2008. LNCS, vol. 4963, pp. 337–340. Springer, Heidelberg (2008)
10. Flake, S., Müller, W.: Past- and Future-Oriented Time-Bounded Temporal Properties with OCL. In: SEFM 2004, pp. 154–163. IEEE Computer Society (2004)
11. Gabmeyer, S., Brosch, P., Seidl, M.: A Classification of Model Checking-Based Verification Approaches for Software Models. In: Proceedings of VOLT 2013 (2013)
12. Gogolla, M., Büttner, F., Richters, M.: USE: A UML-Based Specification Environment for Validating UML and OCL. Science of Computer Programming 69 (2007)
13. Gogolla, M., Büttner, F., Cabot, J.: Initiating a Benchmark for UML and OCL Analysis Tools. In: Veanes, M., Viganò, L. (eds.) TAP 2013. LNCS, vol. 7942, pp. 115–132. Springer, Heidelberg (2013)
14. Gogolla, M., Hamann, L., Hilken, F., Kuhlmann, M., France, R.B.: From Application Models to Filmstrip Models: An Approach to Automatic Validation of Model Dynamics. In: Fill, H.G., Karagiannis, D., Reimer, U. (eds.) Proc. Modellierung (MODELLIERUNG 2014), Gesellschaft für Informatik, LNI (2014)
15. Haedicke, F., Frehse, S., Fey, G., Großbe, D., Drechsler, R.: metaSMT: Focus on your application not on solver integration. In: DIFTS 2012 (2012)
16. Jackson, D.: Software Abstractions: Logic, Language, and Analysis. The MIT Press, Cambridge (2006)
17. Kuhlmann, M., Gogolla, M.: From UML and OCL to Relational Logic and Back. In: France, R.B., Kazmeier, J., Breu, R., Atkinson, C. (eds.) MODELS 2012. LNCS, vol. 7590, pp. 415–431. Springer, Heidelberg (2012)
18. Kyas, M., Fecher, H., de Boer, F.S., Jacob, J., Hooman, J., van der Zwaag, M., Arons, T., Kugler, H.: Formalizing UML Models and OCL Constraints in PVS. Electr. Notes Theor. Comput. Sci. 115, 39–47 (2005)
19. Queralt, A., Artale, A., Calvanese, D., Teniente, E.: OCL-Lite: Finite reasoning on UML/OCL conceptual schemas. Data Knowl. Eng. 73, 1–22 (2012)
20. Snook, C., Butler, M.: UML-B: A Plug-in for the Event-B Tool Set. In: Börger, E., Butler, M., Bowen, J.P., Boca, P. (eds.) ABZ 2008. LNCS, vol. 5238, p. 344. Springer, Heidelberg (2008)
21. Soden, M., Eichler, H.: Temporal Extensions of OCL Revisited. In: Paige, R.F., Hartman, A., Rensink, A. (eds.) ECMDA-FA 2009. LNCS, vol. 5562, pp. 190–205. Springer, Heidelberg (2009)
22. Soeken, M., Wille, R., Drechsler, R.: Encoding OCL Data Types for SAT-Based Verification of UML/OCL Models. In: Gogolla, M., Wolff, B. (eds.) TAP 2011. LNCS, vol. 6706, pp. 152–170. Springer, Heidelberg (2011)
23. Soeken, M., Wille, R., Drechsler, R.: Verifying dynamic aspects of UML models. In: DATE, pp. 1077–1082. IEEE (2011)
24. Soeken, M., Wille, R., Kuhlmann, M., Gogolla, M., Drechsler, R.: Verifying UML/OCL models using Boolean satisfiability. In: DATE, pp. 1341–1344. IEEE (2010)
25. Straeten, R.V.D., Puissant, J.P., Mens, T.: Assessing the Kodkod Model Finder for Resolving Model Inconsistencies. In: France, R.B., Kuester, J.M., Bordbar, B., Paige, R.F. (eds.) ECMFA 2011. LNCS, vol. 6698, pp. 69–84. Springer, Heidelberg (2011)
26. Torlak, E., Jackson, D.: Kodkod: A Relational Model Finder. In: Grumberg, O., Huth, M. (eds.) TACAS 2007. LNCS, vol. 4424, pp. 632–647. Springer, Heidelberg (2007)
27. Ziemann, P., Gogolla, M.: OCL Extended with Temporal Logic. In: Broy, M., Zamulin, A.V. (eds.) PSI 2003. LNCS, vol. 2890, pp. 351–357. Springer, Heidelberg (2004)

Generating Classified Parallel Unit Tests

Ali Jannesari[1,2], Nico Koprowski[1,2], Jochen Schimmel[3], and Felix Wolf[1,2]

[1] German Research School for Simulation Sciences, Aachen, Germany
[2] RWTH Aachen University, Aachen, Germany
[3] Karlsruhe Institute of Technology (KIT), Germany

Abstract. Automatic generation of parallel unit tests is an efficient and systematic way of identifying data races inside a program. In order to be effective parallel unit tests have to be analysed by race detectors. However, each race detector is suitable for different kinds of race conditions. This leaves the question which race detectors to execute on which unit tests. This paper presents an approach to generate classified parallel unit tests: A class indicates the suitability for race detectors considering low-level race conditions, high-level atomicity violations or race conditions on correlated variables. We introduce a hybrid approach for detecting endangered high-level atomic regions inside the program under test. According to these findings the approach classifies generated unit tests as low-level, atomic high-level or correlated high-level. Our evaluation results confirmed the effectiveness of this approach. We were able to correctly classify 83% of all generated unit tests.

1 Introduction

Today, unit testing is an essential part of software development. A software artifact may consist of billions of lines of code. A full error analysis can be very time consuming and is often unnecessary. Usually, only new and modified code regions have to be tested. For this, developers create unit tests for the considered software. By creating unit tests, small parts of the program can be effectively tested without executing redundant code regions to find new bugs. From unit testing, a new field of research and work has emerged: automatic unit test creation [1]. One remarkable aspect of this work is the parallel unit test generator which focuses on creating unit tests for concurrency bugs.

However, parallel unit tests have to be analysed by external concurrency bug detectors. In general, each of these tools has varying suitability for different classes of concurrency bugs. Today, parallel unit tests do not come with any information on the potentially contained class of bug. Therefore, applying the correct concurrency bug detector is left to the user and mostly results in trial-and-error application.

In this work we present a parallel unit test generator which produces classified unit tests for race detection. We generally distinguish tests by whether they are suited for low-level or high-level race detectors. Additionally, we further classify high-level unit tests according to their suitability for race detectors for

M. Seidl and N. Tillmann (Eds.): TAP 2014, LNCS 8570, pp. 117–133, 2014.

correlated variables. In order to realise this, our work builds on the existing unit test generator AutoRT [2] which analyses and creates parallel unit tests from method pairs. In the scope of this paper we want to introduce an extension of this work: AutoRT+. We enhance AutoRT by identifying and analysing possibly violated high-level atomicity inside the method pairs.

For a total of 10 applications AutoRT+ automatically generated and classified 130 parallel unit tests for low-level and 106 parallel unit tests for high-level race detectors. From these 106 high-level tests AutoRT+ classified 52 for race detectors on correlated variables. We analysed the generated unit tests with four different race detectors. During our evaluation we observed that 83% of all unit tests were correctly classified.

2   Background

In this section we introduce terms which we use in the scope of this paper.

2.1   High-level Data Races

In our work, we define a race condition as an atomicity violation when accessing variable values. We further divide race conditions into *high-level* and *low-level* race conditions, according to the number of variables that are part of the data race.

Low-level races violate the atomicity of a single variable access. A low-level data race occurs when two concurrent threads access a shared variable without synchronization and when at least one of these accesses is a write.

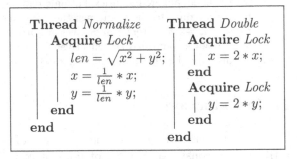

Fig. 1. A high-level data race violating the semantics of the vector (x, y)

High-level races violate the atomicity between several variable accesses. A high-level race condition is generally harder to detect, since identifying high-level atomicity requires an understanding of the program semantics. Figure 1 gives an example for such a high-level data race: All accesses have been secured by locks. However, if we have the interleaving in which the vector is normalized in between the doubling operation, the values of x and y are not correctly tuned to each other any more. We recognize that the semantics of those variables has been violated.

There are different approaches for identifying high-level atomic regions. In our work, AutoRT+ relies on the following two approaches.

Variable Correlations. Two variables are correlated iff their values are, or are meant to be, in a semantic relationship during the entire program execution [9]. Therefore, accesses to correlated variables form high-level atomic regions. Violations of this atomicity lead to correlation violations: the semantic relationship between the correlated variables becomes violated. We already introduced an example of a variable correlation in figure 1, where the two variables x and y constitute a vector. Here, the high-level atomicity inside *Double* is endangered.

Region Hypothesis. The region hypothesis [3] employs the concept of computational units in order to identify high-level atomic regions. Thereby, a computational unit is the longest sequence of instructions which satisfies the following two conditions:

1. The instructions are data and control dependent on one another. Thus, there exist no independent computations inside a single computational unit.
2. Inside a single computational unit a shared variable is not read after it has been written to.

The concept assumes that a typical atomic operation on a shared data structure consists of three parts: reading, computing and storing. The high-level atomic region to be protected inside a computational unit is called the shared region. It starts with the first access to a shared variable and ends with the last.

2.2   Parallel Unit Tests

Unit testing has become a common practice in the field of software engineering. The idea of unit testing is to concentrate debugging on small parts at a time instead of the whole program. This promises better precision and shorter testing times since bug detection can be focussed on the relevant code without analysing or executing the whole program. A unit test verifies the correctness of the corresponding part of the program informs about and reports any anomalous behaviour. For this verification we have to execute the unit test. During execution the program part to be tested

```
Function Parallel Unit Test()
   // Initializing context

   // Concurrent invocation
   Thread1.Start(Method1);
   Thread2.Start(Method2);

   // Wait for methods to
      finish
   Thread1.Wait();
   Thread2.Wait();
end
```

Fig. 2. General structure of a parallel unit test

is invoked and the results of the invocation are compared to the expected results.

Parallel unit tests are a special subclass of unit tests which distinguish themselves in the following ways:

1. A parallel unit test contains the parallel invocation of two methods, a method pair.

2. It should not be executed directly but is intended to be analysed by tools for concurrency bug detection.
3. The parallel unit test is independent with respect to execution. This means it can be executed without any additional support. This is an important feature for dynamic concurrency bug detection tools which need to execute the code for analysis.

Figure 2 illustrates the generic structure of a parallel unit test, divided into three parts: Initializing the necessary context, concurrently invoking the methods and synchronizing with the main thread.

3   Related Work

We present some approaches for the automatic generation of parallel unit tests and race detection approaches used in the scope of this paper. ConCrash [4] uses a static race detection approach to identify methods for unit test generation. The actual generation process is done by employing a Capture-And-Replay technique. ConCrash only considers methods in which race conditions have been found. Katayama et al. [5] explain an approach for the automatic generation of unit tests for parallel programs. The approach uses the Event InterAction Graph (EIAG) and Interaction Sequence Test Criteria, ISTC. Musuvathi et al. [10] use reachability graphs to generate unit tests for parallel programs. The approach proved to be very effective on small programs. However, it is not scalable regarding programs with a large amount of parallelism. A. Nistor et al. [7] generate parallel unit tests for randomly selected public class methods. The approach appends complex sequential code to the unit tests in order to increase the precision of concurrency bug detection. The approach only considers some parts of the program for unit test generation and neglects multiple class interactions.

MUVI [8] is a hybrid race detector for correlated variables. The algorithm employs a static correlation detection analysis based on data mining techniques. Subsequently, MUVI executes a dynamic race detection on the program under test. The correlation detection does not consider data dependencies between correlated variables and the race detection cannot identify continuous locks for high-level atomic regions. $Helgrind^+$ for correlated variables (H^{Corr}) [9] is a dynamic race detection approach. Parallel to the race detection the approach dynamically detects correlated variables by identifying computational units. H^{Corr} considers variables correlated if they are accessed in the same computational unit. CHESS [10], [11] dynamically searches a program for concurrency bugs including races, deadlocks and data errors. Through user annotations CHESS is also able to identify high-level races. However, for whole coverage the approach needs to perform a dynamic analysis for each interesting thread scheduling. This naturally leads to comparatively high analysis times for large programs. The Intel Thread Checker is a commercial dynamic race detector for low-level race conditions. It is part of the Intel Inspector [12], which is a known tool for detecting conventional concurrency bugs as well as memory leaks. [13] presents a dynamic race detector (NDR) which is able to detect low-level and high-level races by identifying non-deterministic reads. Thereby, a non-deterministic read is a read access on a value which is written dependent on the scheduling of threads. NDR also dynamically identifies correlated variables by detecting patterns of data and control dependencies. Finally, NDR reports for each found race condition the violated variable correlations.

4 Approach

This section presents AutoRT+, a parallel unit test generator which produces classified unit tests. The approach extends the parallel unit test generator AutoRT [2] by classification analysis techniques. First, we shortly introduce the original AutoRT approach. Thereafter, we present our new methods and describe the new features of AutoRT+.

4.1 AutoRT

AutoRT is a proactive unit test generator for parallel programs which uses both dynamic and static approaches for program analysis. For a given program the algorithm considers all possible method pairs as candidates for unit testing. In its generation steps AutoRT filters this candidate set to the most significant method pairs and generates unit tests based on them. Figure 3 gives an overview of the approach.

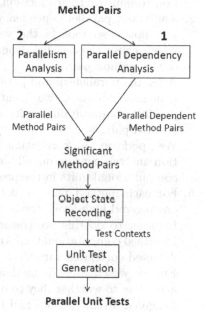

The algorithm identifies significant method pairs in two independent analyses:

1. A static analysis filters the candidate set to parallel dependent method pairs, i.e. method pairs containing accesses to the same variables.
2. A dynamic analysis reduces the candidate set to method pairs which truly run in parallel.

Fig. 3. Overview of AutoRT

Having obtained a significant candidate set, AutoRT employs a Capture-and-Replay technique: It dynamically records the object states which are necessary for invoking each method pair in parallel, called the test context. After AutoRT has filtered out equivalent contexts, the algorithm creates a parallel unit test for each different context of a method pair. Since the Capture-and-Replay technique reconstructs only contexts which actually existed during program execution, the generated unit test cases do not depict situations which never happen during runtime.

4.2 Overview of AutoRT+

AutoRT+ introduces an approach for producing classified unit tests. It distinguishes between three classes of parallel unit tests: (a) low-level unit tests which are suited for low-level race detectors, (b) high-level atomicity unit tests, which should be analysed by high-level race detectors in general, and (c) high-level correlation unit tests which are suitable for high-level race detectors considering correlated variables.

Figure 4 gives an overview of the unit test generator. Extensions are colored and are detailed in the following:

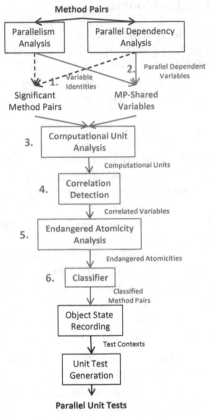

1. We have extended the dynamic parallelism analysis to protocol the encountered variable identities. This information is used in the subsequent computational unit and correlation detection to improve their precision.
2. The static parallel dependency analysis now also reports the variables which cause the parallel dependency of the method pair.
3. After the parallelism and parallel dependency analysis, we identify all possible computational units of each method pair.
4. We perform a correlation detection analysis considering all identified computational units in the program.
5. For each method pair we determine endangered high-level atomic regions. In order to do this, we consider the identified computational units and the detected correlated variables.
6. Finally, we classify the method pairs according to whether they contain endangered atomic regions and in what way they are endangered.

Fig. 4. Overview of AutoRT+

Then, AutoRT+ employs the Capture-and-Replay technique for generating the parallel unit tests. Finally, the class of the unit test is determined by the class of the method pair it is based on.

4.3 Shared vs. Method Pair-Shared (MP-Shared)

A variable is shared iff multiple threads access the variable during program execution. We further differentiate method pair shared (mp-shared) variables.

A variable is mp-shared for a method pair iff each of the two methods in the pair accesses the variable from a different thread. Obviously, an mp-shared variable is also a shared variable but a shared variable is not necessarily mp-shared for every method pair.

In the context of AutoRT+ we can identify mp-shared variables with the help of the dynamic parallelism and static parallel dependency analysis. The mp-shared variables of a parallel method pair are the members of the set of variables on which the two methods are parallel dependent.

4.4 Identifying Computational Units

For a given method pair we perform a static approach to identify the computational units for each method. In order to do so, we need information about the data and control dependencies between instructions and the shared variables. For this reason, we employ an analysis on the method to detect the data and control dependencies between its contained instructions. Further on, for the shared region we do not regard shared variables in general but only the mp-shared variables of the method pair. We use the information gained by the preceding parallelism and parallel dependency analysis in order to determine the mp-shared variables.

By traversing the control flow graph of the method on a specific path we are now able to identify the computational units a method consists of. However, different paths may lead to different computational units. In principle, for all possible computational units we would need to traverse all possible paths. But a method includes an infinite number of possible control flow paths for traversal when it contains loops. Therefore we follow a more relaxed branch coverage, mean-

```
Function SetSize(newSize)
    SizeFt = newSize;
    if SizeFt > 6 then
    |   Big = true;
    end
    SizeCm = SizeFt * 30, 48;
    MethodCount + +;
end
CU₁ = {newSize, SizeFt, SizeCm};
CU₂ = {newSize, SizeFt, Big, SizeCm};
CU₃ = {Count};
```

Fig. 5. All three possible computational units for the method *SetSize*

ing that for every branch in the method there exists a path we traverse which covers that branch. For each encountered instruction on a path we perform the following operations:

- An instruction without a data or control dependency is initially assigned its own computational unit.
- The same goes for an instruction which accesses a previously written mp-shared variable.
- For other instructions, we merge the computational units of the instructions on which they are data and control dependent and assign the resulting merged computational unit to the instruction.

Figure 5 shows an example for the computational units detection. The presented method contains two possible control flow paths. Our first path skips the control flow branch of the if-statement. As a result, we identify CU_1 and CU_3. Since we demand a full branch coverage of the control flow, our second path follows the control flow branch and identifies CU_2 and CU_3. Thus, we have identified all three possible computational units of the method.

4.5   Identifying Correlated Variables

For identifying correlations between variables we perform an analysis on the given computational units of the whole program. Our approach is based on the concepts of H^{Corr} [9] and MUVI [8]. According to H^{Corr}, variables are correlated if they are accessed within the same computational unit. This implies a strong relationship between data/control dependencies and variable correlations. However, this criterion seems to be too weak for successfully detecting correlated variables. Variables that may be initialized in the same computational unit but bear no further connection during the rest of the program can hardly be called correlated. We expect correlated variables to be in relation to each other during most of the program's execution. The approach MUVI uses is based upon this assumption. Here it is assumed that variables which are accessed relatively often near to each other are likely to be correlated. However, it does not additionally regard data and control dependencies for its analysis.

We introduce a hybrid approach for identifying correlated variables which combines the ideas of H^{Corr} and MUVI. As a result, we consider variables whose accesses appear relatively often in the same computational units to be correlated. The more frequently variables are accessed in the same computational units, the higher the probability that these variables are actually correlated. We call this probability the correlation probability. In order to compute the correlation probability for a variable pair, we sum up the total number of accesses to these variables inside the program. Then, the correlation probability is the percentage of accesses that appear inside a computational unit accessing both variables of the pair.

We only identify correlations between shared variables. Trivially, a correlation consisting only of local variables cannot be involved in an atomicity violation; there is just one thread accessing the participating variables.

Figure 6 gives an example for the correlation detection approach, in which we consider only two methods accessing shared variables. In this situation the variables $SizeFt$ and $SizeCm$ are correlated. During the method $Initialize$ the data dependencies between $Count$ and $SizeFt$ is just arbitrary since they have the same initial values. The computational unit obtained from $SetSize$ gives a better representation of the semantic relationships between the variables. When we apply our correlation detection algorithm on the two methods, we identify the correlated variables $SizeFt$ and $SizeCm$ with a correlation probability of 100%. The correlation probabilities involving the uncorrelated variable $Count$ are significantly lower.

```
Function Initialize()                 CU(Initialize) = {SizeFt, SizeCm, Count};
    SizeFt = 0;                        CU₁(SetSize) = {SizeFt, SizeCm};
    SizeCm = SizeFt;                   CU₂(SetSize) = {Count};
    Count = SizeFt;                    #Accesses(SizeFt) = 5;
end                                    #Accesses(SizeCM) = 2;
Function SetSize(newSize)              #Accesses(Count) = 3;
    SizeFt = newSize;
    SizeCm = SizeFt * 30, 48;          CorrelationProb(SizeFt, SizeCm) = 7/7 = 1;
    Count = Count + 1;                 CorrelationProb(SizeFt, Count) = 4/8 = 0.5;
end                                    CorrelationProb(SizeCm, Count) = 2/5 = 0.4;
```

Fig. 6. Correlation probabilities for the variable pairs accessed in two methods

4.6 Endangered Atomicity

After we have identified computational units and correlated variables, we determine endangered high-level atomic regions. Therefore, we consider the synchronisation instructions of the method pair. Any kind of synchronization instruction inside the mp-shared region of a computational unit suggests a possible atomicity violation. For this reason, we regard the atomicity of that computational unit as being endangered. We determine endangered correlated variables in a similar manner. A synchronization instruction which separates two accesses to correlated variables hints at a high-level atomicity violation.

If we do not detect any synchronization instructions, we can assume that the accesses in consideration are either fully and continuously synchronized or not synchronized at all. Of course, the latter case may lead to low-level race conditions and, if applicable, a violation of a high-level atomic region. Despite that, we do not consider this case an endangerment of high-level atomicity, since totally unsynchronized accesses naturally come with low-level race conditions. Therefore, the flaws can be found by low-level race detectors. Thus, a generated unit test for such a method pair should be classified as low-level and analysed by a low-level race detector. Figure 7 illustrates examples for high-level atomic regions we consider endangered or safe.

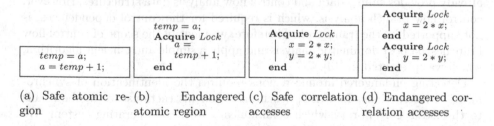

(a) Safe atomic region   (b)   Endangered atomic region   (c) Safe correlation accesses   (d) Endangered correlation accesses

Fig. 7. Examples of safe and endangered high-level atomic regions. Note: All variables are shared and the variables x and y are correlated.

4.7   Unit Test Classification

After we have determined the endangered high-level atomic regions we classify the method pairs accordingly:

Low-Level: The method pair should not contain any high-level race conditions. Therefore, it does not include computational units or correlated variables, which are endangered.

Atomic High-Level: The method pair contains at least one endangered computational unit. However, there are no endangered accesses to correlated variables.

Correlated High-Level: The method pair contains at least one endangered variable correlation.

In this kind of classification we willingly allow the possibility of low-level race conditions to be present inside high-level method pairs. This is because high-level race detectors are generally able to also identify low-level race conditions. On the other hand, low-level race detectors are unable to identify high-level race conditions. Therefore, we assign method pairs which may contain low-level and high-level race conditions to a high-level class.

5   Implementation

We implemented AutoRT+ in C# which runs within the .NET runtime. For data and control flow analysis as well as the code instrumentation we employed the Common Compiler Infrastructure (CCI) framework. Therefore, the presented analysis works on the Common Intermediate Language (CIL) which underlies every .NET program.

The dynamic parallelism analysis protocols encountered field variable accesses. We identify each field variable by its unique field identifier (acquired from the CCI framework) and the hash code of its parent object.

For our approach we need to identify data and control dependencies. CCI already provides simple data and control flow analysis data structures. However, control flow branch analysis, which is required for the control dependencies, is not supported by the framework. Therefore, we identify the scope of control flow branches via post dominator analysis and apply a simple and efficient algorithm, which was presented in [14].

Detecting endangered atomic regions requires the identification of synchronization instructions. In .NET, synchronization instructions are method calls to the .NET core library which communicate with the operating system. We are able to detect these method calls inside the CIL code of the program by their distinctive namespace: *System.Threading.* All methods belonging to that namespace manage synchronization operations between threads. Also, as our analysis does not distinguish between the types of synchronization, it is therefore able to identify synchronization instructions in general.

6   Evaluation

We use sample programs as well as real-world applications for our evaluation purposes. Table 1 lists the programs and provides an overview of their most important characteristics and evaluation results.

We used the programs *Bank Account*, *BoundedQueue* and *Dekker* from CHESS, which provides small programs containing high-level data races. We chose an order-system from MSDN Code Gallery [15]. We implemented an alternative version containing various correlated variables. Furthermore, we evaluated the following open source programs:

Table 1. Summary of the evaluation programs

Program	LOC	Meth.	Thrds	Par. Meth.	Par. Meth. Pairs	Corr. Vars	Unit Tests	Gen. Time (ms)
Bank Acc.	25	4	2	4	4	0	2	1030
Queue	31	6	3	6	14	2	10	451
Dekker	15	3	3	3	5	2	3	238
Order Sys.	360	7	5	5	15	13	15	1820
Corr Sys.	480	18	5	10	27	18	14	1923
Petri Dish	1070	35	7	35	230	12	24	23050
Kee Pass	1240	58	16	58	478	18	18	49300
STP	1120	46	12	37	315	25	53	29400
.Net Zip	14k	2366	19	63	1343	35	87	93900
Cosmos	78k	12k	19	269	5660	35	87	224600

- PetriDish [16], a simulation of three categories of organisms, all growing, mating, and eating each other.
- KeePass [17], a password manager.
- SmartThreadPool (STP) [18], a thread pool library.
  DotNetZip [19], a toolkit for manipulating zip files.
- Cosmos [20], an operating system toolkit.

6.1   Correlation Detection Efficiency

We compare the efficiency of different thresholds for the correlation probability in order to obtain the most suitable threshold. For this reason, we consider the number of variables falsely identified as being correlated, the false positives, and the number of missed correlated variables, the false negatives. In our evaluation we tested thresholds for 50% to 100% correlation probability.

In our 10 evaluation programs we detected 134 correlations in total. The efficiency of our correlation detection analysis depends highly on the chosen threshold for the correlation probability. Generally, we expected and observed that a low threshold leads to many false positives and fewer false negatives. A high threshold, on the other hand, prevents false positives but also drastically increases the number of false negatives.

Figure 8a shows the overall distribution of false positives and false negatives and relation to the correlation probability threshold. The break-even point between false positives and false negatives are approximately 80%. At this point,

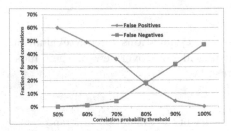
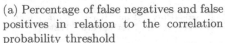

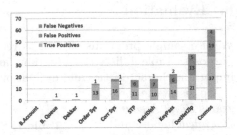

(a) Percentage of false negatives and false positives in relation to the correlation probability threshold

(b) Distribution of false negatives and false positives for a correlation probability threshold of 70%

Fig. 8. Efficiency of the correlation detection

we observed 18% false positives and false negatives. However, we rate false negatives more critically than false positives. As a result, we regard a threshold of 70% to be ideal according to our observations. At this threshold the percentage of false negatives is less than 5%. But as a major drawback we have to deal with an average of 35% false positives.

Figure 8b shows the distribution of false positives and false negatives in regard to the single evaluation programs with a 70% correlation probability threshold. In the smaller test programs we observe far fewer false negatives and false positives, each less than 5%. Some programs do not contain many correlations and due to the small program size the contained correlations are rather obvious. The open source programs prove to be more representative: Only with KeePass was there a relatively low amount of false positives at 22%. The other programs are close to the average of 35%. Considering false negatives, only DotNetZip stands out, having 12% false negatives.

6.2 Classification Precision

We identify falsely classified unit tests based on the contained atomic regions and the detected race conditions inside tests.

1. Low-level unit tests should not contain endangered high-level atomic regions or high-level race conditions.
2. High-level unit tests in general should not only contain low-level race conditions. Either they contain no race conditions or an arbitrary amount of race conditions from which at least one is a high-level race condition.
3. High-level atomic unit tests should not contain endangered variable correlations or race conditions on correlated variables.
4. High-level correlation unit tests should either contain no race conditions or an arbitrary amount of race conditions from which one is at least a race condition on correlated variables.

We consider unit tests which differ from the specification above as falsely classified. In order to identify race conditions we analysed the generated unit tests with four different race detectors: CHESS, ITC, H^{Corr} and NDR (see section 3).

CHESS and ITC are unable to detect high-level race conditions and were used to determine strictly low-level race conditions. H^{Corr} and NDR on the other hand are both able to detect high-level atomic and correlation race conditions.

AutoRT+ generated 236 parallel unit tests in total. Our approach was able to categorize these tests as shown in figure 9a. According to the observed distribution, the majority, roughly 55% of all unit tests, were categorized as low-level. Furthermore, our approach classified 25% of all generated unit tests as high-level atomic and 25% as high-level correlated.

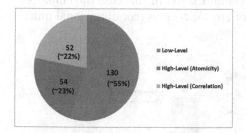
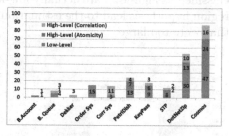

(a) Proportions of generated unit tests in total

(b) Proportions of generated unit tests for each evaluation program

Fig. 9. Distribution of generated parallel unit tests

Figure 9b shows the distribution of unit tests with regard to the evaluation programs. Again, we can observe a significant difference from the average distribution in the smaller test programs. The test program 'order system' was designed not to contain any high-level race conditions which naturally resulted in generating exclusively low-level unit tests. On the other hand, 'corr system' mainly consists of accesses to correlated variables. A higher amount of high-level unit tests was therefore expected. The unit tests for the open source programs follow the average distribution.

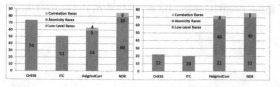
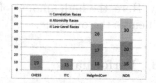

(a) Results for low-level tests   (b) Results for high-level atomicity tests   (c) Results for high-level correlation tests

Fig. 10. Results of the race detectors applied to the classified unit tests

Figure 10 shows the findings of the race detectors which we applied on the classified unit tests. In the low-level tests we observed about 18% high-level findings. Furthermore, of the reported findings of the high-level atomicity test, 29% were low-level and 7% were correlated high-level findings. Finally, the high-level correlation tests included 28% low-level and 29% uncorrelated high-level findings.

The validity of the classification between low-level and high-level unit tests is illustrated by figure 11a. We observed that 11 of the unit tests (8%) which were classified as low-level are actually high-level unit tests. In these cases, the region hypothesis has failed to identify correct high-level atomic regions resulting in computational units that are too small. In this way, our approach was unable to identify the related atomic regions as endangered. Finally, 5 of the unit tests (3%) classified as high-level are actually low-level unit tests. In this case the employed region hypothesis lead to the estimation of atomic regions (computational units) that were too large.

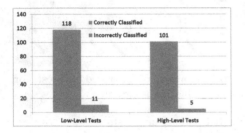
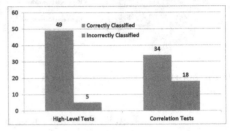

(a) Differentiation between low-level and high-level unit tests

(b) Differentiation between high-level and correlated unit tests

Fig. 11. Precision of the categorization approach

The distinction between regular high-level unit tests and unit tests containing endangered correlations turned out to be far more imprecise, as figure 11b illustrates. 5 unit tests (9%) contained undetected endangered variable correlations. A major influencing factor is the false negatives of the correlation detection. Additionally, we have a high amount of unit tests falsely categorised as unit tests for correlated variables. In total, 18 unit tests (35%) were falsely categorized this way. Here, the high amount of false positives in the correlation detection heavily influences the outcome.

6.3   Performance

Figure 12 shows the time our analysis takes for classifying and ultimately generating the unit test in relation to the execution time. Since our approach analyses method pairs, the time of classification is heavily dependent on the number of parallel method pairs inside the program. The time for unit test generation is a sum of different partial times including the static parallel dependency analysis, the correlation analysis, the dynamic parallelism analysis and the capture-and-replay technique. Our experience is that the most critical performance impact lies in the dynamic analysis. Multiple executions of the same program code and expensive object recording cause a major slow down. The ratio between the overall unit test generation time and the execution time of the program varies wildly by a factor between 16 and 266. Large programs with many objects and many parallel methods like Cosmos cause a high state recording time. The static correlation analysis only takes a small part of the overall generation time. Therefore, the categorization time only takes a small part of the total unit test generation time. In average about 5% of the total time goes into our additional analysis. In the smaller test programs we can even report a rate under 1%.

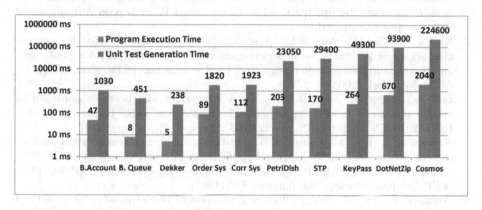

Fig. 12. Comparison between the unit test generation times of AutoRT+ and the execution times of the evaluation programs

7   Conclusion

In this paper we introduced an approach which enhances automatic parallel unit test generation and execution with a totally new dimension: classified unit tests. Our analysis is able to distinguish between unit tests that should be analysed by low-level race detectors, detectors for correlated variables or high-level race detectors in general. This supports testing of parallel software by reducing the number of unnecessary unit tests or unsuitable employed race detectors. Overall for ten different applications, we were able to classify 83% of the generated unit tests correctly.

In the future, we want to introduce new classes to AutoRT+. Generally, different race detectors vary in their effectiveness to detect specific kinds of concurrency bugs. Even detectors for correlated variables vary in precision depending on the structure of the code. Therefore, as a next step we want to provide additional classification analysis and clustering metrics which state how method pairs are suited for specific race detectors. Furthermore, we can extend our heuristics to other concurrency bugs like deadlocks and order violations.

Another direction for our future work would be to pass the results of our correlation detection to the race detectors executing the generated parallel unit tests. This would be especially useful for detectors which normally rely on the user annotation for correlation specifications e.g. CHESS [10] or [21]. However, race detectors with automatic correlation detection may profit from a reduced performance overhead and increased precision by our preceding correlation analysis.

References

1. Hamill, P.: Unit Test Frameworks: Tools for High-Quality Software Development. O'Reilly Series. O'Reilly Media (2008)
2. Schimmel, J., Molitorisz, K., Jannesari, A., Tichy, W.F.: Automatic generation of parallel unit tests. In: 8th IEEE/ACM International Workshop on Automation of Software Test (AST) (2013)
3. Xu, M., Bodík, R., Hill, M.D.: A serializability violation detector for shared-memory server programs. In: Proceedings of the 2005 ACM SIGPLAN Conference on Programming Language Design and Implementation, PLDI 2005, pp. 1–14. ACM, New York (2005)
4. Luo, Q., Zhang, S., Zhao, J., Hu, M.: A lightweight and portable approach to making concurrent failures reproducible. In: Rosenblum, D.S., Taentzer, G. (eds.) FASE 2010. LNCS, vol. 6013, pp. 323–337. Springer, Heidelberg (2010)
5. Katayama, T., Itoh, E., Ushijima, K., Furukawa, Z.: Test-case generation for concurrent programs with the testing criteria using interaction sequences. In: Proceedings of the Sixth Asia Pacific Software Engineering Conference, APSEC 1999. IEEE Computer Society, Washington, DC (1999)
6. Wong, W.E.: Yu Lei, X.M.: Effective generation of test sequences for structural testing of concurrent programs. In: 10th IEEE International Conference on Engineering of Complex Computer Systems, ICECCS 2005, pp. 539–548. IEEE Computer Society, Richardson (2005)
7. Nistor, A., Luo, Q., Pradel, M., Gross, T.R., Marinov, D.: Ballerina: Automatic generation and clustering of efficient random unit tests for multithreaded code. In: Proceedings of the 2012 International Conference on Software Engineering, ICSE 2012, pp. 727–737. IEEE Press, Piscataway (2012)
8. Lu, S., Park, S., Hu, C., Ma, X., Jiang, W., Li, Z., Popa, R.A., Zhou, Y.: Muvi: Automatically inferring multi-variable access correlations and detecting related semantic and concurrency bugs. In: SOSP 2007: Proceedings of Twenty-First ACM SIGOPS Symposium on Operating Systems Principles, pp. 103–116. ACM, New York (2007)
9. Jannesari, A., Westphal-Furuya, M., Tichy, W.F.: Dynamic data race detection for correlated variables. In: Xiang, Y., Cuzzocrea, A., Hobbs, M., Zhou, W. (eds.) ICA3PP 2011, Part I. LNCS, vol. 7016, pp. 14–26. Springer, Heidelberg (2011)
10. Musuvathi, M., Qadeer, S.: Chess: Systematic stress testing of concurrent software. In: Puebla, G. (ed.) LOPSTR 2006. LNCS, vol. 4407, pp. 15–16. Springer, Heidelberg (2007)
11. Musuvathi, M., Qadeer, S., Ball, T., Basler, G., Nainar, P.A., Neamtiu, I.: Finding and reproducing heisenbugs in concurrent programs. In: Proceedings of the 8th USENIX Conference on Operating Systems Design and Implementation, OSDI 2008, pp. 267–280. USENIX Association, Berkeley (2008)

12. Intel (Intel Inspector XE) (2013),
    http://software.intel.com/en-us/intel-inspector-xe
13. Jannesari, A., Koprowski, N., Schimmel, J., Wolf, F., Tichy, W.F.: Detecting correlation violations and data races by inferring non-deterministic reads. In: Proc. of the 19th IEEE International Conference on Parallel and Distributed Systems (ICPADS). IEEE Computer Society, Seoul (2013)
14. Cooper, K.D., Harvey, T.J., Kennedy, K.: (A simple, fast dominance algorithm)
15. Microsoft: Code gallery for parallel programs,
    http://code.msdn.microsoft.com/Samples-for-Parallel-b4b76364
16. Butler, N.: Petridish: Multi-threading for performance in c#,
    http://www.codeproject.com/Articles/26453/
    PetriDish-Multi-threading-for-performance-in-C
17. Reichl, D.: Keepass password safe, http://keepass.info/
18. Smart thread pool, http://smartthreadpool.codeplex.com/
19. Dotnetzip, http://dotnetzip.codeplex.com/
20. C# open source managed operating system, https://cosmos.codeplex.com/
21. Vaziri, M., Tip, F., Dolby, J.: Associating synchronization constraints with data in an object-oriented language. In: POPL 2006: Conference Record of the 33rd ACM SIGPLAN-SIGACT Symposium on Principles of Programming Languages, pp. 334–345. ACM, New York (2006)

JTACO: Test Execution for Faster Bounded Verification

Alexander Kampmann[2], Juan Pablo Galeotti[1], and Andreas Zeller[1]

[1] Software Engineering Chair, Saarland University, Saarbrücken, Germany
{lastname}@cs.uni-saarland.de
[2] Saarbrücken Graduate School of Computer Science
Saarland University
Saarbrücken, Germany
kampmann@st.cs.uni-saarland.de

Abstract. In bounded program verification a finite set of execution traces is exhaustively checked in order to find violations to a given specification (i.e. errors). SAT-based bounded verifiers rely on SAT-Solvers as their back-end decision procedure, accounting for most of the execution time due to their exponential time complexity.

In this paper we sketch a novel approach to improve SAT-based bounded verification. As modern SAT-Solvers work by augmenting partial assignments, the key idea is to *translate* some of these partial assignments into JUNIT test cases during the SAT-Solving process. If the execution of the generated test cases succeeds in finding an error, the SAT-Solver is promptly stopped.

We implemented our approach in JTACO, an extension to the TACO bounded verifier, and evaluate our prototype by verifying parameterized unit tests of several complex data structures.

1 Introduction

Bounded verification [5] is a fully automatic verification technique. Given a program P and its specification $\langle Pre, Post \rangle$, a bounded verification tool exhaustively checks correctness for a finite set of executions. In order to constrain the number of program executions to be analyzed, the user selects a scope of analysis by choosing: (a) a bound to the size of domain (e.g., LinkedList, Node, etc.), and (b) a limit to the number of loop unrollings or recursive calls.

Bounded verification tools [3,5,8,10,12,16] rely on translating P, precondition Pre and postcondition $Post$ into a propositional formula ψ such that

$$\psi = Pre \wedge P \wedge \neg Post.$$

If an assignment of variables exists such that ψ is true, ψ is *satisfiable*, and the satisfying assignment represents an execution trace violating the specification $\langle Pre, Post \rangle$. On the other hand, if ψ is *unsatisfiable* (i.e. there is no satisfying assignment for ψ), the specification holds within the user-selected scope of analysis. However, a violation might still be found if a greater scope of analysis is chosen. In order to decide on the satisfiability of ψ, the bounded verifier relies on a SAT-Solver, a program specialized in solving the satisfiability problem for propositional formulas.

M. Seidl and N. Tillmann (Eds.): TAP 2014, LNCS 8570, pp. 134–141, 2014.
© Springer International Publishing Switzerland 2014

```
1 public static void testRemove(int v1, int v2, int v3) {
2     BinarySearchTree t = new BinarySearchTree();
3     t.add(v1);
4     t.add(v2);
5     t.add(v3);
6     assert t.find(v2);
7     t.remove(v2);           // should remove all occurrences
8     assert !t.find(v2);
9 }
```

Fig. 1. A parameterized unit test for a binary search tree class

TACO [8] targets the bounded verification of sequential Java programs. For example, for the parameterized unit test shown in Figure 1, TACO will search for values for the integer parameters v1, v2 and v3 to falsify any of the assertions. Apart from checking regular `assert` statements, TACO also verifies more complex program specifications written in behavioural formal languages such as JML [2] or JFSL [17]. Although TACO is specially tailored for verifying complex specifications in linked-data structures (such as the well-formedness of red-black trees), the burden of writing such specifications is by no means small. As a light-weight alternative, applying bounded verifiers to parameterized unit tests might still help finding errors, but requires less effort from the user.

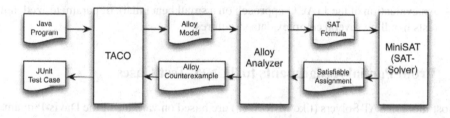

Fig. 2. A high-level view of the TACO architecture

Figure 2 presents a high-level overview of the TACO architecture. In order to translate the Java program into a propositional formula ψ, TACO uses the ALLOY language [11] as an intermediate representation. The analysis starts when the target Java program and its specification are translated into an ALLOY model. The ALLOY analyzer is then invoked to check the correctness of the model. This is done by translating the ALLOY representation into a propositional formula that is later solved using the MINISAT SAT-Solver. In case MINISAT [7] finds a solution to ψ, the satisfying assignment is returned to the ALLOY analyzer, that builds an ALLOY instance as a counterexample to the violated property. Finally, TACO translates the ALLOY counterexample into a JUNIT test case for later inspection by the user.

Given n propositional variables, there are 2^n possible assignments of values to those variables. SAT-Solvers are programs designed for efficiently deciding the satisfiability of a formula (i.e., either it is satisfiable or it is unsatisfiable). Nevertheless, as the worst-case time complexity of SAT is exponential on the number of propositional variables in ψ, it is often the case that most of the verification budget is spent in the execution of the SAT-Solver. On many occasions, when the time bound or the resources at hand are exhausted, the verification effort has to be cancelled. This leads to the unpleasant situation that significant computational resources might have been spent, while the user obtained no feedback from that investment.

In previous work [6], we already explored the idea of profiting from observing the internal state of the SAT-Solver during its execution. By assuming the ψ is unsatisfiable we approximate an UNSAT core [15] by measuring the activity of the SAT-Solver during the progress of the SAT-Solving process. In this paper, we aim at optimizing the bounded verifier when the underlying ψ is satisfiable. More specifically, we try to *lift* a partial assignment collected from the SAT-Solver into a JUNIT [1] test case. If the execution of the JUNIT test case leads to a violation of the specification, the whole SAT-Solver could be stopped. The intuition behind this is that in some cases the SAT-Solving process might not be as performant as executing the code in order to check the validity of ψ.

The contributions of this article include:

- An approach to combine SAT-Solving and JUNIT test case execution based on monitoring the internal state of the SAT-Solver.
- JTACO, an extension to the TACO bounded verifier implementing the aforementioned approach.
- An evaluation of the JTACO approach on a small benchmark of parameterized unit tests handling several complex data structures.

2   From Partial Assignments to JUNIT Test Cases

Most modern SAT-Solvers (like MINISAT) are based on variants of the Davis-Putnam-Logemann-Loveland (DPLL) algorithm [4]. The DPLL algorithm maintains and extends a partial assignment of the propositional variables to binary values. Each propositional variable can be *assigned* (meaning the algorithm has determined a provisional binary value for this variable), or *unassigned*.

In Figure 3 we show the pseudocode of the DPLL algorithm. It starts by calling procedure `search_new_value()` to extend the current assignment by deciding a new binary value for an unassigned variable. The function `propagate()` applies boolean constraint propagation (BCP) until no more values for variables can be inferred or the current decisions led to an unsatisfiable clause (namely, a *conflict*). The function `analyze_conflict()` determines the set of variable assignments that implied the conflict, returning the highest level of decision for all the variables involved (i.e., the `conflict_level` variable). Finally, `backtrack()` undoes the current assignment to the conflict level. This is usually referred to as *back jumping*.

Any partial assignment that led to a conflict during the `propagate()` phase is known to be unsatisfiable. In our previous work [13], we observed that only a fraction of the propositional variables of ψ are actually modelling the initial state of the execution trace. This is due to the fact that, given the *static* nature of the ALLOY language, TACO

```
1  while (true) {
2      search_new_value();
3      propagate();
4      if (status==CONFLICT) {
5          conflict_level = analyze_conflict();
6          if (conflict_level==0) {
7              return UNSAT;
8          } else {
9              backtrack(conflict_level);
10         }
11     } else if (status==SAT) {
12         return SAT;
13     }
14 }
```

Fig. 3. A sketch of the Davis-Putnam-Logemann-Loveland (DPLL) algorithm

models field and variable updates by introducing several versions of the same variable (much like in a SSA-like form[1]).

JTACO extends MINISAT by dumping the partial assignment whenever a conflict occurs (line 5 of Figure 3). Then, JTACO tries to *lift* the obtained partial assignment to a JUNIT test case. In order to lift a partial assignment v, JTACO first removes all those variables in v that are not used to model the initial state of the execution trace. However, the resulting filtered partial assignment might be insufficient for generating a JUNIT test case if any of the propositional variables modelling a given initial value is missing. For example, consider the argument v1 of the parameterised unit test shown in Figure 1. If k propositional variables model the initial value of v1 (namely $v1_0, v1_1, \ldots, v1_{k-1}$[2], we need to know the value of all the propositional variables to conclude the initial value of v1.

```
1  @Test
2  public void test1() {
3      int int0 = -8;
4      int int1 = -8;
5      int int2 = 0;
6      try {
7          BinarySearchTree.testRemove(int0, int1, int2);
8      } catch (AssertionError err) {
9          fail("An assertion did not hold:" + err);
10     }
11 }
```

Fig. 4. A failing JUNIT test case generated by JTACO

---

[1] In the Single Static Assignment (SSA) form, each variable is assigned exactly once.
[2] Alloy encodes integer values using two's complement.

If all the propositional variables encoding the initial state (i.e., arguments and field values) are assigned, then JTACO writes a JUNIT test case by decoding the values from the partial assignment (as the one shown in Figure 4). Subsequently, JTACO compiles the written test case and executes it. By construction, if the test case fails then the initial state led to a violation of the specification (in this case, failing the assert statement in line 8 of Figure 1). We refer to the original partial assignment that led to a failing test case as a *failing* partial assignment. The importance of finding such a partial assignment relies on the fact that, as soon as it is detected, the entire SAT-Solving process can be stopped.

To conclude, whenever a conflict occurs during the execution of the MINISAT's DPLL algorithm, JTACO filters those variables from the partial assignment that are not modelling initial values of the execution trace. If all the variables of the initial state are assigned in the resulting filtered partial assignment, a JUNIT test case is written, compiled and executed. If the JUNIT test case fails, then a violation to the specification has been found, and the verification process is stopped. In any other scenario (i.e., unassigned initial variables, JUNIT execution succeeding) the DPLL algorithm resumes.

3 Evaluation

We ran our prototype of JTACO on an Intel Core Duo T6600 with a scope of analysis of 4 elements per domain and 3 loop unrollings. We selected a benchmark of container classes taken from [8]. Since all these classes have already been verified using TACO, we wrote 9 additional faulty parameterized unit tests that are expected to fail (like asserting an AVL tree is empty after an insertion). Additionally, we add a faulty implementation of binary search trees plus a parameterized unit test capable of exhibiting the failure. The rationale behind these decisions is twofold: first, by aiming at the case where the formula ψ is satisfiable, we focus on the scenario in which our approach could make gains. Secondly, by resorting to parameterized unit tests (instead of regular JML or JFSL specification violations) we avoid the problem of synthesizing runtime predicates for asserting the validity of the specifications.

We evaluate our approach by addressing the following research questions:

- **RQ1:** During the MINISAT execution, when does the first failing partial assignment occur (i.e. the first partial assignment leading to a failing JUNIT test case)?
- **RQ2:** Does JTACO outperform TACO in terms of execution time?

Experimental Results. Figure 5 presents the average results of 10 executions of TACO and JTACO on the subjects of the selected case study. The first and second column list the subject name and the parameterized unit test. The third column shows the average time for verifying the program using TACO (only MINISAT time is considered). The fourth column presents the point in time when the first failing partial assignment was found during the MINISAT execution. The fifth column shows the total JTACO time (i.e. MINISAT time plus the time for collecting partial assignments, lifting them to JUNIT test cases and executing them). The last column presents the speed-up of JTACO with respect to TACO.

In all cases the failing partial assignment occurs very early during the MINISAT execution: ranging from 0.5% to 56% of the total solver time. Under these circumstances,

Subject	parameterized Unit Test	TACO time (ms)	1st Failing Partial Assignment (ms)	JTACO time (ms)	Speed-up
SinglyLinkedList	testRemove	144.7	81.1 (56.0%)	1545.7	0.09x
DoublyLinkedList	testRemove	496.2	202.4 (40.0%)	1940.3	0.25x
	testIndexOf	167.8	17.7 (10.0%)	408.4	0.41x
NodeCachingLinkedList	testIndexOf	1065.5	16.7 (1.5%)	150.5	7.07x
	testRemove	1823.9	20.7 (1.1%)	172.6	10.56x
BinaryTree	testRemove	567.4	7.9 (1.3%)	101.0	5.61x
BuggyBinaryTree	parameterized	315.2	10.4 (3.3%)	176.9	1.78x
	parameterizedSmall	136.5	9.0 (6.5%)	163.0	0.83x
AvlTree	testFindMax	3886.3	1072.5 (27.0%)	12928.9	0.30x
	testIsEmpty	2743.9	16.0 (0.5%)	146.2	18.76x
BinaryHeap	testFindMinDecrease	679.3	10.7 (1.5%)	100.0	6.76x

Fig. 5. Average execution times for 10 runs of TACO and JTACO on the benchmark

the fundamental idea of lifting these partial assignments into JUNIT test cases seems validated.

Regarding the performance of TACO and JTACO, surprisingly JTACO is outperformed on half of the subjects. A closer inspection revealed that, although a failing partial assignment was indeed found very quickly, the MINISAT process was mostly delayed by JTACO's generation and execution of test cases. In other words, the cost of generating and executing JUNIT test cases was higher than the benefit of stopping the SAT-Solver execution sooner, at least in a single-core environment. Observe that JTACO was faster if the first failing partial assignment occurred within the first 5% of the MINISAT execution time.

4 Conclusions and Further Work

Given the exponential complexity of the SAT-solving process, techniques for decreasing the execution time of bounded verification tools are paramount. In this work we presented an approach for generating JUNIT test cases from partial assignments collected during the SAT-Solver execution.

Besides general improvements such as robustness and maturity for the JTACO tool, our future work will focus on the following issues:

- **Runtime-checking of JML/JFSL Specifications:** The current prototype of JTACO only handles properties that are expressed as assert statements. In order to fully support JML and JFSL specifications we need to automatically synthesize runtime predicates for a significant fragment of the specification language (e.g., handling the runtime-checking of all the constructs used in [8]). Additionally, we also need to extend the lifting mechanism (introduced in Section 2) for handling initial values that do not satisfy the precondition of the method under analysis.
- **Bounded Verification of Correct Programs:** If ψ happens to be unsatisfiable, all the overhead invested in dumping partial assignments is lost. Due to this fact, JTACO could become a practical approach only if the SAT-Solver's overhead is reasonable in case the formula is unsatisfiable.

– **A Multi-core JTACO:** In a multi-core environment, several processes could be spawned for lifting different partial assignments without blocking the main MI-NISAT process. We expect that a multi-core JTACO might boost JTACO performance. Our future work will include a comparison against other parallel SAT-solving tools [9,14].

The current prototype of the JTACO tool, as well as all subjects required to replicate the results in this paper are publicly available. For details, see:

```
http://www.st.cs.uni-saarland.de/jtaco/
```

Acknowledgments. This work was funded by an European Research Council (ERC) Advanced Grant "SPECMATE – Specification Mining and Testing" and MEALS 295261. Eva May provided helpful comments about this work. We thank the anonymous reviewers for their comments and suggestions.

References

1. Bech, K., Gamma, E.: JUnit: A programmer-oriented testing framework for Java (May 2014), http://junit.org
2. Chalin, P., Kiniry, J.R., Leavens, G.T., Poll, E.: Beyond assertions: Advanced specification and verification with JML and ESC/Java2. In: de Boer, F.S., Bonsangue, M.M., Graf, S., de Roever, W.-P. (eds.) FMCO 2005. LNCS, vol. 4111, pp. 342–363. Springer, Heidelberg (2006)
3. Clarke, E., Kroning, D., Lerda, F.: A tool for checking ANSI-C programs. In: Jensen, K., Podelski, A. (eds.) TACAS 2004. LNCS, vol. 2988, pp. 168–176. Springer, Heidelberg (2004)
4. Davis, M., Logemann, G., Loveland, D.W.: A machine program for theorem-proving. Commun. ACM 5(7), 394–397 (1962)
5. Dennis, G., Yessenov, K., Jackson, D.: Bounded verification of voting software. In: Shankar, N., Woodcock, J. (eds.) VSTTE 2008. LNCS, vol. 5295, pp. 130–145. Springer, Heidelberg (2008)
6. D'Ippolito, N., Frias, M.F., Galeotti, J.P., Lanzarotti, E., Mera, S.: Alloy+HotCore: A fast approximation to unsat core. In: Frappier, M., Glässer, U., Khurshid, S., Laleau, R., Reeves, S. (eds.) ABZ 2010. LNCS, vol. 5977, pp. 160–173. Springer, Heidelberg (2010)
7. Eén, N., Sörensson, N.: An extensible SAT-solver. In: Giunchiglia, E., Tacchella, A. (eds.) SAT 2003. LNCS, vol. 2919, pp. 502–518. Springer, Heidelberg (2004)
8. Galeotti, J.P., Rosner, N., Pombo, C.L., Frias, M.F.: Analysis of invariants for efficient bounded verification. In: Tonella, P., Orso, A. (eds.) ISSTA, pp. 25–36. ACM (2010)
9. Hamadi, Y., Jabbour, S., Sais, L.: ManySAT: a parallel SAT solver. JSAT 6(4), 245–262 (2009)
10. Ivančić, F., Yang, Z., Ganai, M.K., Gupta, A., Shlyakhter, I., Ashar, P.: F-Soft: Software verification platform. In: Etessami, K., Rajamani, S.K. (eds.) CAV 2005. LNCS, vol. 3576, pp. 301–306. Springer, Heidelberg (2005)
11. Jackson, D.: Software Abstractions: Logic, Language, and Analysis, revised edition. The MIT Press (2012)
12. Near, J.P., Jackson, D.: Rubicon: bounded verification of web applications. In: Tracz, W., Robillard, M.P., Bultan, T. (eds.) SIGSOFT FSE, p. 60. ACM (2012)

13. Parrino, B.C., Galeotti, J.P., Garbervetsky, D., Frias, M.F.: TacoFlow: optimizing sat program verification using dataflow analysis. SoSyM: Software and Systems Modeling (2014)
14. Rosner, N., Galeotti, J.P., Bermúdez, S., Blas, G.M., Rosso, S.P.D., Pizzagalli, L., Zemín, L., Frias, M.F.: Parallel bounded analysis in code with rich invariants by refinement of field bounds. In: Pezzè, M., Harman, M. (eds.) ISSTA, pp. 23–33. ACM (2013)
15. Torlak, E., Chang, F.S.H., Jackson, D.: Finding minimal unsatisfiable cores of declarative specifications. In: Cuellar, J., Sere, K. (eds.) FM 2008. LNCS, vol. 5014, pp. 326–341. Springer, Heidelberg (2008)
16. Xie, Y., Aiken, A.: Saturn: A scalable framework for error detection using boolean satisfiability. ACM Trans. Program. Lang. Syst. 29(3) (2007)
17. Yessenov, K.: A light-weight specification language for bounded program verification. Master's thesis, MIT (2009)

Explicit Assumptions - A Prenup for Marrying Static and Dynamic Program Verification

Johannes Kanig[2], Rod Chapman[1], Cyrille Comar[2], Jerôme Guitton[2], Yannick Moy[2], and Emyr Rees[1]

[1] Altran UK, 22 St Lawrence Street, Bath BA1 1AN, United Kingdom
{rod.chapman,emyr.rees}@altran.com
[2] AdaCore, 46 rue d'Amsterdam, F-75009 Paris, France
{comar,guitton,kanig,moy}@adacore.com

Abstract. Formal modular verification of software is based on assume-guarantee reasoning, where each software module is shown to provide some guarantees under certain assumptions and an overall argument linking results for individual modules justifies the correctness of the approach. However, formal verification is almost never applied to the entire code, posing a potential soundness risk if some assumptions are not verified. In this paper, we show how this problem was addressed in an industrial project using the SPARK formal verification technology, developed at Altran UK. Based on this and similar experiences, we propose a partial automation of this process, using the notion of explicit assumptions. This partial automation may have the role of an enabler for formal verification, allowing the application of the technology to isolated modules of a code base while simultaneously controlling the risk of invalid assumptions. We demonstrate a possible application of this concept for the fine-grain integration of formal verification and testing of Ada programs.

Keywords: Formal methods, Program Verification, Test and Proof, Assumptions.

1 Introduction

Formal modular verification of software is based on assume-guarantee reasoning, where each software module is shown to provide some guarantees under certain assumptions, and an overall argument linking results for individual modules justifies the correctness of the approach. Typically, the assumptions for the analysis of one module are part of the guarantees which are provided by the analysis of other modules. The framework for assume-guarantee reasoning should be carefully designed to avoid possible unsoundness in this circular justification. For software, a prevalent framework for assume-guarantee reasoning is Hoare logic, where subprograms[1] are taken as the software modules, and subprogram contracts (precondition and postcondition) define the assumptions and guarantees.

---

[1] In this paper, we use the term *subprogram* to designate procedures and functions, and reserve the more common term of *function* to subprograms with a return value.

M. Seidl and N. Tillmann (Eds.): TAP 2014, LNCS 8570, pp. 142–157, 2014.

Formal verification tools based on Hoare logic analyze a subprogram without looking at the implementation of other subprograms, but only at their contract.

Although verification is done modularly, it is seldom the case that the results of verification are also presented modularly. It is tempting to only show which components have been verified (the guarantees), omitting the assumptions on which these results depend. This is indeed what many tools do, including the SPARK tools co-developed by Altran UK and AdaCore. In theory, the correctness of the approach would depend, among other things, on formal verification being applied to all parts of the software, which is never the case for industrial projects. Even when considered desirable to maximize formal verification, there are various reasons for not applying it to all components: too difficult, too costly, outside the scope of the method or tool, *etc.* In practice, expertise in the formal verification method and tool is required to manually justify that the implicit assumptions made by the tool are valid.

The care with which this manual analysis must be carried out is an incentive for system designers to minimize boundaries between formally verified modules and modules that are verified by other means. For example, this can be achieved by formally verifying the entire code except some difficult-to-verify driver code, or by formally verifying only a very critical core component of the system. However, such a monolithic approach is hindering a wider adoption of formal methods. Modules that are not formally verified are usually verified using other methods, often by testing. If combining verification results of *e.g.,* proof and test was easy, projects could freely choose the verification method to apply to a given component, based on tool capabilities and verification objectives. We propose to facilitate the effective combination of modular formal verification and other methods for the verification of critical software by extending the application of assume-guarantee reasoning to these other methods.

1.1   SPARK

SPARK is a subset of the Ada programming language targeted at safety- and security-critical applications. SPARK builds on the strengths of Ada for creating highly reliable and long-lived software. SPARK restrictions ensure that the behavior of a SPARK program is unambiguously defined, and simple enough that formal verification tools can perform an automatic diagnosis of conformance between a program specification and its implementation. The SPARK language and toolset for formal verification has been applied over many years to on-board aircraft systems, control systems, cryptographic systems, and rail systems [3,11].

In the versions of SPARK up to SPARK 2005, specifications are written as special annotations in comments. Since version SPARK 2014 [10], specifications are written as special Ada constructs attached to declarations. In particular, various contracts can be attached to subprograms: data flow contracts (introduced by global), information flow contracts, and functional contracts (preconditions and postconditions, introduced respectively by pre and post). An important difference between SPARK 2005 and SPARK 2014 is that functional contracts are executable in SPARK 2014, which greatly facilitates the combination between test and proof (see Section 4). The definition of the language subset is motivated by the simplicity and feasability of formal analysis and the need for an unambiguous semantics. Tools are available that provide flow analysis and proof of SPARK programs.

Flow analysis checks correct access to data in the program: correct access to global variables (as specified in data and information flow contracts) and correct access to initialized data. Proof is used to demonstrate that the program is free from run-time errors such as arithmetic overflow, buffer overflow and division-by-zero, and that the functional contracts are correctly implemented.

The different analyses support each other - for example, proof assumes that data flow analysis has been run without errors, which ensures that all variables are initialized to a well-defined value before use, that no side-effects appear in expressions and function calls, and that variables are not aliased. The latter point is partly achieved by excluding access (pointer) types from the language, and completed by a simple static analysis. For the purposes of this paper, we consider the SPARK analysis as a whole in Section 4 and will discuss interaction between the different analyses in Section 5.

1.2 Related Work

Neither the idea of explicit assumptions nor the idea of combining different types of analyses on a project are new. However, the focus of this line of research has been to show how different verification techniques can collaborate *on the same code* and support each other's assumptions. Examples are the explicit assumptions of Christakis *et al.* [5], the combination of analyses [7] in Frama-C [9], the EVE tool for Eiffel [13] and the work of Ahrendt *et al.* [1]. In contrast, we focus on the combination of verification results for *different* modules. Another line of research is the Evidential Tool Bus (ETB [8]), which concentrates on how to build a safe infrastructure for combining verification results from different sources and tracking the different claims and supporting evidence. An ETB could be used as the backbone for the framework that we describe in this paper.

1.3 Outline

In Section 2, we describe how the problem of heterogeneous verification was addressed in an industrial project using the SPARK formal verification technology, developed at Altran UK, using an ad-hoc methodology. In Section 3, we propose a framework for combining the results of different verification methods that can be partly automated, and thus lends itself to a more liberal combination of verification methods. In Sections 4 and 5, we present our experiments to combine at coarse-grain and fine-grain levels proof and test on Ada programs, using the SPARK technology that we develop.

2   Assumptions Management in a Large Safety-Critical Project

Project X^2 is a large, mission-critical, distributed application developed by Al-tran UK, and now in operational service. The software consists of several programs that execute concurrently on a network of servers and user workstations. The latter machines include a user-interface that is based on the X11/Motif UI framework.

Almost all of the software for Project X is written in SPARK 2005 and is subject to extensive formal verification with the SPARK 2005 toolset. Two other languages are used, though:

- Ada (not SPARK subset, but still subject to a project coding standard) is used where SPARK units need to call operating-system or compiler-defined run-time libraries.
- C code is used to form a layer between the SPARK code and the underlying X11/Motif libraries, which is implemented in C.

One program, called the UI Engine, is a multi-task SPARK program that uses the RavenSPARK subset of Ada's tasking features [3]. This mitigates many common problems with concurrent programming, such as deadlock and priority inversion. The C code is only ever called from a single task of the main SPARK program - a major simplification which prevents interference between the implementation languages, because the C code does not have global side effects. Also, in this way the C code does not need to worry about reentrance. The UI engine component is 87kloc (logical lines of code), comprising of 61kloc SPARK and 26kloc MISRA C.

2.1   The Requirements Satisfaction Argument

The fitness-for-purpose of Project X is justified at the top-level by a "Requirements Satisfaction Argument". This is essentially structured as a tree of goals, justifications, assumptions, and evidence, expressed in the Goal Structured Notation (GSN).

A large section of the GSN is devoted to non-interference arguments that form the core of the safety argument for Project X. Part of that non-interference argument includes detailed justifications for the integration of software written in multiple languages, and the prevention of defects that could arise. The leaves of the GSN typically refer to verification evidence (*e.g.*, test specifications, results, provenance of COTS components, static analysis results and so on) or standards (such as the coding standards for SPARK and C used by the project).

2.2   From SPARK to C (and Back Again)

In Project X, SPARK code calls C code to implement various user-interface elements. Beyond that point, the formal analyses offered by the SPARK toolset

---

[2] This is not its actual name, which we cannot mention.

Table 1. SPARK to C assumptions and verification

Assumption	How verified
Parameter types match	AUTO
Variables initialized	MISRA
Outputs in expected subtype	REVIEW, TEST
No side effects	MISRA
No aliasing	MISRA, REVIEW
Data flow contract respected	REVIEW
No thread/task interaction	REVIEW
No dynamic allocation	MISRA
Functional contract respected	REVIEW, TEST
Absence of run-time errors	TEST

are not available, so we cannot rely on these analyses to prove the assumptions made to analyze the SPARK code. Instead, the project manages an explicit list of assumptions that must be enforced across each such boundary. Essentially, the SPARK code assumes that the called C function is "well-behaved" according to a set of implicit project-wide rules (*e.g.*, the function terminates, and parameters are passed using the expected types and mechanism) and the explicit SPARK contract (*e.g.*, precondition and postcondition) applied to the SPARK specification of that function.

Each of these assumptions is verified on the C code through a combination of one or more of:

- AUTO. Automated code generation. In particular, the Ada and C type declarations that are used to communicate across the language boundary are automatically generated from a single description.
- MISRA. Automated static analysis using the MISRA C:2004 rules [2].
- REVIEW. Checklist-driven manual code review. In particular, parameter passing mechanisms and types are carefully reviewed to ensure they match across such a language boundary.
- TEST. Specific unit test objectives.

The set of MISRA rules enforced and the review checklist items were chosen to cover the assumptions needed to support the verification of the SPARK units. The project maintains a detailed analysis of every MISRA rule and how its use meets the assumptions required by the SPARK analysis. A small number of MISRA rules are not used by the project, or deviations may be justified on a case-by-case basis. Again, detailed records are maintained to make sure that these deviations do not undermine the analysis of the SPARK code. Table 1 shows how each major assumption made by the SPARK code is verified in the C code.

```
procedure Set_Off_Button
    (Button_Enabled    : Boolean;
     Background_Colour : Background_Colour_T);
--# global in out Shutdown.Error_Flag;
--#        in out Shutdown.Do_Shutdown_SO;
```

(a) The SPARK specification of Set_Off_Button

```
void TB_Set_Off_Button_SC (
    const bool                               Button_Enabled ,
    const HMI_Types__Background_Colour_T  Background_Colour,
          HMI_Types__Status_T*              Error);
```

(b) The C specification of TB_Set_Off_Button_SC

```
procedure Set_Off_Button
    (Button_Enabled    : Boolean;
     Background_Colour : Background_Colour_T)
is
    Button_Enabled_C    : C_Base_Types.C_Bool;
    Background_Colour_C : HMI_Types.C.Background_Colour_T;
    Error               : HMI_Types.C.Status_T;

    -- Here is the interface to C function TB_Set_Off_Button_SC
    procedure TB_Set_Off_Button
        (Button_Enabled_C   :       C_Base_Types.C_Bool;
         Background_Colour_C :       HMI_Types.C.Background_Colour_T;
         Error              : out HMI_Types.C.Status_T);
    pragma Import (C, TB_Set_Off_Button, "TB_Set_Off_Button_SC");
begin
    Button_Enabled_C := C_Base_Types.To_C_Bool (Button_Enabled);
    Background_Colour_C :=
        HMI_Types.C.To_C.Background_Colour_T (Background_Colour);

    -- Call to C here
    TB_Set_Off_Button
        (Button_Enabled_C   => Button_Enabled_C ,
         Background_Colour_C => Background_Colour_C,
         Error              => Error);

    Common_Error.Log_And_Handle_If_Error
        (Message => Error,
         Gate    => HMI_DM_Fatal_Error_In_C_Code);
end Set_Off_Button;
```

(c) The SPARK body of Set_Off_Button

Fig. 1. Excerpt of mixed SPARK/C code in Project X

```
/* PRQA S:R14_1_S002 1503 1 */
void TB_Set_Off_Button_SC (
    const bool                              Button_Enabled ,
    const HMI_Types__Background_Colour_T    Background_Colour ,
          HMI_Types__Status_T*              Error)
{
    CF_Set_OK (Error);
    CF_Set_Widget_Sensitivity(tb_OffButton , Button_Enabled);

    switch (Background_Colour)
    {
        case HMI_Types__Active_Colour:
        {
            XtVaSetValues (tb_OffButton ,
                           XmNbackground ,      /* PRQA S:R11_5_S001 0311 */
                           Alert_Colour ,
                           NULL);
            break;
        }
        case HMI_Types__No_Colour:
        {
            XtVaSetValues (tb_OffButton ,
                           XmNbackground ,      /* PRQA S:R11_5_S001 0311 */
                           Background_Colour ,
                           NULL);
            break;
        }
        default:  /* PRQA S:R14_1_S001 2018 */
        {
            CF_Set_Not_OK_Str_Int (Error ,
                                   "Invalid Off Background Colour, Enum ",
                                   (int) Background_Colour);
            /* Note that analysis deemed that a failure to decode an */
            /* enumeration is likely to have been caused by a memory */
            /* corruption, and to continue processing would be unsafe. */
            /* Assign the category as force shutdown. */
            CF_Set_Category (Error ,
                             HMI_Common_Types__Force_Shutdown ,
                             CF_On_Error_Abort);
        } break;
    }
}
```

(d) The C implementation of **TB_Set_Off_Button_SC**

Fig. 1. (*Continued.*)

2.3   Example

This section shows an example of how SPARK code interfaces to a UI function that is written in C. The SPARK specification is given Listing 1a. Note the data flow contract introduced by **global**. This specifies the frame condition of the procedure - stating exactly the set of objects that may be referenced and/or updated by the procecure and (implicitly) defining that *no other* objects are used. In this case, we see that the procedure may read and update two objects in package Shutdown, both of which record the need to terminate the system in response to a fatal error.

The SPARK implementation is given in Listing 1c. Ada's pragma Import here specifies Convention "C" for the nested procedure - this instructs the compiler to pass parameters as would be expected in C, according to a set of rules given in the Ada Reference Manual.

The corresponding C header is provided in Listing 1b. Note the careful use of naming conventions here to ease the task of both generating and reviewing the Ada/C interface. Finally, the C implementation is given in Listing 1d. Note that the coding is overtly defensive, dealing with the possibility of a memory corruption leading to the default branch of the switch statement being executed. The "PRQA" comments are instructions to the MISRA analysis tool to suppress particular warnings. All of these comments are collated and verified as part of the satisfaction argument.

Consider one particular verification objective for this code: the output parameter **Error** on the SPARK declaration of the imported procedure **TB_Set_Off_Button**. In SPARK, output parameters *must* be defined by the called procedure in all cases. This ensures that **Error** is properly initialized when calling **Log_And_Handle_Error** inside the body of **Set_Off_Button**. If the body of **TB_Set_Off_Button** were written in SPARK, then the flow analysis engine would verify this obligation, but since the body is in C, additional steps are needed. In this case, an explicit review checklist item requires C function parameters that correspond to SPARK output parameters to be unconditionally initialized - hence the call to **CF_Set_OK** that initializes **Error** at the top of the function body, for cases which do not result in an error.

2.4   Summary

This approach has proven reliable in practice, owing to judicious architectural design, a strong desire to minimize the volume of C code (although 26kloc does still feel a little too large for comfort in an 87kloc application), and strict adherence to design and coding disciplines through automated analysis, review checklists and focussed testing.

The main drawback is the time, expense and paperwork required to maintain the satisfaction argument and its supporting evidence across a long-lived project, which has absorbed several major UI re-designs in its lifetime.

3   Tool Assisted Assumptions Management

Reading the previous section, the reader may ask the questions of how we came up with the left column of Table 1 and how all subprograms at the interface have been identified. This is in fact the result of expert knowledge of the SPARK technology as well as specificities of the project. We want to present here a more systematic way to achieve the same goal.

The work done on Project X to develop Table 1 and to apply it at the boundary between formal verification and other methods can be broken down into three steps:

- listing all assumptions of formal verification,
- verifying the non-formally-verified modules using some other method, so that the previous assumptions are verified, and
- checking that all assumptions have been taken care of.

It is clear that for the first and the last step, tool support is possible and welcome, and this is the topic of this paper. We propose to enhance formal verification tools to not only output verification results, but also the assumptions these results rely on - a more detailed version of the left column of Table 1. As non-formal methods may rely on assumptions as well, we may also require that these other methods explicitly list all their assumptions and guarantees when applied to a module. These should be precise enough to avoid holes in the justification, or subtly different interpretations of the properties in different methods. As an extreme example, "module M is correct" is not at the appropriate level of precision. For formal methods, this requires an explicit enumeration of the usually implicit assumptions made for the verification of a component, like non-aliasing of subprogram parameters, non-interference of subprogram, validity of the data accessed, *etc.* For informal methods, this requires defining methodological assumptions and guarantees that the method relies upon.

Formally, each verification activity is a process whose output is a list of Horn clauses, that is, implications of the form

$$A_1 \wedge A_2 \wedge \cdots \wedge A_n \rightarrow C$$

where C is a claim[3], and the A_i are assumptions. The exact form of claims and assumptions differs for each method and tool. The next sections will provide examples based on SPARK.

Compared to the manual process in the previous section, the advantage is that the "checklist" of verification activities at the boundary between verification methods is simply provided by each tool, and does not require that users possess this level of expertise about the tool. The assumptions still need to be verified of course - that is the right column of Table 1.

---

[3] We prefer to use the word "claim" here over "guarantee", as it more clearly conveys the idea that until the corresponding assumptions are verified, no guarantee can be given.

If explicit assumptions are gathered for all verification activities on the project, we can simply consider together all Horn clauses, and simple queries such as

– Is claim C completely verified?
– On which unverified assumptions is claim C based on?
– Which verification activities are left to do to verify claim C?
– If assumption A turns out to be invalid, which claims does this impact?

can be answered simply by analyzing these Horn clauses.

Other forms of explicit assumptions are possible. Christakis *et al.* [5] and Correnson and Signoles [7] describe assumptions and claims as formulas at program points, which is more precise than our approach. The drawback is the complexity to generate and exploit these assumptions, as their formulation implies the use of a weakest precondition calculus in the former work, or trace semantics in the latter work, in order to interpret the meaning of a formula at a program point. Also, simply formulating these formulas already requires choosing a memory model. Instead, we prefer to see claims and assumptions as well-defined, parameterized properties uniquely identified by a tag. For example, where Christakis *et al.* use the formula $c \neq d$ to express non-aliasing of two parameters at subprogram entry, we prefer to write it as the property *Nonaliased*(c, d) where the names c and d are given in a format which allows their unique identification, and *Nonaliased* is a tag which is unambiguously defined to mean that two variables do not share any memory. Similarly, to denote an assumption on the precondition of some subprogram p, we would write $Pre(p)$ instead of the formula which constitutes the precondition.

This choice, together with the choice of Horn clauses as data format, makes it much simpler to feed assumptions to existing tools such as the ETB [8] and opens the door to tool assisted assumptions management.

4 Coarse-Grain Assumptions Management

We have described in some previous work [6] a coarse-grain application of the framework described in the previous section, to combine the results of test and proof on Ada programs (proof being restricted to SPARK subprograms) in the context of certification of avionics software following the DO-178C [12] certification standard. In this context, tests with MC/DC coverage [4] or proofs are two acceptable methods to verify a module, where modules here are subprograms. We can reexpress the goal of verifying a subprogram P using Horn clauses as described in the previous section:

$$Tests\_Passed(P) \wedge MCDC\_Covered(P) \rightarrow Verified(P)$$
$$Contract\_Proved(P) \wedge No\_Runtime\_Errors(P) \rightarrow Verified(P)$$

Note that assumptions made during proof are still implicit in the Horn clauses above. Assumptions related to functional contracts, like the guarantee that called subprograms respect their postcondition, or that the subprogram proved is only called in a context where its precondition holds, are discharged either by the proof of the callees/callers, or by executing the corresponding contracts during the test of the callees/callers. Thus, it is essential for the combination that functional contracts are executable. Other assumptions related to non-aliasing of parameters, or validity of variables, are discharged by having the compiler instrument the tested programs to check the assumptions. Finally, the assumptions that cannot be tested are guaranteed by the combination of a coding standard and a static analysis on the whole program. The coding standard forbids in particular calls through subprogram pointers, so that the call-graph is statically known. The static analysis forbids aliasing between parameters of a call and global variables that appear in the data flow contract for the called subprogram.

We built a prototype tool in Python implementing this approach, allowing users to specify the generic Horn clauses above in some special syntax. This monolithic specially crafted approach for SPARK was not completely satisfying, as it was not easily extensible or customizable by users. This is why we switched to a finer-grain approach where assumptions are explicit.

5   Fine-Grain Assumptions Management

We consider now the combination of verification results for individual subprograms whose declaration is in SPARK. As described in Section 1.1, various contracts can be attached to such subprograms: data flow contracts, information flow contracts, and functional contracts (preconditions and postconditions).

5.1   Claims and Assumptions

We provide a detailed definition of claims and assumptions for SPARK. We assume subprograms are uniquely identified, for example by using their name and the source location of the declaration. We also assume that *calls* to subprograms are uniquely identified, again using *e.g.,* the source location of the call. We use capital letters such as P for subprograms, and write $P@$ to indicate a specific call to a subprogram.

It should be noted that some fundamental assumptions, *e.g.,* correctness of the verification tool, compiler and hardware, are out of scope of this framework and are not taken into account here.

SPARK formal verification tools may be used to ensure that the following claims are satisfied by a subprogram P or a call to P:

- *Effects*(P) - the subprogram P only reads input variables and writes output variables according to its data flow contract.
- *Init*(P) - the subprogram P is only called when all its input parameters, and all the input variables in its data flow contract, are initialized.
- *Init*$(P@)$ - in this specific calling context of P, all its input parameters, and all the input variables in its data flow contract, are initialized.
- *Nonaliasing*(P) - the subprogram P is not called with parameters which would create aliasing.

- *Nonaliasing*(P @) - in this specific calling context of P, the values of parameters do not create aliasing.
- *AoRTE*(P) - the subprogram P is free of run-time errors.
- *Contract*(P) - the subprogram P respects its contract, that is, the precondition is sufficient to guarantee the postcondition.
- *Pre*(P) - the subprogram P is only called in a context that respects its precondition.
- *Pre*(P @) - in this specific calling context of P, its precondition is respected.
- *Term*(P) - the subprogram P terminates.

The output of the SPARK tools can then be described as follows. Given a subprogram P which contains the calls R_i @, if flow analysis is applied without errors, then the following set of Horn clauses holds:

$$Effects(R_i) \wedge Init(P) \wedge Nonaliasing(P) \longrightarrow Effects(P) \wedge$$
$$Init(R_i @) \wedge$$
$$Nonaliasing(R_i @) \qquad (1)$$

and if proof is applied without unproved properties being reported, then the following set of Horn clauses holds:

$$Effects(R_i) \wedge Init(P) \wedge Nonaliasing(P) \wedge$$
$$AoRTE(R_i) \wedge Contract(R_i) \wedge Pre(P) \longrightarrow AoRTE(P) \wedge$$
$$Pre(R_i @) \qquad (2)$$
$$Effects(R_i) \wedge Init(P) \wedge Nonaliasing(P) \wedge$$
$$Contract(R_i) \longrightarrow Contract(P) \qquad (3)$$

For the sake of succinctness, we have taken the liberty to merge Horn clauses with different conclusions, but identical premises - this is only a shortcut for the equivalent expansion using only Horn clauses. The result of successful flow analysis of subprogram P, as expressed in Formula 1, is that, assuming P's callees respect their data flow contract, and assuming P is always called on initialized inputs and non-aliased inputs/outputs, then P respects its data flow contract, and calls inside P are done in a context which does not introduce uninitialized inputs or aliasing for the callee. For proof, there are in fact two different sets of results and assumptions. The first one, expressed in Formula 2, is that, assuming P's callees respect their data flow contract and their pre/post contract, and they do not raise run-time errors, and assuming P is always called on initialized inputs and non-aliased inputs/outputs, in a context where its precondition holds, then P does not raise run-time errors, and calls inside P are done in a context where their precondition holds. The second one, expressed in Formula 3, is that assuming P's callees respect their data flow contract and their pre/post contract, and assuming P is always called on initialized inputs and non-aliased inputs/outputs, then P also respects its pre/post contract.

Note that the precondition of P is *not* an assumption of Formula 3, because the tag *Contract* already includes the precondition. In this manner, as can be easily seen, Formula 3 propagates assumptions about contracts *down* the call graph, while Formula 2 propagates the assumptions on preconditions *up* the call graph.

Note that *Pre*, *Init* and *Nonaliasing* applied to a subprogram are a bit special: they only appear as assumptions and not as claims. They are in fact assumptions on the calling context, and the only way to discharge them is to verify that they hold for all calling contexts. As a consequence, a non-modular analysis is needed here to identify all calls to a subprogram, so we add Horn clauses of the form:

$$tag(\overline{P@}) \longrightarrow tag(P) \tag{4}$$

where *tag* is any of *Pre*, *Init* and *Nonaliasing* and $\overline{P@}$ are all calls to a given subprogram P. An important special case is that, for main subprograms (which are not called by any other subprogram), we obtain the immediate guarantees of the form:

$$tag(P) \tag{5}$$

By combining Formulas 1, 4, and 5, it can be checked easily that, if formal verification is applied to the entire program[4], then *Effects*(P), *Init*(P) and *Nonaliasing*(P) hold for every subprogram P. Similarly, by combining Formulas 2 to 5 together with the guarantees just obtained, it can be checked easily that, if formal verification is applied to the entire program, then *AoRTE*(P), *Pre*(P) and *Contract*(P) hold for every subprogram P. As we did not check termination here, this corresponds exactly to partial correctness of the program.

But, as we argued earlier, it is almost never the case that formal verification is applied to a complete program. In that very common case, it is not immediately clear what guarantees the application of formal verification gives. In particular, a user is probably interested in knowing that no run-time errors can be raised, which corresponds in our formalization to *AoRTE*(P) and *Pre*$(P@)$ and that the subprogram contracts are respected, which corresponds in our formalization to *Effects*(P) and *Contract*(P). With our formulation of formal verification results as Horn clauses, we can precisely compute on which unverified assumptions these claims depend.

Termination. We have not discussed termination (represented by the tag *Term*) yet. In fact, termination is *not* an assumption of Formulas 2 and 3, because the properties claimed there are formulated in terms of partial correctness. For example, the most precise formalization of *Contract* is: if the precondition holds, and *if* the control flow of the program reaches the end of the subprogram, then the postcondition holds. Assuming absence of recursion, the SPARK tools can in fact establish termination by adding the following set of Horn clauses for each subprogram:

$$Term(R_i) \wedge Term(L_k) \longrightarrow Term(P)$$

where the R_i are the subprograms called and the L_k are the loops occurring in the subprogram P. Termination of loops can be established in SPARK by two means: `for`-loops terminate by construction in Ada, and more general loops can be annotated with a variant, wich allows to prove termination of the loop.

---

[4] We are assuming absence of recursion in the program. Recursion requires a more advanced treatment.

Table 2. Assumptions and possible verification strategies

assumption	verification strategy
assumption on call	
$Init(P@)$	coding standard, run-time initialization checking
$Nonaliasing(P@)$	static analysis, run-time non-aliasing checking, review
$Pre(P@)$	unit testing with assertions enabled
assumption on subprogram	
$Effects(P)$	static analysis, review, coding standard
$AoRTE(P)$	unit testing with run-time checks enabled
$Contract(P)$	unit testing with assertions enabled
$Term(P)$	unit testing, review

5.2 Discharging Assumptions

As visible from Formulas 1 to 3, the SPARK tools provide claims for the formal verification of one subprogram that discharge assumptions for the formal verification of another subprogram. It remains to see how to discharge assumptions at the boundary between formally verified and non-formally verified code.

Table 2 summarizes the assumptions of SPARK and presents possible verification strategies when the SPARK tools cannot be applied to the code on which the assumption is issued. The possibility in Ada to perform exhaustive run-time checking allows applying unit testing for verifying the absence of run-time errors. The possibility to also execute functional contracts is only available with SPARK 2014, not SPARK 2005, and it allows applying unit testing for verifying functional contracts.

Assumptions on the calling context are a bit more difficult to verify. Table 2 does not contain entries for assumptions on the calling context, so the first step is to find out all callers. Once all call points are identified, one needs to verify that each call verifies the assumptions that have been made for the verification of the called subprogram. This poses another interesting challenge: How to verify by testing that, *e.g.,* the precondition of a call deep inside the tested subprogram holds? How can one be sure that enough testing was applied? We are not answering these questions in this paper, but raising the issue.

Finally, SPARK lets the user insert assumptions inside the program for both flow analysis and proof. A typical example is a counter whose incrementation could overflow in theory, but never does in practice because it would require that the system runs for longer that its longest foreseen running time. In that case, the user can insert a suitable code assumption before the counter is incremented:

```
pragma Assume (Cnt < Integer'Last, "system is rebooted every day");
Cnt := Cnt + 1;
```

Such assumptions can also be part of the output of the tools, so that a review of all remaining assumptions can assess their validity.

5.3　A Concrete Example

In this section, we exercise the assumptions mechanism on the example provided in Section 2. Let us assume that we apply the SPARK tools only to Set_Off_Button, and in the remainder of this section we assume that flow analysis and proof have been applied successfully. We therefore obtain the following verification results:

$$Effects(R_i) \wedge Init(P) \longrightarrow Effects(P) \wedge Init(R_i@)$$
$$Effects(R_i) \wedge Init(P) \wedge AoRTE(R_i) \longrightarrow AoRTE(P)$$

where P is Set_Off_Button and the R_i are the subprograms called by Set_Off_Button: To_C_Bool, Background_Color_T, TB_Set_Off_Button, and Log_And_Handle_If_Error.

Note that the above statement is somewhat shorter than the general one because the tags *Pre* and *Contract* do not apply (no preconditions or postconditions appear in the example), just as the tag *Nonaliasing*. In fact, it is impossible for aliasing to occur in the example, partly due to the types of parameters that cannot alias in some calls, and partly because scalar input parameters are passed by copy in Ada, and thus cannot alias with anything. The other claims that SPARK could provide do not apply, because Set_Off_Button doesn't have a postcondition, and the called subprograms do not have preconditions.

There are three assumptions in the above Horn clauses, for which we can find both which verification was actually performed in Project X, in Table 1, and to which general verification strategy this corresponds, in Table 2, as summarized in Table 3:

Table 3. Discharging assumptions by other methods in a concrete example

Assumption	How verified in Project X	Verification strategy applied
$Effects(R_i)$	MISRA	coding standard
$Init(P)$	MISRA	coding standard
$AoRTE(R_i)$	TEST	unit testing

In fact, most assumptions from Table 1 also appear in Table 2. Those that do not appear are project-specific. For example, the use of SPARK tools does not prevent the use of dynamic allocation in other parts of the program, in general. It happens to be a requirement of the project described in this paper.

6　Conclusion

We have presented the current state of the art in industrial software when applying formal verification on part of the code only. We reused the notion of explicit assumptions, which has already been present in other works, but used differently and for different purposes, to show how to render formal verification truly modular by proper tool support. We have experimented with a coarse-grain variant of explicit assumptions to realize the combination of proof and test, and have presented a more fine-grain model.

Future Work. Our immediate plan is to implement explicit assumptions in the SPARK technology, using the evidential tool bus as the back-end for assumptions management. More work is required to make the application of the framework truly usable. For example, all the presented tags simply have a subprogram name or call as argument. To increase precision, it would be better to also include tags with variable arguments, *e.g.*, a tag such as *Nonaliasing*(x, y). Such support is not very different from what we describe here, but much more complex to write down, and the non-modular analysis to match call guarantees with calling context assumptions requires more work.

Our ultimate goal is to provide support for assumptions management and a smooth combination of test and proof in a future version of the commercial SPARK tools.

References

1. Ahrendt, W., Pace, G.J., Schneider, G.: A unified approach for static and runtime verification: framework and applications. In: Margaria, T., Steffen, B. (eds.) ISoLA 2012, Part I. LNCS, vol. 7609, pp. 312–326. Springer, Heidelberg (2012)
2. M. I. S. R. Association. MISRA C:2004 - Guidelines for the use of the C language in critical systems (2004)
3. Barnes, J.: SPARK: The Proven Approach to High Integrity Software. Altran Praxis (2012)
4. Chilenski, J.J.: An Investigation of Three Forms of the Modified Condition/Decision Coverage (MCDC) Criterion. Technical Report DOT/FAA/AR-01/18 (April 2001)
5. Christakis, M., Müller, P., Wüstholz, V.: Collaborative verification and testing with explicit assumptions. In: Giannakopoulou, D., Méry, D. (eds.) FM 2012. LNCS, vol. 7436, pp. 132–146. Springer, Heidelberg (2012)
6. Comar, C., Kanig, J., Moy, Y.: Integrating formal program verification with testing. In: Proc. ERTS (2012)
7. Correnson, L., Signoles, J.: Combining Analyses for C Program Verification. In: Stoelinga, M., Pinger, R. (eds.) FMICS 2012. LNCS, vol. 7437, pp. 108–130. Springer, Heidelberg (2012)
8. Cruanes, S., Hamon, G., Owre, S., Shankar, N.: Tool integration with the evidential tool bus. In: Giacobazzi, R., Berdine, J., Mastroeni, I. (eds.) VMCAI 2013. LNCS, vol. 7737, pp. 275–294. Springer, Heidelberg (2013)
9. Cuoq, P., Signoles, J., Baudin, P., Bonichon, R., Canet, G., Correnson, L., Monate, B., Prevosto, V., Puccetti, A.: Experience report: OCaml for an industrial-strength static analysis framework. SIGPLAN Not. 44(9), 281–286 (2009)
10. Dross, C., Efstathopoulos, P., Lesens, D., Mentré, D., Moy, Y.: Rail, space, security: Three case studies for spark 2014. In: Proc. ERTS (2014)
11. O'Neill, I.: SPARK – a language and tool-set for high-integrity software development. In: Boulanger, J.-L. (ed.) Industrial Use of Formal Methods: Formal Verification. Wiley (2012)
12. RTCA. DO-178C: Software considerations in airborne systems and equipment certification (2011)
13. Tschannen, J., Furia, C.A., Nordio, M., Meyer, B.: Usable verification of object-oriented programs by combining static and dynamic techniques. In: Barthe, G., Pardo, A., Schneider, G. (eds.) SEFM 2011. LNCS, vol. 7041, pp. 382–398. Springer, Heidelberg (2011)

A Case Study on Verification of a Cloud Hypervisor by Proof and Structural Testing*

Nikolai Kosmatov[1], Matthieu Lemerre[1], and Céline Alec[2]

[1] CEA, LIST, Software Reliability Laboratory, PC 174, 91191 Gif-sur-Yvette, France
{firstname.lastname}@cea.fr
[2] LRI, CNRS UMR 8623, Université Paris-Sud, France
lastname@lri.fr

Abstract. Complete formal verification of software remains extremely expensive and often reserved in practice for the most critical products. Test generation techniques are much less costly and can be used in combination with theorem proving tools to provide high confidence in the software correctness at an acceptable cost when an automatic prover does not succeed alone. This short paper presents a case study on verification of a cloud hypervisor with the Frama-C toolset, in which deductive verification has been advantageously combined with structural all-path testing. We describe our combined verification approach, present the adopted methodology and emphasize its benefits and limitations.

Keywords: deductive verification, test generation, specification, Frama-C.

1 Introduction

Deductive verification can provide a rigorous mathematical proof that a given annotated program respects its specification, but remains relatively expensive, whereas testing can find counter-examples or increase confidence in the program correctness at a much lower cost. This short paper describes how both techniques have been combined during the verification of a critical module of a cloud hypervisor using the FRAMA-C toolset [1]. This case study has focused on combining automatic theorem proving and automatic structural testing in order to provide a high confidence in the system within limited time and costs. In particular, we address the question of how to share the roles between formal proof and testing in order to take the best of each technique and to increase the final level of confidence. The contributions of this paper include the presentation of the combined verification approach, the proposed methodology, its evaluation and results.

2 The Anaxagoros Hypervisor and Its Virtual Memory Module

Since the usage of cloud becomes pervasive in our lives, it is necessary to ensure the reliability, safety and security of cloud environments [2]. Anaxagoros [3,4] is a secure

---

* This research work has received funding from the FUI-AAP14 SYSTEM@TIC Paris-Région project "PISCO" partially funded by bpifrance.

M. Seidl and N. Tillmann (Eds.): TAP 2014, LNCS 8570, pp. 158–164, 2014.

microkernel and hypervisor developed at CEA LIST, that can virtualize preexisting operating systems, for example, Linux virtual machines. It enables execution of hard real-time tasks or operating systems, for instance the PharOS real-time system [5], securely along with non real-time tasks, on a single chip. This goal has required to put a strong emphasis on security in the design of the system.

A critical component to ensure security in Anaxagoros is its *virtual memory system* [4]. The x86 processor (as many other high-end hardware architectures) provides a mechanism for *virtual memory translation*, that translates an address manipulated by a program into a real physical address. One of the goals of this mechanism is to help to organize the program address space, for instance, to allow a program to access big contiguous memory regions. The other goal is to control the memory that a program can access. The physical memory is split into same-sized regions, called *frames* or *physical pages*, that we will simply call *pages* in this paper. Pages can be of several types: data, pagetable, pagedirectory. Basically, page directories contain mappings (i.e. references) to page tables, that in turn contain mappings to data pages. The page size is 4kB on standard x86 configurations.

Anaxagoros does not decide what is written to pages; rather, it allows tasks to perform any operations on pages, provided that this does not affect the security of the kernel itself, and of the other tasks in the system. To do that, it has to ensure only two simple properties. The first one ensures that a program can only access a page that it "owns". The second property states that pages are used according to their types.

Indeed, the hardware does not prevent a page table or a page directory from being also used as a data page. Thus, if no protection mechanism is present, a task can change the mappings and, after realizing a certain sequence of modifications, it can finally access (and write to) any page, including those that it does not own.

The virtual memory module should prevent such unauthorized modifications. It relies on recording the type of each page and maintaining counters of mappings to each page (i.e. the number of times the page is referred as a data page, page table, or page directory). The module ensures that pages can be used only according to their role. In addition, to allow dynamic reuse of memory, the module should make it possible to change the type of a page. To avoid possible attacks, changing the page type requires that we ensure even more complex additional properties. (Simplified) examples of properties include: page contents should be cleaned before any type change; still referred pages cannot be cleaned; the cleaning should be correctly resumed after an interruption; the counters of mappings (references) should be correctly maintained; cleaned pages are never referred to; etc.

3   The Verification Approach and Methodology

3.1   Context and Objectives

The verification target of this case study was a simplified sequential version of the Anaxagoros virtual memory system containing a significant subset of its features (pages of all three types, read-only and writable mappings, page cleaning with possible interruptions, page type changes, counters of mappings, etc.). Our objective was to study how such different verification techniques as automatic theorem proving and structural

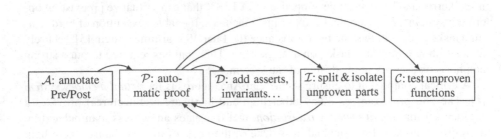

Fig. 1. Methodology of combined verification

testing could be combined together in order to provide the best trade-off between correctness guarantees obtained by rigorous formal proof and low cost of automatic structural testing.

We used verification tools offered by the FRAMA-C framework for verification of C programs [1], in particular, the JESSIE plugin [6] for Hoare logic based deductive verification with the automatic provers Alt-Ergo and Simplify, and the concolic test generator PATHCRAWLER [7,8]. FRAMA-C also offers an expressive specification language for C programs called ACSL [1]. Therefore we needed to annotate the C code in ACSL, apply whenever possible automatic theorem proving using JESSIE and complete verification using PATHCRAWLER. The ACSL specification was derived from informal specification of the code and an earlier formalization and (paper-and-pencil) proof of properties for the Anaxagoros virtual memory system detailed in [9].

3.2 The Methodology

Very soon after the beginning of the project, when the first proof failures occurred (along with the difficulties of their analysis) and the first naive attempts to complete verification with testing appeared to be inconclusive, it became clear that we needed to elaborate a structured methodology that would allow to advantageously combine proof and testing. The adopted methodology is outlined in Fig. 1.

Step ($\mathcal{A}$) consists of writing initial Annotations including e.g. function contracts with pre-/postconditions and auxiliary predicates with global invariants necessary to express function contracts. Step ($\mathcal{P}$) applies automatic Proof. When proof failures occur, the specification Detailing step ($\mathcal{D}$) consists in analysis of failures and adding further annotations (assertions, loop invariants, revised function contracts). Several iterations between Steps ($\mathcal{P}$) and ($\mathcal{D}$) can be necessary to help an automatic prover to prove as many properties as possible, and to identify the origin of each remaining proof failure, for instance, by surrounding relevant statements by appropriate assertions. The first steps ($\mathcal{A}$), ($\mathcal{P}$), ($\mathcal{D}$) are commonly used in deductive verification practice.

When the origin of each proof failure is identified (in terms of particular statements that cannot be traversed by the proof, and particular parts of the global property whose proof fails), we apply the Isolation step ($\mathcal{I}$). It consists of splitting an unproven function into simpler ones in order to isolate an unproven part in a smaller annotated function.

So, if a function f is not proven and a (block of) statement(s) s is identified as the origin of a proof failure, we isolate s in a separate annotated function g, and a call to g will now replace s in f. Since modular deductive verification of f relies on the contract of g, it allows us to prove f (under hypothesis that g is correct). The original function f is now proven, and we isolated proof failures in simpler functions.

Finally, each remaining unproven function g is verified using Step ($\mathcal{C}$) that applies all-path testing w.r.t. a specification, sometimes also called *Cross-checking*. Assume the specification of a function g is translated into a C function u. In cross-checking, the user runs all-path testing on a new function h that calls the function under test g and its specification u, in order to check whether it is possible to cover a path which conjoins a path in g and a path in u which fails to satisfy the specification (see [10, "Bypassing the limits..." section] for more detail). When cross-checking is used with an all-path testing tool ensuring completeness like PATHCRAWLER [8, Sec. 3.1] and when the tool manages to explore all paths (hence, the resulting function h has a finite number of paths), the absence of a counter-example provides a guarantee of correctness.

In general, the number of paths in h can be however too big to be explored. In this case, testing cannot provide any guarantee of correctness. Hence, we propose to *limit the program input domain so that the number of paths becomes finite but remains representative* of the behavior of the function under test (cf discussion below). Absence of counter-examples for the remaining unproven functions established by automatic cross-checking on a reduced input domain provides the verification engineer with additional confidence in correctness of these unproven parts when an automatic prover fails to complete the proof.

3.3   Benefits and Limitations of the Approach

We applied and evaluated the proposed methodology on the present case study. The results are very encouraging. First of all, relying only on automatic verification techniques, our approach could be acceptable for most software developers and validation engineers. Indeed, the present case study was performed within 2 months, and was mainly conducted by a junior software engineer who did not have any experience in software verification before this project. The complete annotated C code contains 2400 lines with 37 functions and the total number of 3915 proof obligations was generated by JESSIE.

Second, Steps ($\mathcal{D}$) and ($\mathcal{I}$) helped to prove as much as possible (98.8% of generated proof obligations were proven by JESSIE), and to identify and isolate actions and properties for which automatic proof failed. Starting from a situation where automatic proof failed for most functions without any clear reason, we were finally able to precisely identify and isolate the real proof issues. Unproven code has been reduced to one-line functions (e.g. changing one element of a page) that impact the counters of mappings.

Maintaining the counters of mappings appeared to be the most difficult issue for automatic proof in this case study so we present it here in more detail. Fig. 2 shows a (simplified) definition of two inductive predicates used to count mappings, where `pData[p*PageSize + i]` represents the element of index `i` in page of index `p`. The predicate `CountOne` states that `N` is the number of occurrences of target page `targ` at index range `0..last` of the page of index `p`. The predicate `CountAll` states that `N` is the number of occurrences of target page `targ` in the pages of index range `0..lastP`. A frequent origin of proof failures in this case study is related to the (simplified) global invariant `Inv` that says that `Mappings[targ]` is indeed the number of occurrences of `targ` in all pages.

Finally, thanks to Steps ($\mathcal{D}$) and ($\mathcal{I}$), the isolated unproven functions were quite appropriate for cross-checking. For instance, consider a simple function writing a new element into a page: `pData[p*PageSize + i]=new`. If true in the precondition, the invariant `Inv` would remain true in the postcondition for all elements except for the new and the old element (if they are different) for which the real number of occurrences becomes greater (resp., less) by 1 than the unmodified counter of mappings. Such elementary unproven functions do not contain any loops, and the C version of its specification contains only fixed-size loops over all page entries to compute the real number of occurrences (specified by `CountAll` in Fig. 2). Therefore, a simple way to limit path explosion for such functions would be to limit the page size and number of pages to smaller constants, say, 5. This limit does not modify the function logic, and is very unlikely to eliminate a counter-example in this case (even if it cannot be excluded). It shows that cross-checking of Step ($\mathcal{C}$) can be run on reduced, but representative input domain, and provide a higher confidence in program correctness at a relatively low cost.

One limitation of the methodology is the need to restructure the code and to move some parts of a function into a separate function at Step ($\mathcal{I}$) that might be not desirable at the verification step. Notice however, that it could often be acceptable because high-level function interfaces (such as microkernel hypercalls) are not modified, since the code restructuring is performed on the sub-function level. Moreover, the proposed methodology can be hopefully adopted by the developers that might find it useful to structure their code in a way that facilitates verification.

The second limitation is related to the need of reducing the input domain for cross-checking at Step ($\mathcal{C}$). When there is no way to reduce the program input domain to a representative smaller subset, it can still be interesting to obtain some confidence after a partial cross-checking.

4   Related Work and Conclusion

Klein et al. [11] presented formal verification for seL4, a microkernel allowing devices running seL4 to achieve the EAL7 level of the Common Criteria. Another formal verification of a microkernel was described in [12]. In both projects, the verification used interactive, machine-assisted and machine-checked proof with the theorem prover Isabelle/HOL. The formal verification of a simple hypervisor [13] used VCC, an automatic first-order logic based verifier for C. The underlying architecture was precisely modeled and represented in VCC, where the mixed-language system software was then proved correct. Unlike [11] and [12], this technique was based on automated methods.

[14] reports on verification of the translation lookaside buffer (TLB) virtualization, a core component of modern hypervisors. As devices run in parallel with software, they require concurrent program reasoning even for single-threaded software. This work gives a general methodology for verifying virtual device implementations, and demonstrate the verification of TLB virtualization code in VCC.

Formal verification nowadays remains very expensive. [15] estimates that the verification of the seL4 microkernel took around 25 person-years, and required highly

```
 1 #define NumPages 10000     // number of memory pages
 2 #define PageSize 1024       // page size (in words)
 3 unsigned int pData[NumPages * PageSize]; // page entries
 4 unsigned int Mappings[NumPages]; // counters of references (mappings) to pages
 5 /*@
 6 inductive countOne{L}(integer p, integer last, integer targ, integer N){
 7   case oneEq: \forall integer p, targ;
 8     0<=p<NumPages && pData[p*PageSize] == targ ==> countOne(p, 0, targ, 1);
 9   case oneNotEq: \forall integer p, targ;
10     0<=p<NumPages && pData[p*PageSize] != targ ==> countOne(p, 0, targ, 0);
11   case severalLastNotEq: \forall integer p, last, targ, N;
12     (0<=p<NumPages && 0<last<PageSize && pData[p*PageSize + last] != targ &&
13     countOne(p, last-1, targ, N) ==> countOne(p, last, targ, N) );
14   case severalLastEq: \forall integer p, last, targ, N;
15     (0<=p<NumPages && 0<last<PageSize && pData[p*PageSize + last] == targ &&
16     countOne(p, last-1, targ, N) ==> countOne(p, last, targ, N+1) );
17 }
18 inductive countAll{L}(integer lastP, integer targ, integer N){
19   case onePage: \forall integer targ, N;
20     ( countOne(0, PageSize-1, targ, N) ) ==> countAll(0, targ, N);
21   case severalPages: \forall integer lastP, targ, N1, N2;
22     ( 0 < lastP < NumPages && countAll(lastP-1, targ, N1) &&
23     countOne(lastP, PageSize-1, targ, N2) ==> countAll(lastP, targ, N1+N2) );
24 }
25 */
26 /*@
27 predicate Inv{L} = \forall integer targ; 0<=targ<NumPages ==>
28     countAll(NumPages-1, targ, Mappings[targ]);
29 */
```

Fig. 2. Simplified ACSL predicates for counting mappings (occurrences) in memory pages

qualified experts. seL4 contains only about 10,000 lines of C code, and verification cost is about $700 per line of code.

Our present work continues these efforts, but in addition fixes a quite different objective: to perform a real-life case study using a combination of automatic theorem proving and automatic all-path testing, and to explore how to find a reasonable trade-off between rigorous proof and cross-checking of the program on a reduced program domain. We described our methodology and evaluated it during this project. In particular, our results suggest that all-path testing of the code w.r.t. a specification on a reduced program domain can be a precious complement to deductive verification allowing any verification engineer (without being a highly qualified expert) to achieve a higher level of confidence within a very limited time and cost and without using more expensive interactive proof.

An ongoing work is aimed at a complete formal verification of the virtual memory module of Anaxagoros by combining automatic and interactive proof tools. The first observations confirm the conclusions of this case study: properties we validated by cross-checking appear so far to be correct and provable in the interactive proof tool Coq, while their interactive proof takes (at least 10x) more time and requires a higher level of qualification of the verification engineer.

Future work includes further evaluation of the proposed combined methodology, as well as verification of the complete code of the Anaxagoros virtual memory module taking into account parallel execution in several threads.

References

1. Cuoq, P., Kirchner, F., Kosmatov, N., Prevosto, V., Signoles, J., Yakobowski, B.: Frama-C - a software analysis perspective. In: Eleftherakis, G., Hinchey, M., Holcombe, M. (eds.) SEFM 2012. LNCS, vol. 7504, pp. 233–247. Springer, Heidelberg (2012)
2. Loulergue, F., Gava, F., Kosmatov, N., Lemerre, M.: Towards Verified Cloud Computing Environments. In: HPCS 2012 (2012)
3. Lemerre, M., David, V., Vidal-Naquet, G.: A communication mechanism for resource isolation. In: IIES 2009 (2009)
4. Lemerre, M., David, V., Vidal-Naquet, G.: A dependable kernel design for resource isolation and protection. In: IIDS 2010 (2010)
5. Lemerre, M., Ohayon, E., Chabrol, D., Jan, M., Jacques, M.B.: Method and Tools for Mixed-Criticality Real-Time Applications within PharOS. In: AMICS 2011 (2011)
6. Moy, Y.: Automatic Modular Static Safety Checking for C Programs. PhD thesis, Univ. Paris 11 (2009)
7. Williams, N., Marre, B., Mouy, P., Roger, M.: PathCrawler: automatic generation of path tests by combining static and dynamic analysis. In: Dal Cin, M., Kaâniche, M., Pataricza, A. (eds.) EDCC 2005. LNCS, vol. 3463, pp. 281–292. Springer, Heidelberg (2005)
8. Botella, B., Delahaye, M., Hong Tuan Ha, S., Kosmatov, N., Mouy, P., Roger, M., Williams, N.: Automating structural testing of C programs: Experience with PathCrawler. In: AST 2009 (2009)
9. Lemerre, M.: Intégration de systèmes hétérogènes en termes de niveaux de sécurité. PhD thesis, Université Paris Sud XI — Orsay (2009) (in French)
10. Williams, N., Kosmatov, N.: Structural testing with PathCrawler. Tutorial synopsis. In: QSIC 2012 (2012)
11. Klein, G., Elphinstone, K., Heiser, G., Andronick, J., Cock, D., Derrin, P., Elkaduwe, D., Engelhardt, K., Kolanski, R., Norrish, M., Sewell, T., Tuch, H., Winwood, S.: seL4: formal verification of an OS kernel. In: SIGOPS 2009 (2009)
12. Alkassar, E., Paul, W.J., Starostin, A., Tsyban, A.: Pervasive verification of an OS microkernel. In: Leavens, G.T., O'Hearn, P., Rajamani, S.K. (eds.) VSTTE 2010. LNCS, vol. 6217, pp. 71–85. Springer, Heidelberg (2010)
13. Alkassar, E., Hillebrand, M.A., Paul, W., Petrova, E.: Automated verification of a small hypervisor. In: Leavens, G.T., O'Hearn, P., Rajamani, S.K. (eds.) VSTTE 2010. LNCS, vol. 6217, pp. 40–54. Springer, Heidelberg (2010)
14. Alkassar, E., Cohen, E., Kovalev, M., Paul, W.J.: Verification of TLB virtualization implemented in C. In: Joshi, R., Müller, P., Podelski, A. (eds.) VSTTE 2012. LNCS, vol. 7152, pp. 209–224. Springer, Heidelberg (2012)
15. Klein, G.: From a verified kernel towards verified systems. In: Ueda, K. (ed.) APLAS 2010. LNCS, vol. 6461, pp. 21–33. Springer, Heidelberg (2010)

Runtime Assertion Checking and Its Combinations with Static and Dynamic Analyses
Tutorial Synopsis*

Nikolai Kosmatov and Julien Signoles

CEA, LIST, Software Reliability Laboratory, PC 174
91191 Gif-sur-Yvette France
{firstname.lastname}@cea.fr

Abstract. Among various static and dynamic software verification techniques, runtime assertion checking traditionally holds a particular place. Commonly used by most software developers, it can provide a fast feedback on the correctness of a property for one or several concrete executions of the program. Quite easy to realize for simple program properties, it becomes however much more complex for complete program contracts written in an expressive specification language. This paper presents a one-hour tutorial on runtime assertion checking in which we give an overview of this popular dynamic verification technique, present its various combinations with other verification techniques (such as static analysis, deductive verification, test generation, etc.) and emphasize the benefits and difficulties of these combinations. They are illustrated on concrete examples of C programs within the Frama-C software analysis framework using the executable specification language E-ACSL.

1 Introduction

Among the most useful techniques for detecting and locating software errors, *runtime assertion checking* (RAC) is nowadays a widely used programming practice [1]. *Assertions* offer one of the most convenient and scalable automated techniques for detecting errors and providing information about their locations, even for errors that are traversed during execution but do not necessarily lead to failures. More and more engineers and researchers today are interested in verification tools allowing to automatically check specified program properties at runtime.

This one-hour tutorial proposes a short survey on runtime assertion checking and focuses on combinations of this technique with other static and dynamic verification approaches (such as abstract interpretation, deductive verification, test generation, etc.). While runtime assertion checking is not so difficult to implement for simple program properties, it becomes much more complex for more evolved specification like full function contracts written in an expressive specification language. We discuss the benefits and the difficulties of runtime assertion checking for expressive specifications, and of its combinations with other analysis techniques.

---

* This work was partially funded by EU FP7 (project STANCE, grant 317753).

M. Seidl and N. Tillmann (Eds.): TAP 2014, LNCS 8570, pp. 165–168, 2014.

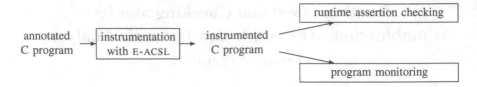

Fig. 1. Basic usages of the E-ACSL plugin translating annotations into C code

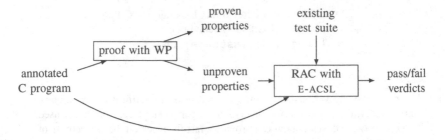

Fig. 2. Combination of deductive verification and runtime assertion checking

Tutorial examples are run in FRAMA-C[1] [2], an open-source software verification toolset, using the executable specification language E-ACSL [3,4]. E-ACSL syntax is intentionally close to C and can be easily learned on-the-fly. FRAMA-C offers various analyzers, such as abstract interpretation based value analysis plugin VALUE, deductive verification plugin WP, test generation plugin PATHCRAWLER [5]. The E-ACSL plugin of FRAMA-C translates E-ACSL annotations into instrumented C code that can be used for runtime assertion checking or program monitoring as illustrated by Fig. 1.

2   Tutorial Outline

In the first part of the tutorial, we give a historical overview of runtime assertion checking and its usage in software engineering. The second part presents runtime assertion checking for E-ACSL, an expressive specification language (including pre- and post-conditions, loop annotations, mathematical integers, quantifications, memory-related constructs, references to specific program points, etc.), and emphasizes the benefits and the issues of this kind of specifications. We also show how different types of errors, sometimes very subtle, can be efficiently detected by runtime assertion checking.

As an illustration of what kind of examples the tutorial provides, Fig. 3 shows a C function which implements binary search and contains E-ACSL annotations enclosed in special comments /*@ ... */. Before the function, we specify the function contract. First, the `requires` clauses define preconditions stating that each cell of the array must be a valid memory location, that the array must be sorted and that its length must be positive. The function has two behaviors: if the searched `key` exists, the result of the function is the index where the `key` is found; otherwise (if the `key` does not exist), the

---

[1] http://frama-c.com/

```
1  /*@ requires \forall integer i; 0 <= i < length ==> \valid(a+i);
2   @ requires \forall integer i; 0 <= i < length-1 ==> a[i] <= a[i+1];
3   @ requires length >= 0;
4   @
5   @ behavior exists:
6   @ assumes \exists integer i; 0 <= i< length && a[i] == key;
7   @ ensures a[\result] == key;
8   @
9   @ behavior not_exists:
10  @ assumes \forall integer i; 0 <= i < length ==> a[i] != key;
11  @ ensures \result == -1; */
12 int binary_search(int *a, int length, int key) {
13   int low = 0, high = length - 1;
14   /*@ loop invariant 0 <= low <= high + 1;
15    @ loop invariant high < length;
16    @ loop invariant \forall integer k; 0 <= k < low ==> a[k] < key;
17    @ loop invariant \forall integer k; high < k < length ==> a[k] > key; */
18   while (low <= high) {
19     int mid = low + (high - low) /2;
20     /*@ assert low <= mid <= high; */
21     if (a[mid] == key) return mid;
22     if (a[mid] < key) { low = mid+1; }
23     else { high = mid - 1; }
24   }
25   return -1;
26 }
```

Fig. 3. Function `binary_search` annotated in E-ACSL

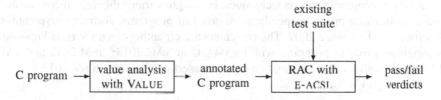

Fig. 4. Combination of value analysis and runtime assertion checking

function returns −1. The body of the function also contains several loop invariants that express invariant properties of the loop, and an assertion.

The last part of the tutorial focuses on combinations of runtime assertion checking with other analyzers. We show the benefits and the limitations of runtime verification used in combination with deductive verification where it can help to quickly check if the program respects an unproven annotation on one or several concrete executions (see Fig. 2). Combinations of abstract interpretation with runtime assertion checking can be beneficial in several ways, for example, by statically validating or invalidating some annotations, avoiding redundant or irrelevant checks to optimize runtime verification, or generating annotations for alarms to be checked (see Fig. 4). Combinations with automatic test generation can be used to check at runtime complex properties on a large test suite even when the properties are too complex to be supported by symbolic test generation techniques directly (see Fig. 5). The combinations will be illustrated on examples of C programs within the FRAMA-C verification framework and using the PATHCRAWLER test generator [5].

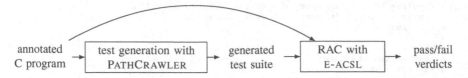

Fig. 5. Combination of test generation and runtime assertion checking

3   About the Presenters

The presenters are researchers at CEA LIST. Nikolai Kosmatov's research interests include software testing, constraint solving and combinations of various software verification techniques. Nikolai gave several theoretical courses and exercise sessions on software testing and proof of programs since 2009. He is the main author of the online testing service pathcrawler-online.com. Nikolai co-organized (with Nicky Williams) tutorials on software testing with PATHCRAWLER at TAP 2012, TAROT 2012, ASE 2012 and QSIC 2012[2].

Julien Signoles is one of the main developers of FRAMA-C. He is also the main author of the E-ACSL plug-in of FRAMA-C and the E-ACSL specification language. His research focused on software security, runtime assertion checking and combination and applications of program analysis techniques. He taught various theoretical courses and exercise sessions on program specification, proof of programs, abstract interpretation and software testing since 2009. The presenters are co-authors (with Virgile Prevosto) of tutorials on proof of programs with FRAMA-C at SAC 2013[2], iFM 2013 and TAP 2013, and the authors of the tutorial on runtime assertion checking at RV 2013.

References

1. Clarke, L.A., Rosenblum, D.S.: A historical perspective on runtime assertion checking in software development. ACM SIGSOFT Software Engineering Notes 31(3), 25–37 (2006)
2. Cuoq, P., Kirchner, F., Kosmatov, N., Prevosto, V., Signoles, J., Yakobowski, B.: Frama-C, a program analysis perspective. In: Eleftherakis, G., Hinchey, M., Holcombe, M. (eds.) SEFM 2012. LNCS, vol. 7504, pp. 233–247. Springer, Heidelberg (2012)
3. Signoles, J.: E-ACSL: Executable ANSI/ISO C Specification Language (2013), http://frama-c.com/download/e-acsl/e-acsl.pdf
4. Delahaye, M., Kosmatov, N., Signoles, J.: Common specification language for static and dynamic analysis of C programs. In: The 28th Annual ACM Symposium on Applied Computing (SAC 2013), pp. 1230–1235. ACM (2013)
5. Williams, N., Marre, B., Mouy, P.: On-the-fly generation of k-paths tests for C functions: towards the automation of grey-box testing. In: The International Conference on Automated Software Engineering (ASE 2004), pp. 290–293. IEEE Computer Society (2004)

---

[2] Tutorial materials available at http://kosmatov.perso.sfr.fr/nikolai/

Generating Test Data from a UML Activity Using the AMPL Interface for Constraint Solvers

Felix Kurth, Sibylle Schupp, and Stephan Weißleder

Hamburg University of Technology, Institute for Software Systems,
Schwarzenbergstr. 95, 21073 Hamburg, Germany
{felix.kurth,schupp}@tu-harburg.de, stephan.weissleder@gmail.com
http://www.sts.tu-harburg.de
www.model-based-testing.de/person/stephan_weissleder

Abstract. Testing is one of the most wide-spread means for quality assurance. Modelling and automated test design are two means to improve effectivity and efficiency of testing. In this paper, we present a method to generate test data from UML activity diagrams and OCL constraints by combining symbolic execution and state–of–the–art constraint solvers. Our corresponding prototype implementation is integrated in the existing test generator ParTeG and generates C++ unit tests. Our key improvement is the transparent use of multiple industry strength solvers through a common interface; this allows the user to choose between an expressive constraint language or highly optimised test data generation. We use infeasible path elimination to improve the performance of test generation and boundary value analysis to improve the quality of the generated test data. We provide an industrial case study and measure the performance of our tool using different solvers in several scenarios.

Keywords: Model–Based Testing, Activity Diagram, AMPL, Constraint Solving, Infeasible Path Elimination, Boundary Value Analysis, Mixed Integer Non–Linear Programming.

1 Introduction

Model–Based Engineering is a promising technology for system engineering. The Unified Modelling Language^{TM} (UML) is the quasi standard for model–based specifications. A UML activity diagram can be used to give a quick and intuitive overview of a system. It can also be used to formally describe details of a procedural implementation. They can be refined in a step-wise manner starting with a vague description of the intended system usage and adding more details later on.

Modelling is not an end in itself. The benefits of Model–Based Engineering are automated subsequent tasks in software development like, for example, testing. We want to automatically generate test data from an activity diagram with embedded constraints described using the Object Constraint Language (OCL). The test model describes the relevant control flows in the system under test

M. Seidl and N. Tillmann (Eds.): TAP 2014, LNCS 8570, pp. 169–186, 2014.

(SUT). The embedded OCL constraints describe interdependencies between the variables and how variables change their value.

In this paper we present a transformation from an activity diagram into an 'A Mathematical Programming Language' (AMPL) program. For that, we symbolically execute control–flow paths in the activity diagram and encode each of them as AMPL program. The solutions of these resulting AMPL programs contain input values and corresponding oracle values that can be used to test the implementation. Since test data at the boundaries of path constraints has a higher probability to detect failures [5], we also integrate boundary value analysis in test generation. Depth–first search is used to find control–flow paths and we introduced *early infeasible path elimination* within the depth–first search to reduce the runtime of our algorithm. The presented transformation is implemented as part of a master thesis [7] in a proof–of–concept, fully automated unit test generation tool called Activity Tester (AcT). The tool is integrated as a feature into the Partition Test Generator (ParTeG) available as Eclipse plug–in.[1]

The paper is structured as follows. Section 2 contains the related work. An introduction to AMPL and the used models is given in Section 3. Section 4 contains a description of the core ideas of the proposed algorithm. The report on our case study is given in Section 5. The paper is concluded in Section 6.

2   Related Work

There are several approaches for test generation based on activity diagrams. For instance, Wang Linzhang et al. propose in [9] a path–search–based method to find test scenarios in an activity diagram. They implemented the proof–of–concept tool UMLTGF. Minsong et al. [11] propose to randomly generate Java unit tests and match the test execution traces to the control–flow paths in the activity diagram. They then select a subset from the test cases that covers all simple paths in the test model. Our method is also path–search–based like [9] and unlike [11] we are using constraint solvers to find test data.

Weißleder and Sokenou presented a data–oriented approach to select test cases [16]. They use abstract interpretation to derive partitions and corresponding boundaries of the domain of input values. Weißleder [15] describes a detailed collection of different model–based structure- and data–oriented coverage criteria including their formal definition. The source code of ParTeG, the proof–of–concept tool associated with this thesis, is freely available.[2] It uses graph search in combination with abstract interpretation and a comprehensive framework, allowing the user to steer which coverage criteria the generated test cases will adhere to. In contrast to the data–oriented test data generation with abstract interpretation we are using symbolic execution. We are also offering boundary value analysis based on mathematical optimisation instead of data partitions.

There are several approaches to integrate the solution of OCL formulas. Ali et al. [1] use evolutionary algorithms to search for potential solutions of OCL

---

[1] ParTeG and AcT are available from: http://parteg.sourceforge.net/

[2] Source code of ParTeG is available from: http://sourceforge.net/p/parteg/code

constraints. Krieger and Knapp [6] use a SAT solver to find instantiations of variables satisfying OCL constraints. They transform OCL formulas into boolean formulas and use a SAT-solver-based model finder for solving these formulas. In contrast, we generate models for OCL formulas not based on a single heuristic or a single solver, but we are using the AMPL frontend to which we can link either a heuristic or an algorithm.

Malburg and Fraser [10] propose a hybrid approach. On the top level they use a genetic algorithm evolving a population of candidate test data. Internally, they provide guidance to the genetic algorithm by providing a special mutation operator performing dynamic symbolic execution. Also the white–box unit test tool PEX [14] from Microsoft® research is based on dynamic symbolic execution. Both [10] and [14] execute the implementation with random input values and generate new input values by collecting path conditions along the executed control flow. Then they negate one of the path conditions and use a constraint solver to find a solution. Like the presented work, we also use symbolic execution. Since we are only performing a static analysis, however, we do not need the source code to generate test cases. So in contrast to the related work, our tool is also suitable for black–box testing.

3   Preliminaries

In this section, we introduce the programming language AMPL and the semantics of the used test models.

3.1   AMPL and Its Solvers

We use 'A Mathematical Programming Language' (AMPL) by Robert Fourer [4] to formalise the execution of a control–flow path in the test model. In this section, we describe AMPL and introduce the solvers we have used to generate test data.[3] In AMPL we can state linear, non–linear, and logical constraints. Variables can be continuous or discrete. The AMPL system serves as a common interface to a variety of solvers. Depending on the constraint satisfaction problem encoded in the AMPL program a suitable solver can be selected to solve

Table 1. List of solvers and problems they can solve

Solver	MILP	NLP	SMT	MINLP	Solver	MILP	NLP	SMT	MINLP
Cplex	✓				Couenne	✓	✓		✓
LPsolve	✓				IlogCP	✓		✓	
Gurobi			✓		GeCoDE			✓	
Minos			✓						

---

[3] A bundle containing AMPL and the solvers Cplex, LPsolve, Gurobi, and Minos is available from: http://ampl.com/try-ampl/download-a-demo-version/

the problem. If all constraints are linear we use a solver that is specialized on mixed integer linear programming (MILP), for example, Cplex or LPsolve [3]. If constraints are non–linear but convex and all variables are continuous we use a non–linear programming (NLP) solver. For problems with non–linear constraints and discrete as well as continuous variables we need a solver capable of solving mixed integer non–linear programming (MINLP), for example, Couenne [4] [2]. If logical operations are used in the constraints, a satisfiability modulo theories (SMT) solver supporting appropriate background theories is used, for example, GeCoDE [5] or IlogCP [6] [8]. In Table 1 we show a selection of solvers interfacing with AMPL. A checkmark in a cell means that we have successfully tested the solver in the row on the problem named in the column.

3.2   Semantics of the Test Models

For the transformation into 'A Mathematical Programming Language' (AMPL) presented in Section 4.2 we clarify the semantics of the expected input model. Modelling elements of the UML such as *Activity* and UML references *name* or *ownedParameter* are typeset in a special font. In this section, we first detail which UML modelling elements we use and will then shortly recapitulate the Petri–Net semantics of activity diagrams (see [12]). Further, we introduce the notion of a *state*, which will be relevant for our algorithm.

As test model we assume an activity diagram with *Action*s, *ControlNode*s, and *ControlFlow*s modelling the control flow of an *Operation*. The *Activity* is linked as *method* to its specifying *Operation*. Each *Action* can contain several textual OCL constraints as *localPostcondition* and each *ControlFlow* can hold a textual OCL constraint as *guard*. The textual OCL in the *guard* and *localPostcondition* will be parsed in the context of the specifying *Operation*. That means the OCL constraints can access all *ownedAttribute*s of the *Class* containing the specifying *Operation*. Further, all *ownedParameter*s of the specifying *Operation* can be referenced in the textual OCL. We interpret every *Property* as variable that can change its value during the execution of an *Action*. A *Parameter* will be interpreted as a parameter that can not change its value during the execution of an *Action*.

When executing a control–flow path, we start with a token in the *InitialNode*. We allow only one *InitialNode* per *Activity*. The token can move along an enabled *ControlFlow*. A *ControlFlow* is enabled when the OCL constraint in its *guard* evaluates to true. We say that an *Action* is being executed when a token resides in the *Action*.

We refer to an assignment of all variables and parameters as *state*. While the token resides in the *InitialNode* there is an initial state. After each execution of an *Action* the current state can change according to the OCL constraints contained

---

[4] Couenne is available from: http://www.coin-or.org/download/binary/Couenne/
[5] GeCoDE is available from: http://www.gecode.org/
[6] IlogCP with AMPL drivers is available on request from:
http://ampl.com/try-ampl/get-a-trial-license/

in the *Action*'s *localPostcondition*. An OCL constraint contained as *localPostcon-dition* can specify a relation between the current state and the previous state. Consequently, the states are interconnected with each other via *localPostconditions*. The set of all relations contained in *localPostconditions* can be seen as state transition function. For a *ControlFlow* to be enabled the OCL constraint in its *guard* has to evaluate to true with respect to the current state. OCL constraints contained in a *guard* can only specify a relation between the variables and parameters within a single state. It is not possible to access the value of a variable in the previous state within a *guard*.

4   The Algorithm

In this section we explain the core ideas of the algorithm that we implemented in AcT. First, we demonstrate with a small example how the execution of a control–flow path can be formalised. Then we show how to acquire test data that is at the boundary of path constraints and, finally, we present an algorithm that efficiently searches for executable control–flow paths.

4.1   Overview

Symbolic execution is done by transforming an activity diagram into a parameterised AMPL model representing all relevant OCL Constraints, *Properties*, and *Parameters*. This transformation preserves the original semantics of the activity diagram.

The parameters of the AMPL model encode a control–flow path. An assignment of each variable in each state is generated by state–of–the–art constraint solvers from an AMPL model with given parameters. The generated variable assignment is suitable test data. A great advantage of a commonly used mathematical programming language is that industrial–strength solvers are available for a wide variety of problems (see Section 3.1).

4.2   AMPL Transformation

An AMPL model encodes the relevant *Properties*, *Parameters*, and OCL constraints contained in an activity diagram. *Properties* and *Parameters* are relevant if they are referenced in a *guard* or *localPostcondition* inside the *Activity* under consideration. We call a sequence of *ControlFlows* *control–flow path*. For two subsequent *ControlFlows* A and B in a control–flow path it holds that A.target=B.source. A control–flow path is encoded in the AMPL data.

We model the execution of a control–flow path as a series of states. Each AMPL model has one parameter called `pathlength` representing the number of *Actions* on a control–flow path. Executing an *Action* changes the state, consequently, there are `pathlength + 1` states. Since a *Property* can have a distinct value in each state, they are modelled as an array of variables. *Parameters* are

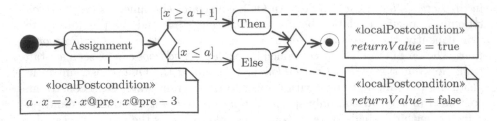

Fig. 1. A simple UML activity diagram

constant and are therefore represented by a single AMPL variable. Every *Property* and *Parameter* has either integer, float, or boolean as *type*; in AMPL we specify the domain of an AMPL variable correspondingly.

The OCL constraints in Figure 1 reference three different OCL variables. We assume a and *returnValue* to be *Parameter*s that are modelled as a single variable in AMPL and we assume x to be a *Property* that is modelled as an array of variables. We further assume that all three UML elements have the *type* integer. Consequently, we generate the following AMPL code for them:

```
var a : integer;
var returnValue : integer;
var x{0..pathlength} : integer;
```

During execution, a *ControlFlow*'s *guard* or an *Action*'s *localPostcondition* is always evaluated with respect to the current state. The set of states in which an *Action* or *ControlFlow* is being executed is called *activation set*. There is one activation set for each *ControlFlow* having an OCL *guard* and each *Action* having an OCL *localPostcondition*. All OCL *localPostcondition*s and OCL *guard*s are contained in the AMPL model as constraints, which can be switched on and off for each state. In the AMPL model states are referenced via their index. For each *Action* and *ControlFlow* the activation set is declared as a subset of the set {0..pathlength}. Each OCL constraint in a *guard* or *localPostcondition* is transformed into an indexed collection of constraints over the activation set.

When a variable reference is marked with @pre we are accessing the variable in the previous state and thus need to subtract one from the index; otherwise we access the variable at the index from the activation set. The AMPL model code generated for the Assignment *Action* in Figure 1 is, for example, as follows:

```
set Assignment within {0..pathlength} default {};
s.t. Assignment_post0 {i in Assignment} : a*x[i]=2*x[i
    -1]*x[i-1]-3;
```

The code generated for the Then and Else *Action*s and *ControlFlow*s with *guard* is analogous. The complete AMPL model consists of the declaration of the parameter `pathlength`, variable declarations and the constraints together with their activation sets. The value of the parameter `pathlength` as well as the elements of each activation set will be specified in the AMPL data. This way, there is one

AMPL model per activity diagram and any control–flow path within the activity diagram can be specified in the AMPL data.

Let us, for example, encode the bold printed control–flow path from Figure 1 as AMPL data. Starting at the *InitialNode*, the current state is the initial state with the index 0. In this state there are no constraints. When we reach the Assignment *Action* our current state switches to 1. Since there is a post–condition for Assignment, we add 1 to the activation set of the Assignment. The next *ControlFlow* has an OCL guard, consequently we add 1 to its activation set. Further, we add 2 to the activation set of the Then *Action*. In AMPL syntax, the data specifying this path is:

```
param pathlength := 2;
set Assignment := 1;
set Cf_Then := 1;
set Then := 2;
```

4.3 Boundary Value Analysis

Test data at the boundaries of the path constraints is more valuable than arbitrary test data causing the given control–flow path to be executed [5]. We will refer to test data at the boundaries of path constraints also as *boundary test data*. Up to now we did not explicitly require the test data to be boundary test data. An additional linear objective function in the AMPL model ensures that generated test data is boundary test data. When solving AMPL programs augmented by such an objective function three things can happen: either the solver generates boundary test data, or the solver reports that the problem is unbounded, or the solving time for the problem increases enormously and the solver exceeds its time limit. The first case is the good case. In the second case we can change the direction of the objective function and try again to hit a boundary. The last case is especially a problem of mixed integer non–linear programming solvers. It is not too hard to find a solution to a mixed integer non–linear program, if there are enough solutions, but finding a solution that is optimal with respect to an objective function is much harder. In fact Couenne will try to find the global optimum although also a locally optimal solution—with respect to a linear objective function—would be suitable as boundary test data. In such a case we can first use a global mixed integer non–linear programming solver to solve the original AMPL program. In a second step we add the linear objective function and use a local search algorithm using the solution generated before as starting point to find a solution at the boundary of the path constraints.

4.4 Early Infeasible Path Elimination

Control–flow paths are stored in a *path tree*. A path tree is a tree data structure consisting of path–tree nodes. Each path–tree node holds a reference to its parent path–tree node, a reference to a *ControlFlow*, and an integer—its depth. The root node points to an *outgoing ControlFlow* of the *InitialNode*. Any path–tree node is a representation of a control–flow path from the *InitialNode* to the *target* of its referenced *ControlFlow*. Leaf path–tree nodes reference a *ControlFlow* that ends in an *ActivityNode* with no *outgoing ControlFlow*. We call the control–flow path represented by a leaf path–tree node an *abstract test case*.

Not every control–flow path is a *feasible path*. A control–flow path is feasible, if there exists test data that causes this control–flow path to be executed. In other words, for an infeasible path the corresponding AMPL program will contain contradicting constraints, for example, $x_0 \leq 5; x_0 \geq 10$. It is quite obvious that if a path–tree node represents an infeasible path any of its children nodes will also represent an infeasible path. Since we are only interested in abstract test cases for which test data can be generated, we prune branches containing no feasible abstract test cases as early as possible.

Pseudo code constructing a path tree with early infeasible path elimination is given in Algorithm 1. Infeasible path check (isFeasiblePath()) is done by running a solver on the AMPL program corresponding to the examined control–flow path. If the solver reports a failure or infeasibility of a problem, we assume the control–flow path to be infeasible. The earlier during construction of the path tree a control–flow path is detected to be infeasible the more control–flow paths are pruned. On the other hand, if we check feasibility for every single path–tree node we will impose unnecessary work. We allow for a customised trade–off by introducing the parameter *unchecked steps* (UchkSteps). Further, our path search algorithm accepts the parameters *maximum path length* (MaxPathLen) bounding the depth of the path tree and *maximum number of test cases* (MaxNoPaths) bounding the number of abstract test cases to find. The function countPathDecisionsTo() in the third last line of Algorithm1 counts the number of path–tree nodes with at least 2 children nodes on the path from its source to its argument.

5   Results

The presented algorithm is implemented as an Eclipse plug–in. The tool is called Activity Tester (AcT) and is integrated into the Partition Test Generator (ParTeG). We built a set of example models with corresponding C implementations to test our implementation. Finally, our tool has also been applied in an industrial case study at Airbus Operations GmbH. The constraint solver based approach presented here has already been adopted by Amin Rezaee for *StateMachine*s [13]. In this section we will first evaluate AcT for a model with mixed integer non–linear constraints and then summarise the results of the industrial case study.

5.1   Mixed Integer Non–linear Example Model

Figure 2 shows an activity diagram modelling the physical process of pumping air into a tyre. The relations between *volume*, amount of air (n), *pressure*, and *temperature* are described by the ideal gas equation. The equations for adiabatic compression of air during one pump stroke states a non–convex relation

---

Algorithm 1. Path search algorithm with early infeasible path elimination

---

Require: root : path–tree node   ▷ the root path–tree node
  MaxPathLen : integer   ▷ maximum path length for each control-flow path
  MaxNoPaths : integer   ▷ maximum amount of leaf path–tree nodes to find
  UchkSteps : integer   ▷ number of path decisions without infeasible path check
Ensure: constructs path tree starting from root using early infeasible path elimination
  decisions : integer ← 0   ▷ count path decisions
  stack : LIFO Buffer ← {root}   ▷ only root node in stack
  while !stack→isEmpty() **and** path tree contains less than MaxNoPaths leaf nodes
  do
      ptn : path–tree node ← stack→pop()   ▷ remove first path–tree node from stack
      f : integer ← ptn.controlFlow.target.outgoing→size()   ▷ fanout of current node
      if f>0 **and** ptn.depth<MaxPathLen **and** (decisions<UchkSteps **or** f<2 **or**
      ptn→isFeasiblePath()) **then** ▷ evaluate isFeasiblePath() only if its value is relevant
          for cf : *ControlFlow* ∈ ptn.controlFlow.target.outgoing **do**
              stack→push(**new path–tree node**(ptn, cf, ptn.depth+1))
          end for
          decisions ← (f≥2 ? (decisions mod UchkSteps)+1 : decisions)
      else
          decisions ← max(decisions − stack→top()→countPathDecisionsTo(ptn), 0)
      end if
  end while

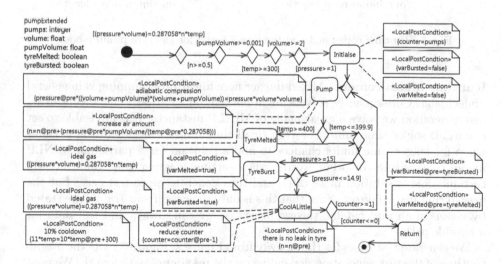

Fig. 2. Activity diagram with mixed integer non–linear constraints

between these physical measures, consequently the resulting AMPL programs will be non–convex. Additionally, we introduced the boolean variables *tyreExploded* and *tyreMelted*, which will be set when the *pressure* or *temperature* inside the tyre raised above a certain threshold. Moreover, we introduce an integer loop counter (*counter*) to count the number of pump strokes. Consequently, the AMPL program is also a mixed integer problem.

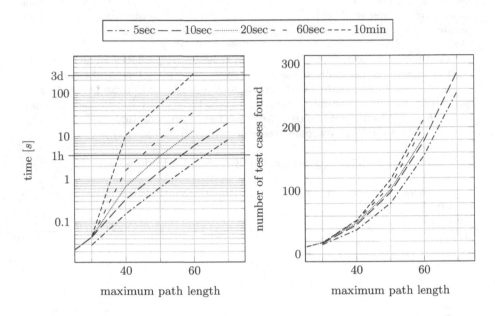

Fig. 3. Runtime consumed and test cases found for the tyre pump model

Runtime Measurement. Mixed integer non–linear programming is in general undecidable. Consequently, solvers might not halt on an MINLP instance. During test generation we solve a great many of MINLP instances. It is advisable to set a suitable solver time limit. For very small time limits test generation is faster while for longer time limits chances to find a solution for a particular MINLP instance are rising. In other words, when setting a larger time limit we will certainly find a solution more often and thus generate more test cases but the overall runtime will grow. Note that this is only the case if constraints are stated by means of an undecidable theory; otherwise we can always find test data for a feasible path.

We generate test cases for the *Activity* from Figure 2. Figure 3 plots the overall runtime of the test generation depending on the maximum path length. We used Couenne as solver and varied the time limit per MINLP instance between 5 seconds and 10 minutes. The right hand side of Figure 3 plots the number of abstract test cases for which we found test data with the given solver time limit.

The number of abstract test cases grows exponentially with the maximum path length and so does the overall computation time and the number of real test cases.

Comparing the runtime of our algorithm with different time limits for the maximum path length 60 we recognise that increasing the time limit from 20 seconds to 60 seconds increased the overall runtime by a factor of 2.78 and generated 17 more real test cases; those are 9.2% more test cases. Increasing the time limit from 60 seconds to 600 seconds increased the overall runtime by a factor of 7.67 and produced 11 additional test cases, which amounts to only 5.4% more test cases. We see that increasing the time limit for the solver massively increases the overall runtime, but we gain only very few additional test cases for that and we doubt that those additional test cases massively increase the quality of the test suite. We therefore recommend using less than 20 seconds as solver time limit for Couenne.

Mutation Testing. We applied selective mutation generate 1000 mutants of our C implementation of the tyre pump model. The mutate.py [7] script used does this by text pattern matching and therefore created 427 non compilable mutants. We generated test suites with a solver time limit of 10 seconds and for a maximum path length of 20,30,40, and 50 and ran them on the 573 compilable mutants. The test suite for path length 50 was mutation adequate. The test suites for path length 20 left 20 mutants alive; that is a mutation score of 96.5%. Table 2 summarises the results of the performed mutation testing.

Table 2. Mutation test results for tyre pump model

maximum path length	20	30	40	50
number of test cases	4	18	47	97
killed mutants	553	569	570	573
alive mutants	20	4	3	0
mutation score	96.5%	99.3%	99.5%	100%

Those high mutation scores have two reasons. First, we produced one test case for every control–flow path up to a given maximum path length which is quite exhaustive testing for a small academic example. Second, due to the interdependency between *temperature, pressure,* and amount of air (n) a small error in one of these measures will propagate to all three of those measures causing a great number of failed tests due to just one wrong statement. Similarly, reordering of statements introduced huge errors in all three measures. And finally, sub–optimal calculation plans resulting in small rounding errors have been detected by almost every test case. For example the C expressions (10 *temp + 300) / 11 and 10 * temp / 11 + 300 /11 have been identified as not equivalent. Even the replacement of < by ≤ has been detected.

---

[7] mutate.py is available from: http://archive.today/wz4TF

5.2 Case Study

We tested our implementation on a model from Airbus Operations GmbH. Out of the model of the complete product we selected a large activity diagram modelling the control flow of a function. The selected *Activity* contains 21 *Actions*, 24 *ControlNodes*, and two *LoopNodes*. Furthermore, there are eight *DataStoreNodes* representing function local variables. The branching conditions and the code body of each *Action* is given in C syntax. All assignments and conditions consist of linear equations and inequalities. All variables are in the integer or boolean domain. Consequently, for test data generation mixed integer linear programs have to be solved. Cplex and LPsolve are perfectly optimised for this kind of problem while Couenne is suitable for a more general class of problems.

The algorithm described in Section 4 has several parameters. We use this case study to evaluate the influence of the parameters maximum path length, the solver to use, unchecked steps, maximum amount of test cases, and boundary value analysis on the runtime.

Manual Adaptation. A bit of manual pre–processing is necessary in order to use the case study model with AcT: import the model, add *guard*s and *localPostconditions* in OCL syntax, flatten the *LoopNodes*, and replace the *DataStoreNodes* by *Properties*.

The model was provided as XMI export from Atego® Artisan Studio. Due to slight differences in the implementation it is not directly possible to load an XMI file from Atego® in Eclipse. We manually removed some objects not recognised by Eclipse and corrected some typing errors in the XMI file. Every *Action* and *ControlFlow* contains C code snippets, but no OCL constraints. We added *guard*s and *localPostconditions* reproducing the semantics of the C code snippets contained in the original model. The function specifying which *ControlFlow* to take after each *Action* is well–defined and defined over the complete domain. The original model used local C struct variables modelled by the *DataStoreNodes* contained by the *Activity*. Our implementation can handle variables modelled as *Property*. Consequently, we created one *Property* per field of a struct variable. The original model also used arrays. We emulated the behaviour of an indexed collection by allowing all variables depending on an index to change to an arbitrary value upon a change of the index. This may produce wrong behaviour but seemed good enough to evaluate the runtime of our algorithm. The *LoopNodes* contain further model elements in their *bodyPart*. We connect those elements from the *bodyPart* to additional *ControlFlow*s and *ActivityNodes* emulating the counter loop semantics. The *LoopNode* is discarded and its augmented *bodyPart* is directly embedded in the *Activity*.

Runtime Measurement Results. We examine the influence of the used solver, the maximum path length, the maximum number of test cases, the unchecked steps, and boundary value analysis on the runtime of our algorithm.

Different Solvers. We found that the runtime grows almost exponentially with the maximum path length: It doubles when the maximum path length increases by 6-7. The solvers LPsolve, Cplex, and GeCoDE are equally fast. Couenne consumed about three times the runtime consumed by LPsolve. This is because Couenne is actually suitable for the much more general mathematical problem of mixed integer non–linear programming; it is not perfectly specialized for mixed integer linear programming.

All constraints in the case study model are instances of mixed integer linear programming and the solvers implement effective methods for mixed integer linear programming. Consequently, we gain test data for every feasible path. The number of test cases grows exponentially with the maximum path length. For a maximum path length of 110 a total of 12,850,000 linear programs had to be solved to find 83,000 sets of test data. The fastest solver, LPSolve, took only 13 hours for this task. This makes 275 solved problems per second and among them 1.8 produced actual test data.

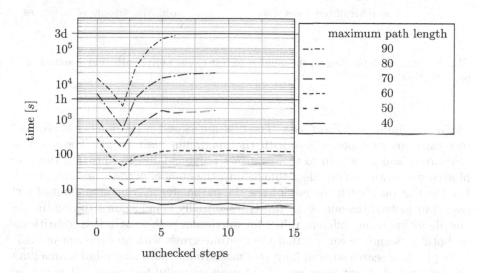

Fig. 4. Runtime of our implementation depending on the unchecked steps

Unchecked Steps. In Figure 4, we plotted the overall runtime of our algorithm depending on the unchecked steps (see Section 4.4). We used Cplex as solver and repeated the experiment for different maximum path lengths. In the plots we see, up to a maximum path length of 50 it is not beneficial to use early infeasible path elimination for the case study model. With longer maximum path lengths the impact of well configured early infeasible path elimination grows. For a maximum path length of 90 our algorithm configured with the optimal value for the unchecked steps parameter — 2 — takes less than one hour, while it takes several days with unchecked steps set to 6.

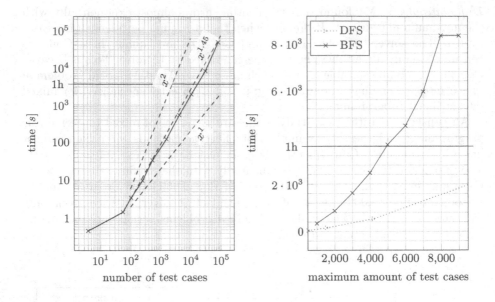

Fig. 5. Runtime depending on the number of test cases. Left: depth–first search. Right: breadth–first search

Maximum Amount of Test Cases. The runtime as well as the number of abstract test cases grows exponentially with the maximum path length. The quotient of runtime and generated test cases grows polynomially. To illustrate that, we plotted the runtime of our algorithm against the number of test cases in Figure 5. For the plot on the left we did not use the parameter maximum amount of test cases but plotted the number of test cases actually found against the runtime of our algorithm using different values for maximum path length. It is logarithmic on both axes and we can see that the runtime grows with an exponent of 1.45.

Depth–first search without limit on the maximum path length but with a limit on the number of test cases, would not produce useful test cases. All generated abstract test cases would over and over share very long common sub–paths and some *ControlFlows* would not be checked at all. Therefore, we implemented a breadth–first search–based alternative to the algorithm explained in Section 4.4. We use this alternative to evaluate the effect of the maximum amount of test cases on the runtime; for all other experiments we use only depth first search.

In Figure 5, right, we plot the runtime of our algorithm with breadth–first search. The dotted line shows a small section of the left plot. As we can see breadth–first search is considerably slower than depth–first search. The reason for that is that breadth–first search can not make such a good use of the warm start capabilities of the solvers as depth–first search can. In depth–first search, usually only a small amount of the constraints change between two subsequent solver invocations. For breadth–first search it happens more often that all constraints have changed between two subsequent solver invocations. Furthermore, we see that the generation of 9,000 test cases took only slightly longer than the generation of 8,000 test cases. We can not explain this last effect.

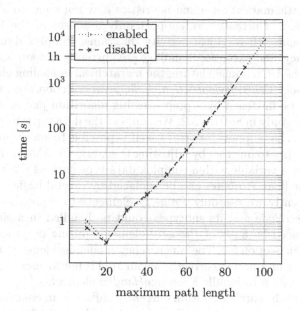

Fig. 6. Comparison of runtime with boundary value analysis enabled and disabled

Boundary Value Analysis Finally, we analysed the impact of boundary value analysis on the runtime of our implementation. As explained in Section 4.3, an additional objective has been added in the AMPL program. We minimise the sum of all variables in the initial state. In Figure 6, we show the runtime of our algorithm depending on the maximum path length. We use LPsolve as solver. The runtime with boundary value analysis and the runtime without boundary value analysis are plotted. The plot clearly shows that there is no difference in runtime between generating boundary test data or arbitrary test data.

This result is plausible because the number of solver invocations where extra work needs to be performed is small compared to the number of total solver calls. For example, for a maximum path length of 70 there are 1568 test cases. The solver performs the optimisation only for them. On the other hand, there are 35044 solver invocations in total including those that recognise a control–flow path as infeasible. Consequently, only 4.5% of all solver invocations are actually performing some extra work. For larger maximum path lengths this fraction is declining further.

5.3   Limitations and Outlook

A natural limitation for constraint-solver-based test data generation is decidability. There is no effective method to generate variable instantiations that satisfy an arbitrary mathematical term and heuristics may not come to a halt on some problem instances. Currently, we support only a subset of the UML activity modelling elements. Hierarchical activity diagrams, complex data types, data flow, concurrency, and exception handling are currently not supported.

In terms of the UCL nomenclature, the hierarchical modelling elements *StructuredActivityNode*, *CallBehaviourAction*, *CallOperationAction* are missing. These elements could be flattened by a preprocessing algorithm just as we did manually for our case study in Section 5.2. We support the data types integer, boolean, and float. AMPL has support for arrays, so it is possible to add support for arrays of those basic types to our tool by adjusting the UML–to–AMPL transformation slightly. Further a variable with a complex data type such as *Class* holding integer, boolean, or float *attributes* can be replaced by several basic typed *Property* elements. Currently we use only *Property* elements to represent a data store; of course, *ObjectNode* and its subtypes could be handled in a similar manner or just be replaced by a set of *Property* elements during preprocessing; this is done manually in Section 5.2. The concurrency modelling elements *ForkNode* and *JoinNode* are not interpreted correctly, as our tool is not focused on concurrency. There is no provision to handle *ExceptionHandler* elements.

Finally, our path search algorithm currently suffers from combinatorial explosion. Generating test cases that adhere to a feasible coverage criterion like, for example, control–flow coverage, would avert this problem. In [15] a comprehensive framework for generating test suites that adhere to model coverage criteria has been presented. At its core it uses a depth first search based algorithm that is supported by abstract interpretation. This search algorithm can be replaced by Algorithm 1, which is supported by symbolic execution and constraint solvers; this has been done by Amin Rezaee in [13]. Further, some adaptations of the framework need to be done to work with an *Activity* instead of a *StateMachine* element.

6   Summary and Recommendation

In this paper, we presented an efficient way to integrate state–of–the–art constraint solvers into a model–based testing tool. Depending on the specific needs of the modeller, a variety of constraints can be used in the model. We showed that the automatic test data generation is especially fast when constraints are specified in terms of a decidable theory and solved with an optimised solver. On the other hand we generated test data for models whose constraints are formulated as instances of an undecidable problem like, for example, mixed integer non–linear programming. Although our approach makes it possible to generate test data for models with undecidable constraints, this can be very time consuming. Furthermore, it is not guaranteed that existing test data will be found.

If possible, one should restrict oneself to linear inequalities or another decidable constraint formulation.

We have presented a concept for early infeasible path elimination during generation of abstract test cases and examined its impact on the overall runtime of our algorithm. Using early infeasible path elimination with two unchecked steps massively reduces the runtime of our algorithm.

Finally, we showed that the presented approach allows steering the generation of test data in a way that boundary values are produced with no additional effort. It is common knowledge that the use of boundary values as test data tends to trigger existing bugs with a higher probability.

References

1. Ali, S., Iqbal, M.Z., Arcuri, A., Briand, L.: A Search-based OCL Constraint Solver for Model-based Test Data Generation. In: 11th International Conference on Quality Software, QSIC 2011, pp. 41–50. IEEE Computer Society (July 2011), http://dx.doi.org/10.1109/QSIC.2011.17
2. Belotti, P., Lee, J., Liberti, L., Margot, F., Wächter, A.: Branching and Bounds Tightening Techniques for Non–Convex MINLP. Optimization Methods and Software 24(4-5), 597–634 (2009), http://dx.doi.org/10.1080/10556780903087124
3. Berkelaar, M., Eikland, K., Notebaert, P.: lpsolve: Open source (Mixed-Integer) Linear Programming system, http://lpsolve.sourceforge.net/5.5/
4. Fourer, R., Gay, D.M., Kernighan, B.W.: AMPL: A Modeling Language for Mathematical Programming, 2nd edn. Duxbury Press (2002), http://ampl.com/resources/the-ampl-book/
5. Kosmatov, N., Legeard, B., Peureux, F., Utting, M.: Boundary coverage criteria for test generation from formal models. In: 15th International Symposium on Software Reliability Engineering, ISSRE 2004, pp. 139–150. IEEE Computer Society (November 2004), http://dx.doi.org/10.1109/ISSRE.2004.12
6. Krieger, M.P., Knapp, A.: Executing Underspecified OCL Operation Contracts with a SAT Solver. Electronic Communications of the EASST 15 (2008), http://journal.ub.tu-berlin.de/eceasst/article/view/176
7. Kurth, F.: Automated Generation of Unit Tests from UML Activity Diagrams using the AMPL Interface for Constraint Solvers. Master's thesis, Hamburg University of Technology, Germany, Hamburg (January 2014), http://www.sts.tuhh.de/pw-and-m-theses/2014/kurth14.pdf
8. Laborie, P.: IBM ILOG CP Optimizer for Detailed Scheduling Illustrated on Three Problems. In: van Hoeve, W.-J., Hooker, J.N. (eds.) CPAIOR 2009. LNCS, vol. 5547, pp. 148–162. Springer, Heidelberg (2009), http://dx.doi.org/10.1007/978-3-642-01929-6_12
9. Linzhang, W., Jiesong, Y., Xiaofeng, Y., Jun, H., Xuandong, L., Guoliang, Z.: Generating Test Cases from UML Activity Diagram based on Gray–Box Method. In: 11th Asia-Pacific Software Engineering Conference, APSEC 2004, pp. 284–291. IEEE Computer Society, Los Alamitos (2004), http://dx.doi.org/10.1109/APSEC.2004.55
10. Malburg, J., Fraser, G.: Combining Search–based and Constraint–based Testing. In: 2011 26th IEEE/ACM International Conference on Automated Software Engineering, ASE 2011, pp. 436–439. IEEE Computer Society (November 2011), http://dx.doi.org/10.1109/ASE.2011.6100092

11. Mingsong, C., Xiaokang, Q., Xuandong, L.: Automatic Test Case Generation for UML Activity Diagrams. In: Workshop on Automation of Software Test, AST 2006, pp. 2–8. ACM, New York (2006), http://dx.doi.org/10.1145/1138929.1138931
12. Object Management Group (OMG): OMG Unified Modeling Language™ (OMG UML), Superstructure (May 2010), http://www.omg.org/spec/UML/2.3/
13. Rezaee, A.: A New Approach to Optimized Generation of Test Cases using UML State Machine. Master's thesis, University of Isfahan, Iran, Isfahan (February 2014)
14. Tillmann, N., de Halleux, J.: Pex-White Box Test Generation for.NET. In: Beckert, B., Hähnle, R. (eds.) TAP 2008. LNCS, vol. 4966, pp. 134–153. Springer, Heidelberg (2008), http://dx.doi.org/10.1007/978-3-540-79124-9_10
15. Weißleder, S.: Test Models and Coverage Criteria for Automatic Model–Based Test Generation with UML State Machines. Ph.D. thesis, Humboldt University Berlin (2010), http://model-based-testing.de/data/weissleder_phd_thesis.pdf
16. Weißleder, S., Sokenou, D.: Automatic Test Case Generation from UML Models and OCL Expressions. In: Maalej, W., Brügge, B. (eds.) Software Engineering 2008 - Workshopband, Fachtagung des GI-Fachbereichs Softwaretechnik. Lecture Notes in Informatics, vol. 122, pp. 423–426. Gesellschaft für Informatik (February 2008), http://pdf.aminer.org/000/231/949/generating_test_
sequences_from_uml_sequence_diagrams_and_state_diagrams.pdf

Lightweight State Capturing for Automated Testing of Multithreaded Programs

Kari Kähkönen and Keijo Heljanko

Helsinki Institute for Information Technology HIIT
Department of Computer Science and Engineering
School of Science, Aalto University
{kari.kahkonen,keijo.heljanko}@aalto.fi

Abstract. We present a lightweight approach to capture abstract state information that can be used to avoid testing redundant interleavings of multithreaded programs. Our approach is based on modeling states that are observed during the test executions as a Petri net. This model is then used to determine if some execution paths lead to an already explored state. In such cases exploring execution paths from the same state multiple times can be avoided. Our approach does not capture the complete global states of programs but instead it relies on particular commutativity of transitions to determine if they lead to already known abstract states. We have combined this lightweight state capture technique with a dynamic symbolic execution based approach to systematically test multithreaded programs. Experiments show that even without complete state information, the lightweight state capturing technique can sometimes reduce the number of redundant test executions substantially.

1 Introduction

Testing multithreaded programs is challenging due to the large number of execution paths caused by input values and interleavings of threads. One way to avoid redundant test executions is to capture program states and stop a test execution when an already explored state is encountered. However, capturing and storing states of real world multithreaded programs can add a considerable time and space overhead to a testing algorithm. Furthermore, matching states can be nontrivial if the states are expressed symbolically as in some testing approaches such as dynamic symbolic execution (DSE) [8]. For example, in a symbolic state a variable x could have any value that satisfies a constraint $x > 0$. If another execution path leads to an identical symbolic state except that the constraint for x is $x > 5$, the first symbolic state *subsumes* the second one (i.e., the first state represents all concrete states of the second symbolic state). To determine if a symbolic state has been visited before, a subsumption check by a constraint solver is needed. This can be computationally expensive if the constraints are complex and therefore we will not use such an approach in this paper.

An alternative to capturing states is to use stateless algorithms that explore execution paths through a program without explicitly storing state information.

M. Seidl and N. Tillmann (Eds.): TAP 2014, LNCS 8570, pp. 187–203, 2014.

A naive way to do such exploration is to consider all possible input values and interleavings. Approaches like DSE and partial order reductions [7,15] can be used to avoid redundant test executions. DSE expresses symbolically the sets of input values that cause the same execution path to be followed. Partial order reduction algorithms avoid redundant tests based on the fact that it is not necessary to explore different interleavings of independent state transitions. However, even with such reduction techniques, stateless algorithms can explore the same subset of the state space multiple times.

In this paper we present a lightweight approach to state capturing that can be combined with DSE without the need for subsumption checks that use constraint solvers or for storing complete global states. Our approach is based on the observation that sometimes it is easy to see that interleavings even with dependent transitions commute and thus lead to the same state. As an example, consider a program that has an array in shared memory and the access to this array is synchronized with a lock. This means that if two threads want to read a value from the array (or to update distinct indexes), both threads need to acquire the same lock. The corresponding transitions are dependent and therefore both ways to interleave the accesses to the array need to be explored even if using partial order reductions. However, after both threads have acquired the lock, read a value and released the lock, the program ends up in the same state regardless of the execution order. In this case it is not necessary to know the exact global states of the program to be able to determine that both interleavings result in the same state. In this paper we detect such cases by constructing a Petri net model of the program under test based on the information collected during test executions. This model is constructed such that any modeled state transitions lead to new abstract states unless it is easy to determine that a transition leads to an already known state.

We also present a systematic testing algorithm that constructs the model on-the-fly and uses it to perform state matching. The new algorithm can be seen as extending our previous unfolding based testing approach [10] with lightweight state matching. Naturally without complete state information, the cases where state matching can be done are limited. Nevertheless, experiments show that in cases where our approach can detect that a given state has been visited before, the savings both in testing time and the number of test executions can be substantial. The main contributions of this paper are: (1) a lightweight approach to match states without capturing complete global states or using symbolic subsumption with a constraint solver, (2) a testing algorithm that combines net unfoldings, dynamic symbolic execution and the lightweight state capturing to reduce unnecessary test executions, and (3) an experimental evaluation of the new approach.

2   Background

To keep the presentation simple we assume that in programs to be tested the number of shared variables is fixed and the only nondeterminism in threads is caused by concurrent access of shared memory or by input data from the environment. We also assume that operations accessing shared memory are sequentially consistent. The state of a multithreaded program consists of the local states of threads and the shared state consisting of the shared variables. The operations on shared memory that are considered in this work are read and write of shared variables and acquire and release of locks. We assume that a read operation reads a value from a shared variable and assigns it to a variable in the local state of the thread performing the operation. Write assigns either a constant or a value from a local variable to a shared variable. Local operations, such as if-statements, are evaluated solely on the values in the local state and therefore cannot access shared variables directly. In real programs the statements can be modified automatically to satisfy these assumptions by using local temporary variables. The algorithms discussed in this work are based on analyzing sequences of operations observed during test executions and therefore language constructs such as loops, goto-statements and function calls are also supported.

2.1 Dynamic Symbolic Execution

Dynamic symbolic execution (DSE) [8,14], which is also known as concolic testing, is a systematic test generation approach in which a program is executed both concretely and symbolically at the same time. The concrete execution corresponds to the execution of the actual program and symbolic execution computes constraints on values of the variables in the program by using symbolic values that are expressed in terms of input values. At each branch point in the program's execution, the symbolic constraints specify the input values that cause the program to take a specific branch. As an example, executing a program x = x + 1; if (x > 0)...; generates constraints $input_1 + 1 > 0$ and $input_1 + 1 \leq 0$ at the if-statement assuming that the symbolic value $input_1$ is assigned initially to x. A path constraint is a conjunction of the symbolic constraints corresponding to each branch point in a given execution path. All input values that satisfy a path constraint will explore the same execution path for sequential programs. If a test execution goes through multiple branch points that depend on the input values, a path constraint can be constructed for each of the branches that were left unexplored along the execution path. These constraints are typically solved using SMT-solvers in order to obtain concrete values for the input symbols. This allows all the feasible execution paths through the program under test to be explored systematically.

2.2 Petri Nets and Unfoldings

In the following we describe Petri nets and their unfoldings that are used in our testing algorithm to model and explore the states of the program under test.

Definition 1. *A net is a triple (P, T, F), where P and T are disjoint sets of places and transitions, respectively, and $F \subseteq (P \times T) \cup (T \times P)$ is a flow relation. Places and transitions are called nodes and elements of F are called arcs.*

The preset of a node x, denoted by $^\bullet x$, is the set $\{y \in P \cup T \mid (y, x) \in F\}$. The postset of a node x, denoted by $x^\bullet$, is the set $\{y \in P \cup T \mid (x, y) \in F\}$. A marking of a net is a mapping $P \mapsto \mathbb{N}$. A marking M is identified with the multiset which contains $M(p)$ copies of p. A Petri net is a tuple $\Sigma = (P, T, F, M_0)$, where (P, T, F) is a net and M_0 is an initial marking of (P, T, F).

Graphically markings are represented by putting tokens on circles that represent the places of a net. A transition t is enabled in a marking that puts tokens on the places in the preset of t.

Definition 2. *The causality relation $<$ in a net is the transitive closure of F. The reflexive and transitive closure of F is denoted by $\leq$.*

Definition 3. *Two nodes x and y are in conflict if there are distinct transitions t_1 and t_2 such that $^\bullet t_1 \cap {}^\bullet t_2 \neq \emptyset$ and $t_1 < x$ and $t_2 < y$.*

Similarly as a directed graph can be unwinded into a tree that represents all paths through the graph, a Petri net can be unfolded into an acyclic net called occurrence net. For acyclic Petri nets the causality relation is a partial order.

Definition 4. *An occurrence net O is an acyclic net (B, E, G), where B and E are sets of conditions (places) and events (transitions) and G is the flow relation. Occurrence net O also satisfies the following conditions: for every b in B, $|^\bullet b| \leq 1$; for every $x \in B \cup E$ there is a finite number of nodes $y \in B \cup E$ such that $y < x$; and no node is in conflict with itself.*

To avoid confusion when talking about Petri nets and their occurrence nets, the nodes B and E are called *conditions* and *events*, respectively. If an occurrence net is obtained by unfolding a Petri net, the events and conditions in it can also be labeled with the corresponding transitions and places.

Definition 5 (Adapted from [11]). *A labeled occurrence net is a tuple $(O, l) = (B, E, G, l)$ where $l : B \cup E \mapsto P \cup T$ is a labeling function such that: (i) $l(B) \in P$ and $l(E) \in T$; (ii) for all $e \in E$, the restriction of l to $^\bullet e$ is a bijection between $^\bullet e$ and $^\bullet l(e)$; (iii) the restriction of l to $Min(O)$ is a bijection between $Min(O)$ and M_0, where $Min(O)$ denotes the set of minimal elements with respect to the causal relation; and (iv) for all $e, f \in E$, if $^\bullet e = {}^\bullet f$ and $l(e) = l(f)$ then $e = f$.*

Different labeled occurrence nets can be obtained by stopping the unfolding process at different times. The maximal labeled occurrence net (possibly infinite) is called *the unfolding* of a Petri net [3]. To simplify the discussion in this paper, we use the term unfolding for all labeled occurrence nets and not just the maximal one. To illustrate the concepts above, let us consider the Petri net shown on the left in Fig. 1. Next to the Petri net are its computation tree and unfolding that represent the computations (sequences of transitions) of the Petri net in an acyclic manner. The nodes in the computation tree represent the reachable markings of the Petri net (i.e., global states) and the edges represent transitions that lead from one marking to another. In the unfolding each event

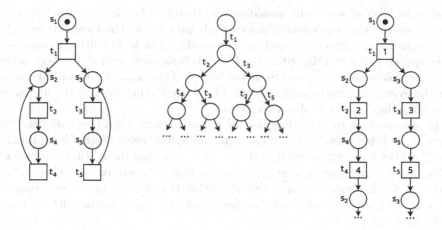

Fig. 1. A Petri net, its computation tree and unfolding

and condition are labeled with the corresponding transition or place of the Petri net. For some Petri nets its unfolding can be exponentially more succinct than the corresponding computation tree.

All the reachable markings of a Petri net can be explored by traversing its computation tree. However, exploring the full computation tree is not always necessary. In our example, the marking reached after firing t_1 is $\{s_2, s_3\}$. Firing transition sequence $t_1 t_2 t_4$ leads to the same marking and therefore there is no need to expand the computation tree further from the node that corresponds to this transition sequence. In a similar way, it is also possible to compute a finite prefix of the unfolding that captures all the reachable markings of a Petri net. However, as an unfolding is a more succinct representation than the computation tree, computing a finite prefix is not as straightforward. In the following we use notation similar to [3].

Definition 6. *The local configuration of an event e in an unfolding is the set* $\{e' \mid e' \le e\}$.

Definition 7. *Let e be an event in the unfolding of Petri net N. St(e) denotes the marking of N reached after firing the transitions corresponding to the events in the local configuration of e.*

Definition 8. *Let $\prec$ be a partial order on the events of an unfolding. An event e in a prefix of the unfolding is a terminal (also known as a cut-off event) if there exists an event e' such that $e' \prec e$ and* **St(e')** = **St(e)**.

A finite prefix of an unfolding can be constructed by leaving out any events that are causally preceded by a terminal event. That is, if an event e' has been added to the unfolding before event e and **St**(e') = **St**(e), the unfolding process can be stopped at event e. To illustrate this, let us consider the unfolding in Fig. 1 again. The numbers on the events in the unfolding denote the order in which they have been added to the unfolding and therefore follow the $\prec$ partial order. Let us assume that e_n denotes the event labeled with n. The local configuration of e_4 consists of events e_1, e_2 and e_4. The marking reached by firing these events corresponds to the marking $\mathbf{St}(e_4) = \{s_2, s_3\}$. Note that event e_1 has been added to the unfolding before e_4 and $\mathbf{St}(e_1) = \mathbf{St}(e_4)$. This means that e_4 is a terminal and no events that are causally preceded by it need to be added to the unfolding. Similarly the event e_5 is also a terminal.

It is important to note that not all partial orders $\prec$ lead to complete prefixes [3]. In other words, if the prefix is not complete, some reachable marking of the Petri net is not represented in the prefix. It has been shown that if events are added to the unfolding in so called *adequate order*, the prefixes are always complete. In the implementation of our algorithm that is used in the experiments, we use the ERV adequate order as described in [4]. For further details about unfoldings, see [3].

3   Modeling Test Executions

Our lightweight state capturing technique is based on modeling behavior observed during test executions as a Petri net. This model can then be used for state matching in a testing algorithm. The initial state of the program is modeled by having a place for each thread, shared variable and lock in the program under test. Places for threads are abstract representations of their local states and places for shared variables represent valuations of that shared variable. To model execution paths through the program, transitions are added to the model such that they correspond to operations that have been observed during test executions. To model these operations we use the constructs shown in Fig. 2. For clarity, the places corresponding to shared variables and locks have a darker color than places for abstract local states.

The intuition behind the modeling constructs is as follows. When a thread is in a local state such that the next operation to be executed is a write, the operation always results in the same subsequent local state and the same value to be written to the shared memory regardless of the current valuation of the shared variable. This is represented in Fig. 2 such that if the write transition marked with dashed lines is added to the model after the transition with solid lines from the same local state, the transitions result in the same places for the local state and the shared variable. For read operations the resulting local states are always different if the shared variable places are different (i.e., in cases where the values being read might be different). This is again illustrated by a second read transition marked with dashed lines in Fig. 2. However, reading a value does not change it and therefore a read operation can be modeled with a transition that returns the token back to the original shared variable place. For each lock there is always only one lock place and acquiring a lock takes a token from this place and releasing the lock puts the token back to the same place. Local operations of threads are not modeled explicitly as a thread executes them always in the same way until the next global operation is encountered. An exception to

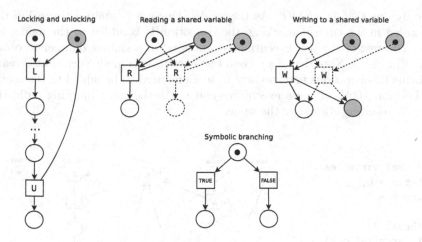

Fig. 2. Modeling constructs

this are branching operations that depend on input values. In our approach we use symbolic execution to collect constraints that describe which input values cause either the true or false branch to be followed at a given local state. These constraints are added to the transitions for the true and false branches. As such constraints restrict the possible values in a local state, branching transitions lead to new abstract local states.

To model a test execution, a marking that corresponds to the initial state is first created. This marking is used to denote the current state of the test execution. The operations enabled in the initial state are then modeled. The test execution then executes one of these operations and the corresponding transition is fired to update the current marking. In the resulting state all the enabled operations are again modeled unless a corresponding transition already exists in the model. This process is then continued until the whole test execution has been processed. Note that as we model sequences of observed operations, loops in the program are unrolled. Also as we do not track the full local states of threads, we cannot determine if a thread can loop its execution back to an earlier abstract local state. This means that any transition in the model can be fired at most once in any given test execution. The only cycles in the Petri net model occur with places for shared variables and locks. As a test execution can be infinite for nonterminating programs, we limit the length of each test execution by a given bound in order to guarantee termination.

Example 1. Let us consider the program shown in Fig. 3 and a test execution that executes the statements on lines 1,2,3,4,5,6 in that order. Modeling this execution starts with an initial marking $\{s_1, s_2, x_1, y_1, l_1\}$. In the initial state the lock acquire operations of both threads are enabled. These are modeled as the transitions t_1 and t_2. The lock transition belonging to thread 1 is then fired to obtain a marking $\{s_3, s_2, x_1, y_1\}$. In this new state the operation x = 1 is the only one that is enabled. As the model does not contain a transition that is enabled in the current marking, the transition t_3 is added to the model and fired. The rest of the test execution is processed in a similar manner to obtain the net in Fig. 3. Note that if a second test execution is made such that thread 2 performs its operations first, no new transitions need to be added to the model. Furthermore, both of these executions end up in the same marking indicating that the resulting states are the same.

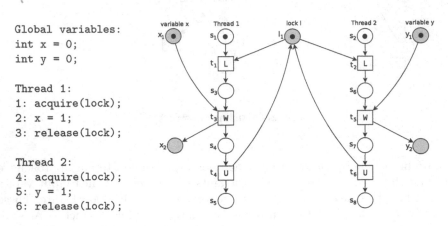

```
Global variables:
int x = 0;
int y = 0;


Thread 1:
1: acquire(lock);
2: x = 1;
3: release(lock);


Thread 2:
4: acquire(lock);
5: y = 1;
6: release(lock);
```

Fig. 3. Locking example

Example 2. Fig. 4 shows another example program where three threads write concurrently to the same shared variable. The partial model on the top of the figure is obtained by performing a test execution where thread 1 is executed first, thread 2 second and thread 3 last. In the initial state the writes for all threads are enabled and this is modeled by the transitions t_1, t_2 and t_3. After executing the write of thread 1, the enabled writes of thread 2 and thread 3 are modeled as transitions t_4 and t_5. The final write of the test execution is modeled as transition t_6. The model on the bottom shows the complete model for the program. In this case there are six possible ways to interleave the write operations. However, there are only three possible end states (markings) for these interleavings and therefore if the program continues after the writes, it is possible to cut the exploration of some of these interleavings.

3.1   Advantages and Limitations for State Matching

As discussed in the examples, test executions following different interleavings can lead to the same marking. This can be used to avoid unnecessary tests in automated testing by storing the visited markings, for example, to a hash table. Naturally the cases where our modeling approach can determine that a test execution leads to an already visited state are limited as it does not do

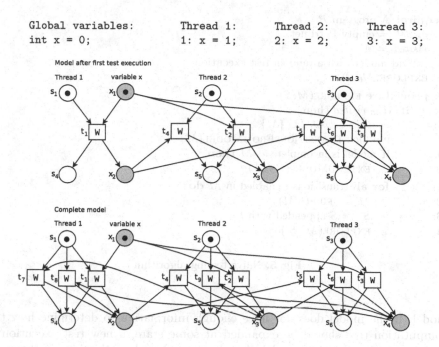

```
Global variables:        Thread 1:      Thread 2:      Thread 3:
int x = 0;               1: x = 1;      2: x = 2;      3: x = 3;
```

Fig. 4. Concurrent writes example

any complex reasoning on the symbolic data values. Furthermore, as in the model the loops in the program are unrolled, it cannot be used to detect cases where a test execution loops back to a state that was already visited during the same execution. However, the model can be in some cases used to detect when different interleavings of the same operations lead to the same state. Cases such as accessing different variables in a shared data structure that is protected by a lock do occur and in such cases our approach has potential to scale much better than stateless testing approaches, even if they reduce interleavings of independent operations. Furthermore, the space requirement of storing markings can be considerably smaller than storing full state information.

4 Systematic Model Construction

Modeling test executions as a Petri net is easy. However, to systematically test a given program, we want to perform test executions that cover the complete model. This can be done by starting with a random initial test execution, modeling it and using the obtained information to compute inputs for subsequent test executions. In this section we present two algorithms to do this.

4.1 Naive Stateful Approach

A simple way to construct a complete model of a program under test is to initially model a random test execution and start traversing the *computation tree* of the

Require: A program P
1: $model :=$ empty Petri net
2: $visited := \emptyset$
3: extend model with a random test execution
4: EXPLORE$(M_0, \emptyset)$

5: **procedure** EXPLORE(M, S)
6:      **if** $M \notin visited$ **then**
7:          $visited := visited \cup \{M\}$
8:          PREDICTTRANSITIONSFROMMODEL(M)
9:          **if** model is incomplete at M **then**
10:             EXTENDMODEL(P, S, k)

11:         **for all** transitions t enabled in M **do**
12:             $M' :=$ FIRE(t, M)
13:             $S' := S$ appended with t
14:             EXPLORE(M', S')

Fig. 5. Naive testing algorithm

model. If the model does not have enough information to determine how the computation tree should be expanded at some state, a new test execution is performed to update the model. An algorithm based on this idea is shown in Fig. 5. It performs a depth-first search on the reachable markings of the model by calling recursively the EXPLORE subroutine that takes the state (marking M of the model) and a sequence S of transitions that lead to this state as input. At each state the algorithm determines that a model is incomplete if it is not known what operations the threads want to perform next or if there are no transitions in the model for these operations. This requires keeping track of the end states of threads observed during test executions (i.e., a thread does not perform any operations after reaching such a state). If the model does not have the necessary information, a test execution to explore the current state is performed. After this the transitions enabled in the current state are known. The algorithm also stores the visited states and backtracks if an already explored state is encountered.

In some cases it is easy to determine from the model which operation a thread wants to perform next even if the corresponding transition in the model is missing. As an example, let us consider the program and the partial model in Fig. 4. Let us assume that we are exploring a marking $m = \{s_1, s_5, s_3, x_3\}$. The model is incomplete at this marking because no transition for thread 1 is enabled in this state. However, each transition from a place representing a local state of a thread has the same type (i.e., from a given local state, the operation the thread wants to perform is always the same). As there is a write transition in the postset of s_1, we know that thread 1 wants to perform a write operation. In cases like this, the missing transition (t_7 in our example) can be added to the model without performing a test execution. The subroutine PREDICT-TRANSITIONSFROMMODEL performs such analysis for each visited marking. To be more precise, PREDICTTRANSITIONSFROMMODEL checks the postsets of the places for local thread states to determine the operations the threads want to perform and adds any missing transitions to the model. For reads and writes this is trivial. For lock operations it needs to be checked that the lock is free in the current state (i.e., the marking contains the respective lock place). Using PREDICTTRANSITIONSFROMMODEL can sometimes significantly reduce the need for test executions. For example, the final model for program in Fig. 4 can be constructed with information obtained from a single test execution.

The EXTENDMODEL subroutine performs a test execution both concretely and symbolically. The subroutine takes as input a sequence S of transitions that leads to the state that is being explored. Bound k for the execution length is used to guarantee termination. To get concrete input values for the test execution, all the symbolic constraints associated with the branching transitions in S are collected and their conjunction is solved using a constraint solver. The sequence S is also given to a runtime scheduler that schedules the execution such that the operations are performed in the same order as the corresponding transitions in S. After reaching the target state, the scheduler is free to follow any schedule.

We call the algorithm in Fig. 5 naive because it explores interleavings of global operations even if they are independent. This is unnecessary to find errors such as assertion violations or reachability of control states. Naturally different interleavings of independent operations lead to the same state and the algorithm backtracks in such cases. To avoid exploring unnecessary interleavings, we present next an algorithm based on unfolding the model. This approach is only guaranteed to cover the reachable local states of threads and to detect all assertion violations. Detecting all deadlocks is not guaranteed. Another approach would be to use partial order reduction algorithms such as DPOR [6]. As using state matching with DPOR requires special care to guarantee the completeness of the algorithm [16], investigating such possibilities is left for future work.

4.2 Unfolding Based Approach

To explore an unfolding of the model instead of the computation tree, we make a small modification to the modeling approach presented in Sect. 3: instead of modeling a shared variable with a single place in each reachable marking, we duplicate the place for each thread. In other words, each shared variable place in the model is replaced with n places, where n is the number of threads in the program. A write transition is made to access each of the n copies while a read transition accesses only the local copy belonging to the thread performing the read. This approach is known as place replication [5] and it has the effect that two concurrent reads of the same shared variable become independent. If place replication is not used, the unfolding process would explicitly explore different interleavings of read transitions. The use of place replication is demonstrated in the example at the end of this section.

The unfolding based testing algorithm is shown in Fig. 6 and the idea behind it is similar as with the naive algorithm. Initially a random test execution is performed to start the model construction. The algorithm maintains a set of events that can be used to extend the unfolding. Initially such events are those that are

Require: A program P
1: *model* := empty Petri net, *unf* := initial unfolding
2: *visited* := ∅
3: extend model with a random test execution
4: *extensions* := events enabled in the initial state
5: **while** *extensions* ≠ ∅ **do**
6:     **choose** ≺-minimal event e from *extensions*
7:     M := $\mathbf{St}(e)$
8:     PREDICTTRANSITIONSFROMMODEL(M)
9:     **if** model is incomplete at M **then**
10:         EXTENDMODEL(P, e, k)
11:     **else**
12:         add e to *unf*
13:         *extensions* := *extensions* \ {e}
14:         **if** $M \notin$ *visited* **then**   // e is not a terminal
15:             *visited* := *visited* ∪ {M}
16:             *extensions* := *extensions* ∪ POSSIBLEEXTENSIONS(e, *unf*)

Fig. 6. Unfolding algorithm

enabled in the initial state. The algorithm then starts adding these extensions to the unfolding in the order specified by the partial order ≺ (lines 5-6). As discussed in Sect. 2, we use the ERV adequate order to guarantee completeness.

To be able to avoid exploring states multiple times, the algorithm computes $\mathbf{St}(e)$ for each event e added to the unfolding. This can be seen as the state that is reached by following the shortest execution path to the event e. For the obtained marking (state), the algorithm performs the same analysis for missing transitions as the naive algorithm does (line 8). If after adding the predicted transitions the model is incomplete at the obtained marking, a new test execution is performed to update the model. Otherwise the algorithm adds the selected event to the unfolding and determines if it is a terminal. This is done by checking if an event with the same marking $\mathbf{St}(e)$ has already been added to the unfolding (line 14). If the event is not a terminal, the algorithm computes a set of new events that can be added to the unfolding and adds these events to the set of possible extensions. To be more precise, a possible extension is an event that has not yet been added to the unfolding but could be fired in some reachable marking.

Computing Possible Extensions. There exists several algorithms for computing possible extensions. Most of these algorithms, however, have been designed for arbitrary Petri nets and are computationally the most expensive part of building unfoldings. Such algorithms can be used in our testing approach but this could adversely affect the performance. Fortunately, the Petri net models constructed in our approach have a restricted structure that makes computing possible extensions more efficient than in the general case. We have recently described an efficient possible extensions algorithm in [10] that works with unfoldings that are constructed in a similar way as in our new testing algorithm. We use this efficient algorithm in the implementation of the algorithm in Fig 6.

Computing Inputs For Test Executions. Extending a model with a test execution can be done similarly as in the naive algorithm. The difference is that with unfoldings we do not have directly a sequence of transitions that leads to the state (i.e., marking M) we want to explore. However, obtaining such a sequence is easy. The state is reached by firing the transitions corresponding to the local configuration of e. If the events in the unfolding have labels that describe the order in which they were added to the unfolding (e.g., the numbers on events in Fig. 1), an event with a larger label cannot causally precede an event with a smaller label. This means that the transitions can be fired in the order given by the labeling of their corresponding events to reach the marking M.

Example 3. To illustrate the unfolding based algorithm, let us consider the Petri net model and its unfolding in Fig. 7. The model represents a program with two threads that acquire a lock and read a shared variable x. The first thread also branches its execution based on input values at the end. Note that the places for x have been replicated for each thread (i.e., x_1 has been replicated to x_1^1 and x_1^2). This makes the read transitions independent as explained earlier. To construct the net in Fig. 7, the algorithm first performs a random test execution. In this example, any execution provides enough information to model all the transitions shown in the Petri net model. However, depending which branch the first thread follows at the end, the model remains incomplete at place s_9 or s_{10} as the corresponding local state is not explored. From the initial state it is possible to fire transitions t_1 and t_2. The events 1 and 2 correspond to these transitions and are added to the set of possible extensions. The algorithm selects event 1 to be added to the unfolding and this results in a new reachable marking where it is possible to fire event 3. The found event is added to the set of possible extensions and the same process is continued until the algorithm selects the event 12 to be added to the unfolding. The marking computed at line 7 is the same for this event as well as for event 11. Therefore event 12 is a terminal (marked with a cross) and possible extensions for it are not computed. Let us assume that the initial test execution did not explore the state corresponding to place s_9. To add event 13 to the unfolding, the algorithm needs first to perform a test execution to explore s_9 so that it has enough information to compute possible extensions for event 13. This is achieved by a test execution that follows the transitions corresponding to the events 1, 3, 5 and 13. Let us assume that the symbolic constraint associated with t_7 is $input_1 > 5$. Solving this constraint gives the test execution a concrete input value (e.g., the value 6). After performing the test execution, the algorithm knows that s_9 corresponds to an end state and can continue the unfolding process by adding event 13 and finally event 14.

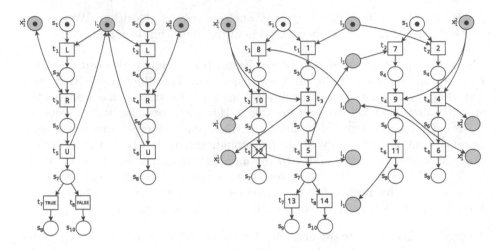

Fig. 7. A model and its unfolding

5   Experiments

We have performed a set of experiments with the new algorithms and compared them with a combination of DSE and DPOR as described in [13] and the stateless unfolding based testing algorithm described in [10]. The naive algorithm described in this paper and DPOR have also been augmented with sleep sets [7] to further reduce the number of test executions needed. The stateless unfolding algorithm constructs similar unfoldings (without constructing the Petri net model) as the new algorithm except that no terminal events are used. In this sense our new approach can be seen as extending the testing approach in [10] by taking some state information into account.

The following benchmarks are used in the experiments. *Fib* and *Szymanski* are from the 1st International Competition on Software Verification except that they have been simplified by limiting how many times some loops are executed. *Filesystem* benchmark is from [6] where it was used to evaluate DPOR. *Dining* implements a dining philosophers problem where each philosopher eats twice. In *Locking* all accesses to shared memory are protected by a single lock. *Updater* contains a set of threads where some threads update values in shared memory and other threads perform work based on these values. *Writes* is similar to the program in Fig. 4 except with more threads and more writes per thread. Finally, synthetic benchmarks perform randomly generated sequences of operations on input values and on global variables. Benchmarks with multiple variants are similar with each other except that the number of threads increases or the program otherwise increases in complexity.

The results of the experiments are shown in Table 1. For each algorithm the table shows the number of test executions needed to fully cover the program under test and the time required to do this. As the algorithms are partially ran-

Table 1. Comparison of different approaches

Benchmark	Stateless unfolding tests	time	Stateless DPOR tests	time	Stateful naive tests	time	Stateful unfolding tests	time
Fib 1	19605	0m 17s	21102	0m 21s	5746	**0m 11s**	4946	0m 15s
Fib 2	218243	4m 18s	232531	4m 2s	53478	3m 45s	46829	**3m 15s**
Filesystem 1	3	**0m 0s**	142	0m 4s	-	(> 30m)	3	**0m 0s**
Filesystem 2	3	**0m 0s**	2227	0m 46s	-	(> 30m)	3	**0m 0s**
Dining 1	798	0m 3s	1161	0m 3s	3	**0m 0s**	4	0m 0s
Dining 2	5746	0m 14s	10065	0m 22s	3	**0m 1s**	3	0m 1s
Dining 3	36095	1m 29s	81527	3m 29s	2	0m 7s	4	**0m 1s**
Dining 4	205161	12m 55s	-	(> 30m)	-	(> 30m)	2	**0m 3s**
Szymanski	65138	2m 3s	65138	**0m 30s**	50264	0m 43s	46679	2m 35s
Locking 1	2520	0m 8s	2520	0m 6s	20	**0m 1s**	18	0m 3s
Locking 2	22680	0m 56s	22680	0m 47s	29	**0m 2s**	26	0m 9s
Locking 3	-	(> 30m)	-	(> 30m)	115	**0m 21s**	89	3m 32s
Updater	33269	2m 22s	33463	2m 6s	13586	**1m 23s**	12259	1m 52s
Writes	-	(> 30m)	-	(> 30m)	1	**0m 0s**	1	**0m 0s**
Synthetic 1	926	0m 3s	1661	0m 4s	68	**0m 1s**	62	0m 1s
Synthetic 2	8205	0m 41s	22462	1m 20s	123	**0m 7s**	97	0m 11s
Synthetic 3	11458	1m 12s	37915	2m 18s	326	1m 8s	298	**0m 30s**

domized (e.g., the random initial execution), the experiments were repeated ten times and the average results are reported. As a sanity check, it was checked that both the naive and the stateful unfolding algorithms generated models of the same size. From the results it can be seen that the stateful algorithms can sometimes greatly outperform the stateless testing approaches. The naive algorithm is more lightweight than the unfolding approach and therefore typically faster for small programs. However, the naive algorithm scales poorly on some benchmarks. The unfolding based algorithm is only guaranteed to cover the reachable local states of threads and therefore it typically scales better. In some cases, such as with *Szymanski*, our new approach does not provide a significant reduction to the number of test executions. In such cases the stateful algorithms can be slower than the stateless counterparts. With stateless unfolding the order in which events are added does not matter and therefore unfolding with terminals has the additional overhead of sorting the possible extensions. One disadvantage of the stateful approaches is that they require more memory as the model and the visited markings need to be stored.

6   Related Work

Stateful approaches have been successful in model checking. However, when systematically testing real-world programs, storing explored states can require a considerable amount of memory. Even though methods to alleviate this problem have been developed (e.g, compression and hashing [9] and selective caching [2]), many testing tools rely on stateless exploration. The problem with stateless testing, even when combined with partial order reductions, is that part of the state space may be explored multiple times. Our work can be seen as balancing between complete state capturing and stateless search.

Yang et al. [16] propose a related lightweight approach to capture states at runtime that is based on tracking changes between successive local states without storing full state information. In their approach the captured local states are abstract but they capture the shared portion of the state concretely. Therefore, unlike our approach, their approach cannot directly be combined with DSE. They also describe a stateful DPOR algorithm based on their state capture approach. To guarantee the soundness of their algorithm, additional computation needs to be performed to make sure that any subset of the state space is not missed. With unfoldings this is handled by adding events in an adequate order.

It is possible to take the valuations of variables into account in state matching. With symbolic execution this leads to subsumption checking of symbolic states. Anand et al. [1] propose a combination of subsumption checking and abstractions for data structures such as lists and arrays. Such approaches are considerably more heavyweight compared to our approach but can match states that our approach cannot. An alternative way to reduce the number of states that need to be explored when using symbolic execution is to use state merging [12], where multiple execution paths are expressed symbolically instead of exploring them separately. This, however, makes path constraints more demanding to solve.

7 Conclusions

We have presented a lightweight approach to capture abstract state information of multithreaded programs. This approach is based on modeling programs under test with Petri nets and using this model to avoid exploring reachable states multiple times. We have presented a testing algorithm that combines the modeling approach with DSE. Based on our experiments, lightweight state matching can greatly improve the scalability of DSE based testing algorithms that target multithreaded programs. Potential directions for future work are combining the state capture approach with other partial order reduction algorithms and implementing modeling constructs for common cases such as waits in while loops that do not change the local state of the waiting thread. Another possibility is to take variable valuations in different states into consideration. As discussed in Sect. 1, capturing full state information can be expensive. However, as the Petri net model contains places for shared variables, it is possible to use the same shared variable place whenever the shared variable has the same concrete value (i.e., the value does not depend on inputs). This could make the model more compact.

Acknowledgments. This work was financially supported by Academy of Finland (project 139402).

References

1. Anand, S., Păsăreanu, C.S., Visser, W.: Symbolic execution with abstract subsumption checking. In: Valmari, A. (ed.) SPIN 2006. LNCS, vol. 3925, pp. 163–181. Springer, Heidelberg (2006)
2. Behrmann, G., Larsen, K.G., Pelánek, R.: To store or not to store. In: Hunt Jr., W.A., Somenzi, F. (eds.) CAV 2003. LNCS, vol. 2725, pp. 433–445. Springer, Heidelberg (2003)
3. Esparza, J., Heljanko, K.: Unfoldings – A Partial-Order Approach to Model Checking. EATCS Monographs in Theoretical Computer Science. Springer (2008)
4. Esparza, J., Römer, S., Vogler, W.: An improvement of McMillan's unfolding algorithm. Formal Methods in System Design 20(3), 285–310 (2002)
5. Farzan, A., Madhusudan, P.: Causal atomicity. In: Ball, T., Jones, R.B. (eds.) CAV 2006. LNCS, vol. 4144, pp. 315–328. Springer, Heidelberg (2006)
6. Flanagan, C., Godefroid, P.: Dynamic partial-order reduction for model checking software. In: Palsberg, J., Abadi, M. (eds.) POPL, pp. 110–121. ACM (2005)
7. Godefroid, P.: Partial-Order Methods for the Verification of Concurrent Systems: An Approach to the State-Explosion Problem. Springer-Verlag New York, Inc., Secaucus (1996)
8. Godefroid, P., Klarlund, N., Sen, K.: DART: Directed automated random testing. In: Proceedings of the ACM SIGPLAN 2005 Conference on Programming Language Design and Implementation (PLDI 2005), pp. 213–223. ACM (2005)
9. Holzmann, G.J.: The model checker Spin. IEEE Trans. Software Eng. 23(5), 279–295 (1997)
10. Kähkönen, K., Saarikivi, O., Heljanko, K.: Using unfoldings in automated testing of multithreaded programs. In: Proceedings of the 27th IEEE/ACM International Conference Automated Software Engineering (ASE 2012), pp. 150–159 (2012)
11. Khomenko, V., Koutny, M.: Towards an efficient algorithm for unfolding Petri nets. In: Larsen, K.G., Nielsen, M. (eds.) CONCUR 2001 LNCS, vol. 2154, pp. 366–380. Springer, Heidelberg (2001)
12. Kuznetsov, V., Kinder, J., Bucur, S., Candea, G.: Efficient state merging in symbolic execution. In: Vitek, J., Lin, H., Tip, F. (eds.) PLDI, pp. 193–204. ACM (2012)
13. Saarikivi, O., Kähkönen, K., Heljanko, K.: Improving dynamic partial order reductions for concolic testing. In: Proceedings of the 12th International Conference on Application of Concurrency to System Design (ACSD 2012), pp. 132–141 (2012)
14. Sen, K.: Scalable automated methods for dynamic program analysis. Doctoral thesis, University of Illinois (2006)
15. Valmari, A.: Stubborn sets for reduced state space generation. In: Proceedings of the 10th International Conference on Applications and Theory of Petri Nets: Advances in Petri Nets 1990, pp. 491–515. Springer, London (1991)
16. Yang, Y., Chen, X., Gopalakrishnan, G., Kirby, R.M.: Efficient stateful dynamic partial order reduction. In: Havelund, K., Majumdar, R. (eds.) SPIN 2008. LNCS, vol. 5156, pp. 288–305. Springer, Heidelberg (2008)

How Test Generation Helps Software Specification and Deductive Verification in Frama-C[*]

Guillaume Petiot[1,2], Nikolai Kosmatov[1], Alain Giorgetti[2,3], and Jacques Julliand[2]

[1] CEA, LIST, Software Reliability Laboratory, PC 174, 91191 Gif-sur-Yvette France
firstname.lastname@cea.fr
[2] FEMTO-ST/DISC, University of Franche-Comté, 25030 Besançon Cedex France
firstname.lastname@femto-st.fr
[3] INRIA Nancy - Grand Est, CASSIS project, 54600 Villers-lès-Nancy France

Abstract. This paper describes an incremental methodology of deductive verification assisted by test generation and illustrates its benefits by a set of frequent verification scenarios. We present STADY, a new integration of the concolic test generator PATHCRAWLER within the software analysis platform FRAMA-C. This new plugin treats a complete formal specification of a C program during test generation and provides the validation engineer with a helpful feedback at all stages of the specification and verification tasks.

Keywords: static analysis, test generation, specification, Frama-C, deductive verification.

1 Introduction

Validation of critical systems can be realized using various verification methods based on static analysis, dynamic analysis or their combinations. Static analysis is performed on the source code without executing the program, whereas dynamic analysis is based on the program execution. Both are complementary and can be advantageously combined [10,3,14,6,7,5,18].

Among static techniques, formal deductive verification allows to establish a rigorous, mathematical proof that a given annotated program respects its specification. The modular verification approach requires a formal specification (contract) for each function describing its admissible inputs and expected results. Modern theorem proving tools can automatically establish many proofs of correctness, but achieving a fully successful proof in practice needs a lot of tedious work and manual analysis of proof failures by the validation engineers. Klein [15] estimates that the cost of one line of formally verified code is about $700. This high cost is explained by the great difficulty of understanding why a proof fails, and of writing correct and sufficiently complete specifications suitable for automatic proof of contracts for which loop variants and invariants can be required.

[*] The research leading to these results has received funding from the ARTEMIS Joint Undertaking under grant agreement N⁰ 269335 and from the French government.

M. Seidl and N. Tillmann (Eds.): TAP 2014, LNCS 8570, pp. 204–211, 2014.

The main motivation of this methodology and tool paper is to study how automatic test generation can help to write a correct formal specification and to achieve its deductive verification. The contributions of this paper include:

- a brief presentation (in Sec. 2) of a combined STAtic/DYnamic tool named STADY. Within the software analysis framework FRAMA-C [11], this tool fills the gap between deductive verification and test generation and allows to treat a complete formal specification (including pre-/postconditions, assertions, loop invariants and variants) during test generation with PATHCRAWLER [4];
- a methodology of iterative deductive verification taking advantage of feedbacks provided by test generation (in Sec. 3). Its benefits are illustrated on a set of frequent verification scenarios;
- a summary of experiments showing STADY's bug detection power (in Sec. 3.4).

2   STADY Tool Overview

The STADY tool integrates the concolic test generator PATHCRAWLER [4] into the software analysis framework FRAMA-C [11], and in particular allows the user to combine it with the deductive verification plugin WP [11].

FRAMA-C [11] is a platform dedicated to analysis of C programs that includes various source code analyzers as separate plugins such as WP performing weakest-precondition calculus for deductive verification, VALUE performing value analysis by abstract interpretation, etc. FRAMA-C supports ACSL (ANSI C Specification Language) [2,11], a behavioral specification language allowing to express properties over C programs. Moreover, ACSL annotations play a central role in communication between plugins: any analyzer can add annotations to be verified by other ones and notify other plugins about results of the analysis it performed by changing an annotation status. The status can indicate that the annotation is valid, valid under conditions, invalid or undetermined, and which analyzer established this result [9].

For combinations with dynamic analysis, we consider the executable subset of ACSL named E-ACSL [12,19]. E-ACSL can express function contracts (pre/postconditions, guarded behaviors, completeness and disjointness of behaviors), assertions and loop contracts (variants and invariants). It supports quantifications over bounded intervals of integers, mathematical integers and memory-related constructs (e.g. on validity and initialization).

PATHCRAWLER [4] is a structural (also known as *concolic*) test generator for C programs, combining *concrete* and *symbolic* execution. PATHCRAWLER is based on a specific constraint solver, COLIBRI, that implements advanced features such as floating-point and modular integer arithmetics support. PATHCRAWLER provides coverage strategies like *k-paths* (feasible paths with at most k consecutive loop iterations) and *all-paths* (all feasible paths without any limitation on loop iterations). PATHCRAWLER is *sound*, meaning that each test case activates the test objective for which it was generated. This is verified by concrete execution. PATHCRAWLER is also *complete* in the following sense: when the tool manages to explore all feasible paths of the program, all features of the program are supported by the tool and constraint solving terminates for all paths, the absence of a test for some test objective means that this test objective is infeasible, since the tool does not approximate path constraints [4, Sec. 3.1].

Given a C program annotated in the executable specification language E-ACSL [11], STADY first translates its specification into executable C code, instruments the program for error detection, runs PATHCRAWLER to generate tests for the instrumented code, and finally returns the results to FRAMA-C. To detect errors, the translation generates additional branches, enforcing test generation to trigger erroneous cases, and thus to generate inputs activating the error if such inputs exist. In this way, STADY treats and triggers errors in assertions, postconditions, loop invariants and variants, and also in pre- and postconditions of called functions (also called *callees*). PATHCRAWLER being complete, whenever test generation terminates without finding any error after an exhaustive "all-path" coverage, we are sure that the translated E-ACSL properties hold. If the coverage is only partial but no error occurred, the test generation increases the confidence that the program respects its specification but cannot guarantee it. However, errors can be found and used to invalidate the annotations in FRAMA-C even when the coverage is incomplete.

STADY currently supports most ACSL clauses. Quantified predicates \exists and \forall and builtin terms as \sum or \numof are translated as loops. Logic functions and named predicates are handled, however recursivity is currently not supported. \old constructs are treated by saving the value of the formal parameters of a function. Validity checks of pointers are partially supported due to the current limitation of the underlying test generator: we can only check the validity when a base address is an input pointer. assert, assumes, behavior, ensures, loop invariant, loop variant and requires clauses are supported as well. assigns clauses and complex constructs like inductive predicates are not handled yet and are part of our future work.

3   Verification Scenarios Combining Proof and Testing

During specification and deductive verification, test generation can automatically provide the validation engineer with a fast and helpful feedback facilitating the verification task. While specifying a program, test generation may find a counter-example showing that the current specification does not hold for the current code. It can be used at early stages of specification, even when formal verification has no chances to succeed yet (e.g. when loop annotations, assertions or callees' contracts are not yet written). In case of a proof failure for a specified program property during program proof, when the validation engineer has no other alternative than manually analyzing the reasons of the failure, test generation can be particularly useful. The absence of counter-examples after a rigorous partial (or, when possible, complete) exploration of program paths provides additional confidence in (resp., guarantee of) correctness of the program with respect to its current specification. This feedback may encourage the engineer to think that the failure is due to a missing or insufficiently strong annotation (loop invariant, assertion, called function contract etc.) rather than to an error, and to write such additional annotations. On the contrary, a counter-example immediately shows that the program does not meet its current specification, and prevents the waste of time of writing additional annotations. Moreover, the concrete test inputs and activated program path reported

```
 1  int delete_substr(char *str, int strlen, char *substr, int sublen, char *dest) {
 2    int start = find_substr(str, strlen, substr, sublen), j, k;
 3    if (start == -1) {
 4      for (k = 0; k < strlen; k++) dest[k] = str[k];
 5      return 0;
 6    }
 7    for (j = 0; j < start; j++) dest[j] = str[j];
 8    for (j = start; j < strlen-sublen; j++) dest[j] = str[j+sublen];
 9    return 1;
10  }
```

Fig. 1. Unspecified function `delete_substr` calling the function of Fig. 2

```
 1  /*@ requires 0 < sublen ≤ strlen;
 2    @ requires \valid(str+(0..strlen-1)) ∧ \valid(substr+(0..sublen-1));
 3    @ assigns \nothing;
 4    @ behavior found:
 5    @   assumes ∃ i ∈ ℤ; 0 ≤ i < strlen-sublen ∧
 6    @     (∀ j ∈ ℤ; 0 ≤ j < sublen ⇒ str[i+j] == substr[j]);
 7    @   ensures 0 ≤ \result < strlen-sublen;
 8    @   ensures ∀ j ∈ ℤ; 0 ≤ j < sublen ⇒ str[\result+j] == substr[j];
 9    @ behavior not_found:
10    @   assumes ∀ i ∈ ℤ; 0 ≤ i < strlen-sublen ⇒
11    @     (∃ j ∈ ℤ; 0 ≤ j < sublen ∧ str[i+j] ≠ substr[j]);
12    @   ensures \result == -1; */
13  int find_substr(char *str, int strlen, char *substr, int sublen);
```

Fig. 2. Verified function `find_substr` with a "pretty-printed" E-ACSL contract

by the testing tool precisely indicate the erroneous situation. Notice that the objective is certainly not *to fit the specification to (potentially erroneous) code*, but *to help the validation engineer to identify the problem (in the specification or in the code)* with a counter-example. Let us illustrate these points on concrete verification scenarios.

Suppose Alice is a skilled validation engineer in charge of specification and deductive verification of the function `delete_substr` (Fig. 1). We follow Alice throughout her validation process. The `delete_substr` function is supposed to delete one occurrence of a substring `substr` of length `sublen` from another string `str` of length `strlen` and to put the result into `dest` (pre-allocated for `strlen` characters), while `str` and `substr` should not be modified. For simplicity, we use arrays rather than usual zero-terminated strings. The `delete_substr` function returns 1 if an occurrence of the substring was found and deleted, and 0 otherwise. We assume Alice has already successfully proved the correctness of `find_substr` (Fig. 2) supposed to return the index of an occurrence of `substr` in `str` if this substring is present, and −1 otherwise.

Alice first writes the following precondition (added before line 1 of Fig. 1):

```
requires 0 < sublen ≤ strlen;
requires \valid(str+(0..strlen-1));
requires \valid(dest+(0..strlen-1));
requires \valid(substr+(0..sublen-1));
requires \separated(dest+(0..strlen-1), substr+(0..sublen-1));
requires \separated(dest+(0..strlen-1), str+(0..strlen-1));
typically strlen ≤ 5;
```

We propose here the new clause **typically** c; that extends E-ACSL and defines the precondition c only for test generation. It allows Alice to strengthen the precondition if she desires to restrict the (potentially too big) number of paths to be explored by test generation to user-controlled partial coverage. Here the clause **typically** strlen ≤5 asks to cover all feasible paths where str is of length 5 or less. Ignored by deductive verification, this clause does not impact the proof. The extension of ACSL with the **typically** keyword is an experimental feature, not available in the distributed version of FRAMA-C.

3.1 Early Validation

Now Alice specifies that the function can assign only the array dest, and defines the postcondition for the case when the substring does not occur in the string. She adds the following (erroneous) clauses into the contract after the precondition defined above:

```
assigns dest[0..strlen-1];
behavior not_present:
 assumes !(∃ i ∈ ℤ; 0 ≤ i < strlen-sublen ∧
   (∀ j ∈ ℤ; 0 ≤ j < sublen ⇒ str[i+j] ≠ substr[j]));
 ensures ∀ k ∈ ℤ; 0 ≤ k < strlen ⇒ \old(str[k]) == dest[k];
 ensures \result == 0;
```

To validate it before going further, Alice applies STADY. It runs test generation and reports that both **ensures** clauses are invalidated by the counter-example strlen = 2, sublen = 1, str[0] = 'A', str[1] = 'B', substr[0] = 'A', dest[0] = 'B' and \result = 0. Alice sees that in this case the string substr has to be found in the string str and the behavior not_present should not apply, so its **assumes** clause must be erroneous. This helps Alice to correct the assumption by replacing ≠ with ==, to get:

```
 assumes !(∃ i ∈ ℤ; 0 ≤ i < strlen-sublen ∧
   (∀ j ∈ ℤ; 0 ≤ j < sublen ⇒ str[i+j] == substr[j]));
```

Running STADY again reports that all feasible paths with strlen ≤5 have been covered (within 3.4 sec.) and 9442 test cases have been successfully generated and executed. Alice is now pretty confident that this behavior is correctly defined.

For the complementary case Alice copy-pastes the not_present behavior and (wrongly) modifies it into the following behavior:

```
behavior present:
 assumes ∃ i ∈ ℤ; 0 ≤ i < strlen-sublen ∧
   (∀ j ∈ ℤ; 0 ≤ j < sublen ⇒ str[i+j] == substr[j]);
 ensures ∃ i ∈ ℤ; 0 ≤ i < strlen-sublen ∧
   (∀ j ∈ ℤ; 0 ≤ j < sublen ⇒ \old(str[i+j]) == \old(substr[j])) ∧
   (∀ k ∈ ℤ; 0 ≤ k < i ⇒ \old(str[k]) == dest[k]) ∧
   (∀ l ∈ ℤ; i ≤ l < strlen ⇒ \old(str[l+sublen]) == dest[l]);
 ensures \result == 1;
```

Again, Alice runs STADY. The tool reports an out-of-bounds error in accessing the element of str at index l+sublen in the last **ensures**. This helps Alice to understand that the upper bound of index l should be strlen-sublen instead of strlen. She fixes this error and re-runs STADY. Test generation reports that 13448 test cases cover without errors the feasible paths for strlen ≤5. Alice is now satisfied with the defined behaviors. Notice that these cases exhibit errors in the specification. In other cases errors could be in the program (cf Sec. 3.4).

3.2 Incremental Loop Validation

Alice now specifies as follows the first for-loop at line 4 in Fig. 1:

```
loop invariant ∀ m ∈ ℤ; 0 ≤ m < k ⇒ dest[m] == \at(str[m],Pre);
loop assigns k, dest[0..strlen-1];
loop variant strlen-k;
```

Then Alice runs WP. The deductive verification tool cannot validate the postcondition of delete_substr, in particular because the other two loops are not yet specified. However, WP could validate the annotations of the first loop. Here it fails, and Alice does not know whether it is because the loop specification is already incorrect, or because it is not complete enough to be verified. She runs STADY, which does not find any error in the loop specification and the postcondition, after 15635 test cases. Alice now believes that loop specification is valid but incomplete. This confidence helps her to add an additional invariant

```
loop invariant 0 ≤ k < strlen;
```

defining the bounds for k. Alice tries again to prove the loop, and WP fails again. She runs STADY and this time the new loop invariant is invalidated. After analyzing the failure on a simple counter-example, Alice understands that the loop invariant k <strlen is not correct. Indeed, k is equal to strlen after the last iteration, so the loop invariant should say k ≤strlen. After fixing this error, WP succeeds to prove the loop annotations. Similarly, Alice iteratively specifies and verifies the other two loops.

The now completely specified function delete_substr can be fully proved by WP. However its default timeout (10 seconds per property) has to be significantly extended (e.g. to 50 seconds per property). The fact that test generation achieves (within only 4 sec.!) a significant partial coverage (restricted by the typically clause for testing) and finds no error convinces Alice to increase the timeout, that could be a waste of time when a counter-example can show why the program does not respect the specification.

3.3 Adaptation of Callees' Contracts for Modular Verification

It often happens that the contract of a called function is fully proved, but is too weak to prove the caller. For instance assume that the clause at line 7 of Fig. 2 is missing. Running WP on the whole program, Alice sees that find_substr is totally proved, but the postcondition and loop annotations of delete_substr are not proved. Since test generation does not find any counter-example, Alice believes that some necessary clause is too weak or missing. Moreover, all properties depending on the behavior not_found being fully proved, Alice reasonably suspects that the found behavior of find_substr is not strong enough.

3.4 Detecting Errors in Source Code

Counter-examples generated by STADY can also help to detect potential errors in the code. To evaluate its bug detection ability, we specified in E-ACSL 26 programs mostly taken from the TACAS 2014 Competition, generated 1088 mutants (that mimic frequent programming errors) and applied STADY to detect errors in them. The E-ACSL contract in mutants was not changed. 96.68% of non equivalent mutants have been successfully reported as buggy.

4 Conclusion and Future Work

We showed by a number of selected verification scenarios how automatic test generation provides a useful feedback that helps the validation engineer to test the conformance of a program to its (even partial) specification, identify errors, understand them thanks to generated counter-examples, and finally find missing, insufficient or wrong annotations, or detect bugs in the code. These scenarios sketch an iterative methodology assisted by test generation that makes deductive verification easier, less costly in time, more interactive and less error-prone. We presented the STADY tool, integrating a concolic test generator into FRAMA-C. A more detailed description of the STADY tool, some verification scenarios and initial experiments are available in [17].

Among previous combinations of static and dynamic analyses, [3,14] developed combinations of predicate abstraction and software testing. [5] described HOL-TestGen, a formally verified test-system extending the interactive theorem prover Isabelle/HOL. The design of JML accommodates both deductive and runtime verification [16]. Combinations of deductive verification and testing for imperative languages were recently studied and implemented for C# programs specified with Boogie in [18], and combining Dafny and Pex in [7]. In [8], the specification-based random testing tool Quickcheck is used to find counter-examples to invariants that have not been formally verified by automated theorem provers. [13] described an approach to show the correctness of a Java program and in case of a verification failure to show a counter-example or to guide the user. A counter-example is found based on information contained in proof trees of failed verification attempts, so the process has to start with a proof attempt. In our approach it is not necessary to start with a proof, the user may start by testing if she thinks the program is more likely to contain bugs. [1] addressed the verification of first-order logic axioms, that are provided by the user to theorem provers and supposed to hold. In this work, model-based random testing is used to find counter-examples to axiomatizations, but no coverage is ensured.

Our work continues these efforts for C programs in the FRAMA-C framework and proposes a methodology of incremental specification and deductive verification assisted by test generation. The SANTE method [6] proposed a combination of value analysis, slicing and test generation in order to detect runtime errors. Our present work combines deductive verification with testing, treats complete E-ACSL specifications (while SANTE treated only simple assertions) and thus handles in addition a large class of functional properties that were not supported in SANTE.

Future work includes further evaluation of the proposed methodology, experiments on real-size programs and a better support of E-ACSL constructs in our implementation (inductive predicates, assigns clauses, validity checks for non-input pointers).

Acknowledgment. The authors thank the FRAMA-C and PATHCRAWLER teams for providing the tools and support. Special thanks to François Bobot, Bernard Botella, Loïc Correnson, Pascal Cuoq, Bruno Marre, Julien Signoles and Nicky Williams for many fruitful discussions, suggestions and advice.

References

1. Ahn, K.Y., Denney, E.: Testing first-order logic axioms in program verification. In: Fraser, G., Gargantini, A. (eds.) TAP 2010. LNCS, vol. 6143, pp. 22–37. Springer, Heidelberg (2010)
2. Baudin, P., Cuoq, P., Filliâtre, J.C., Marché, C., Monate, B., Moy, Y., Prevosto, V.: ACSL: ANSI/ISO C Specification Language, http://frama-c.com/acsl.html
3. Beyer, D., Henzinger, T., Theoduloz, G.: Program analysis with dynamic precision adjustment. In: ASE (2008)
4. Botella, B., Delahaye, M., Hong Tuan Ha, S., Kosmatov, N., Mouy, P., Roger, M., Williams, N.: Automating structural testing of C programs: Experience with PathCrawler. In: AST (2009)
5. Brucker, A.D., Wolff, B.: On theorem prover-based testing. FAC (2012)
6. Chebaro, O., Kosmatov, N., Giorgetti, A., Julliand, J.: Program slicing enhances a verification technique combining static and dynamic analysis. In: SAC (2012)
7. Christakis, M., Müller, P., Wüstholz, V.: Collaborative verification and testing with explicit assumptions. In: Giannakopoulou, D., Méry, D. (eds.) FM 2012. LNCS, vol. 7436, pp. 132–146. Springer, Heidelberg (2012)
8. Claessen, K., Svensson, H.: Finding counter examples in induction proofs. In: Beckert, B., Hähnle, R. (eds.) TAP 2008. LNCS, vol. 4966, pp. 48–65. Springer, Heidelberg (2008)
9. Correnson, L., Signoles, J.: Combining analyses for C program verification. In: Stoelinga, M., Pinger, R. (eds.) FMICS 2012. LNCS, vol. 7437, pp. 108–130. Springer, Heidelberg (2012)
10. Csallner, C., Xie, T.: DSD-Crasher: A hybrid analysis tool for bug finding. In: ISSTA (2006)
11. Cuoq, P., Kirchner, F., Kosmatov, N., Prevosto, V., Signoles, J., Yakobowski, B.: Frama-C - a software analysis perspective. In: Eleftherakis, G., Hinchey, M., Holcombe, M. (eds.) SEFM 2012. LNCS, vol. 7504, pp. 233–247. Springer, Heidelberg (2012)
12. Delahaye, M., Kosmatov, N., Signoles, J.: Common specification language for static and dynamic analysis of C programs. In: SAC (2013)
13. Gladisch, C.: Could we have chosen a better loop invariant or method contract? In: Dubois, C. (ed.) TAP 2009. LNCS, vol. 5668, pp. 74–89. Springer, Heidelberg (2009)
14. Godefroid, P., Nori, A.V., Rajamani, S.K., Tetali, S.D.: Compositional may-must program analysis: unleashing the power of alternation. In: POPL (2010)
15. Klein, G.: From a verified kernel towards verified systems. In: Ueda, K. (ed.) APLAS 2010. LNCS, vol. 6461, pp. 21–33. Springer, Heidelberg (2010)
16. Leavens, G.T., Cheon, Y., Clifton, C., Ruby, C., Cok, D.R.: How the design of JML accommodates both runtime assertion checking and formal verification. In: de Boer, F.S., Bonsangue, M.M., Graf, S., de Roever, W.-P. (eds.) FMCO 2002. LNCS, vol. 2852, pp. 262–284. Springer, Heidelberg (2003)
17. Petiot, G., Kosmatov, N., Giorgetti, A., Julliand, J.: StaDy: Deep Integration of Static and Dynamic Analysis in Frama-C. Tech. rep. (2014), http://hal.archives-ouvertes.fr/hal-00992159
18. Polikarpova, N., Furia, C.A., West, S.: To run what no one has run before: Executing an intermediate verification language. In: Legay, A., Bensalem, S. (eds.) RV 2013. LNCS, vol. 8174, pp. 251–268. Springer, Heidelberg (2013)
19. Signoles, J.: E-ACSL: Executable ANSI/ISO C Specification Language, http://frama-c.com/download/e-acsl/e-acsl.pdf

Author Index